SEX
WITHIN REASON

SEX
WITHIN REASON

Anne Kelleher

JONATHAN CAPE
THIRTY-TWO BEDFORD SQUARE LONDON

To Edwin ... for all the rewards of being his wife

First published 1987
Copyright © 1987 by Anne Kelleher
Jonathan Cape Ltd, 32 Bedford Square, London WC1B 3EL

British Library Cataloguing in Publication Data

Kelleher, Anne
Sex within reason.
1. Sex
I. Title
306.7   HQ21

ISBN 0-224-02394-2

Phototypeset by Falcon Graphic Art Ltd
Wallington, Surrey
Printed in Great Britain by
Ebenezer Baylis & Son Ltd
The Trinity Press, Worcester and London

CONTENTS

ACKNOWLEDGMENTS

My thanks are due to all those who shared their views with me and allowed me to use the results of our discussions in this book. I am also indebted to Maggie Allen who patiently typed the manuscript; to Dr John Hickey and Dr Jean Fanchette who ensured that my medical facts were accurate; to my husband Edwin for his indispensable support and help and to the philosopher Professor Mark Sainsbury, my friend and former tutor whose guidance saved me from many errors.

INTRODUCTION

Everyone cherishes fundamental beliefs about the rights and wrongs of sexual behaviour. These beliefs range from the apparently trivial – should women wear make-up? is it acceptable to describe sex as screwing? – to the undeniably serious – is it wrong to have sex with a child? is abortion ever justified? Our responses to these questions affect the choices we make in our sex lives, as well as the way we view ourselves and others. A woman who accepts the Roman Catholic view that contraception is a sin is unlikely to munch oestrogen pills in the interests of family planning, while those who find masturbation abhorrent may find themselves sentenced to abstinence, or even joyless copulation. If you believe that homosexuality is an abomination, you are almost certain to recoil from the confessed homosexual – and if you sense such tendencies in yourself, as Freud says we all will, the disgust will be turned inwards. The vitriol which accompanies people's condemnation of any sexual preference that differs from their own is witness to the power of individual sexual beliefs.

For all those who claim that abortion is morally acceptable, there are as many who are convinced that it is murder. The law emphatically states that sex with a child is iniquitous, but this does not prevent paedophiliacs from arguing that it is not. For Christians, adultery is an act 'thou shalt not commit'; nevertheless, it is not only non-Christians who practise it, and see nothing wrong in doing so. This state of passionate confusion suggests that we should haul our beliefs into the open and ask ourselves whether we have good reason to subscribe to them, or whether they are merely prejudices. Are we justified in believing that anal sex is immoral, that promiscuity is degrading, that men who think of women as sex objects are pigs? Is monogamy nothing but the restricting remnant of a religious morality that has little application today? Is the taboo on incest simply a superstition?

I have tried to clarify some of these questions about sex by exploring the reasons people offer in support of their most cherished convictions. In all, I have talked to some four hundred people – sex therapists, psychiatrists, marriage-guidance counsellors, students, priests, colleagues, members of self-help and women's groups, family and friends – asking them why they hold the beliefs they do, why they are so sure that some sexual attitudes are right while others are wrong. People are forever discussing sexual issues – at dinner parties and conferences, in talks with their children or letters to newspapers. Ideas are pressed upon us from the political platform, the classroom and the pulpit. Opinions are aired in radio phone-ins and agony columns. Every one of these beliefs is supported by reasons of one kind or another. Sound or fragile, generous or bigoted, hedonistic or killjoy, they are invariably offered as irrefutable grounds for condemning or approving certain types of sexual behaviour. But how many of them are, in fact, good reasons? And how many are based on nothing more than confusion, prejudice, and obfuscation?

_1_

SEX . . . WITH OR WITHOUT LOVE

'Sex without love is dirty ashes.'

This pithy denunciation was the sum total of the sex education given to my mother by my grandmother. Since she was
speaking some sixty years ago, it is perhaps not surprising that
her words reek of a conviction that characterised Victorian
morality – the conviction that there is something troubling, not
to say corrupt, about sex for its own sake. This is an attitude of
which we are not yet free. Indeed, it would be remarkable if we
were, for the distinction between 'good' sex, which involves
the heart as well as the body, and 'bad' sex, which does not,
permeates our culture and powerfully conditions our thinking
on the subject.

The distinction is based on the dichotomy between our
nature as animals and our nature as human beings. Humanity
sees itself as endowed with features that raise it above the other
animals: we are, for example, rational, capable of choice, and
therefore capable of moral thinking. But we also have bodies,
and through them we share the instincts of other creatures. In
particular, it is our bodies that are the vehicles for our sexuality, and it is through the passions of sex that all that is rational –
and thus human – in us may be conquered. We are overcome by
desire. Sex, then, seems to epitomise all that humanity strives
to transcend.

It is not surprising that St Paul and St Augustine had a horror
of concupiscence, nor that they should have embraced celibacy. No man who could write, as Augustine did, 'Lust requires
for its consummation darkness, secrecy; and this not only when

1

unlawful intercourse is desired, but even such fornication as the earthly city has legalised,' could feel anything but shame at the mere thought of sex. For those that could not, or would not, eschew this problematic activity, however, humanity had in some way to be reconciled to its physical condition. Traditionally, the best way to remove sex from the province of the beasts has been through the redeeming power of love.

The affirmation of love as a redeeming quality resounds through our culture in poetry, literature, art, religion and philosophy. Its most popular expression today is in the conviction that desire is physical while love is spiritual. Thus sex with love is finer, more worthy, than sex without love, which is likely to be crude, exploitative, selfish and mechanical. Even Freud, who regarded sex as essentially a release of tension, believed that sex with love was vastly superior.

But what precisely does this superiority consist of? In what ways is sex for its own sake inferior to sex with love?

A 19-year-old girl engaged to be married to her first and only lover took a rather pragmatic line. She told me she believed the benefit, in sexual terms, of loving your partner was heightened sensual pleasure. 'When you're lying with the man you love the pleasures must be so much sweeter than when you're having casual sex, or sex with someone you aren't in love with.' It is certainly true that in the pages of romantic novels the first kiss signals the beginning of perpetual rapture. But is there any reason to suppose that this is an inevitable benefit of love, or that it cannot be experienced by those who are not in love?

The answer to the first question must be 'no'. There are too many loving couples for whom sex, for a variety of reasons, is arid and joyless. It would be absurdly arrogant to insist that these couples cannot love each other, so we are left to conclude what seems obviously true – that love can go hand in hand with indifferent sex.

The second question is less easily answered, and it needs a distinction to be made between two types of pleasure: those that are pure sensation and those that grow out of our view of what causes our sensations.

In sex a great deal of our pleasure is caused by physiological changes in our sexual organs – changes that occur in arousal and orgasm. These changes are not dependent on the presence of a sexual partner: they occur during masturbation, watching a blue movie or even in non-sexual situations. It is frequently alleged, for example, that girls feel intense pleasure when on the back of a horse. Certain sexual pleasures, then, are sensations experienced in the sexual organs, and these may be caused by a variety of objects and circumstances.

This view of sexual pleasures naturally gives support to a common conviction that all that is needed to achieve and induce delight is a knowledge of sexual technique and the physical coordination to apply it. Good sex will be the result of efficiently employing a more or less mechanical skill which aims at giving and receiving pleasure.

There is obviously some truth in this; one who is quite devoid of knowledge of the human anatomy and who is deficient in technique is not likely to be a satisfactory lover. Thus Ovid's *Ars Amatoria* and Burton's *Kama Sutra* and *The Perfumed Garden* all celebrate the importance of technique to one pursuing the erotic life. Some people believe this is all there is to good sex. Professor Alfred Kinsey, for example, seemed to display this conviction when he argued that all a woman needs to be as orgasmic as a man is sufficient stimulation: if you do the right thing you will get optimum results.

If this is true – that technique is all that is needed to produce all the great pleasures of sex – then clearly love is not a vital ingredient in the sexual experience. All you need is expertise. However, many sensations are not simply caused by physical stimulation of the senses. They are also the product of the beliefs you have about what – or who – is doing the stimulating. The plum you grew in your own garden may taste infinitely sweeter than any identically sweet plum that was grown by someone else. Similarly, part of the joy of sex is an awareness of the author of your delight. A vibrator may generate intense sensations, but there is no joy – or at least not usually – in awareness of the vibrator itself. Our pleasure does not derive from knowing that it is *this* that causes the pleasurable sensations. But when sex is with another person, pleasure can be intensified by the acute awareness that it is *this* person one is being kissed or caressed by. A partner is not simply a convenient means of getting delicious sensations; the delight produced by just the right touch and pressure will be the sweeter for your recognition that it is the one you love who is doing the delighting.

It may be true, then, that if your partner is one you love and cherish these pleasures are heightened; the delight you take in your beloved is greater than the delight you would take in anyone else. The ideal must therefore be that technical competence and love will combine.

Delight in the beloved, however, is not the only attitude that can enhance sensual pleasure, and neither is it inevitable that it will do so. Erica Jong's 'zipless fuck' is an encounter in which delight is intensified by the fact that the partner is not only unloved but also unknown, and will never be seen again. Someone else may get intense pleasure from the reflection that the lover is famous, or dangerous, or about to die. Noble ladies once paid vast sums of money to Newgate jailors in order to spend the night with the highwayman who was to be hanged the next morning. Love is not essential to sensual pleasure. Indeed, it may be positively inimical. Some men, it is said, cannot enjoy sex with a woman they love and respect. Their perception of sexual activity is such that they can engage in it only with those they see as in some way degraded or inferior. People are highly individual when it comes to what excites them. As a sex therapist told me: 'Too many people think if you're in love you can let the sex take care of itself. Somehow it will be all right on the night. The trouble is . . . it often isn't.'

The importance of good sex to a relationship will depend very largely on the nature of that relationship. If you have a one-night stand and someone asks you if you have enjoyed it, you can answer only in terms of sexual satisfaction. If the sex was disappointing the whole venture was a waste of time. But in the context of a longer relationship a night can be more than satisfactory, even if the sex is pretty poor. A failure in a one-night stand is the end of everything; the occasional failure with your beloved is only an off night. So sexual performance matters much more in a one-night stand than in an 'on-going' relationship. It is what the one-nighter is all about, after all.

Aristotle believed that human beings were essentially cooperative; he likened us to honey bees —insects that enchanted him by the intricate ways they work together. For humans, a loving relationship can be one of the most enduring and moving forms of cooperation: a couple join in giving each other care and support, in affirming each other's value, sharing interests, perhaps making a home together or planning a family. Such a relationship is clearly set in a framework that embraces much more than sex. These other aspects of life cannot be under-estimated, and can sustain a relationship even when some aspects of it have collapsed. It may easily be sex that goes. There are many solid marriages in which delight in each other's bodies has all but withered; still, it may take years before such a marriage collapses in any other way – and it may never do so. Some people may find the end of physical pleasure dispiriting and that the acid of dissatisfaction eats away at the whole relationship. Nevertheless, the emphasis on sex in marriage is quite different from that in a relationship where all that matters is sex. If sex is all you have going for you, then once it is in ruins everything is over.

A tantalising possibility of sex with love is that of achieving a rare intimacy with another person. A man who describes his wife as his best friend said to me, 'If you love someone you give much more of yourself to the sexual relationship – you can be truly intimate. Without love you hold things back.' Even a purely physical relationship has its intimacies, for the couple surrender to each other a very important privacy: they allow an access to each other's bodies that is usually denied. In unveiling yourself before your lover you allow – encourage – that person to see you as one who has joyfully submitted to sexual desire, who is, as it were, taken over by their body. Jean-Paul Sartre described the process of embodiment this way: 'I make myself flesh in order to impel the other to realise for herself and for me her own flesh and my caresses cause my flesh to be born for me.' The woman who may undress quite freely before her doctor may – in this state of being flesh – feel modest before her lover. She is inviting a different perception of herself, one that sees her as sexual.

In desiring someone we want more than acquiescence; a lover who is unconscious or asleep will be unsatisfactory for most of us. We want consent, a person aroused, filled with desire. In submitting to this desire one is certain to be in some disarray – quite out of control. So in sex there is the danger of

all sorts of weaknesses or sensibilities being exposed as they
are not in any other way. Sex is more than a physical union, it
is also a revelation . . . and a risk. Stendhal describes a woman
'who woos the most well-bred man in the world; she soon
learns that he has certain ridiculous physical misfortunes; he
immediately becomes unbearable to her'.

If you go to bed with someone that person will learn a variety of
things about you, whether you like it or not. Now this may not
matter if you love your partner, for love breeds a certain
confidence. You may find your feelings cancel out a very common
anxiety about exposure. Perhaps, then, love makes it easier to
achieve intimacy – to allow yourself to be known. However, it is
not the only way. A couple, though not in love, may be such good
friends that they are unconcerned about self-revelation. Or maybe
they simply do not worry about such things.

Rembrandt's great marriage portrait *The Jewish Bride* cele-
brates a deep conviction that there is some essential connection
between love and tenderness. Rembrandt shows a couple
leaning towards each other, their faces suffused with love. It is
a moment of silence, and in this silence tenderness says it all.
We must all have delighted in the tender kiss or caress that
assures us we are loved. At its most basic, sex is a biological
need, but the touch of a hand on a face or a glance across a room
tells you that you do more than merely fulfil a need. There is in
these gestures an emphasis on the importance of *you*. Tenderness is the absolute denial of any impersonality in sex; it is the
affirmation that you as a person matter. As Theodore Reik
describes it in *The Psychology of Sexual Relations*, 'The object
of sex is desired only during the short time of excitement and
appears undesirable otherwise; the beloved person is the object
of continued tenderness.' This certainty is so much a part of us
that a sexual relationship that lacks tenderness seems shocking.
To quote Sartre: 'Intercourse counterfeits masturbation.'

Of course, not everyone who loves – perhaps no one – will be
tender every moment. Anger or irritation intrudes into even the
most loving relationship. But, in general, there must surely be
some propensity towards tenderness for us even to begin to
think of the relationship as love. It would be absurd to profess
that one loved another if one was unwilling ever to be tender.

Because tenderness is typically expressed physically it is easy to see sex as a natural vehicle for its expression. But must we conclude that relationships that are sexually sado-masochistic are not loving ones? Havelock Ellis argued that the paradigm of sado-masochism is the relationship in which the woman surrenders to the force she apparently flees but in reality desires. So the aggressive male/submissive female is the archetype of the sado-masochistic encounter. Clearly, many loving and tender relationships contain some of the elements of this archetype: the vigorous thrusting of the penis, the love bites and pinches, one partner pinned beneath the weight of the other – all connote aggression, dominance and submission. But there is room in these for the tender caress, the kiss or the smile. A touch of sadism does not entirely cancel out tenderness.

What, then, of relationships where nothing is intended but the infliction of pain? Where, for example, one partner is tied up and beaten by the other?

If there is some special pleasure that two people enjoy within a loving set-up – if, for example, the 'aggressor' knows that the 'victim' loves bondage and has agreed to it – then tenderness may be put in abeyance for the sake of that pleasure. This is not at all the same as tenderness being entirely missing. Nevertheless, some special explanation of the lack is required. Compare tenderness to jealousy. If your lover is not jealous – then they are simply not the jealous type. You do not have to root around for some explanation of it in order to hang on to the idea that they love you. But unless there is some special explanation for the absence of tenderness there are strong – overwhelming – grounds for thinking that love is not there.

One such explanation was offered me by a psychiatrist who said, 'Many people feel adrift from real contact with others because they recognise that people don't communicate honestly. There's the smile before the Judas kiss. But the expression of pain is invariably genuine because it is involuntary.' Rather surprisingly, Emily Dickinson wrote:

> I like a look of agony
> Because I know it's true:
> Men do not sham convulsion
> Nor simulate a throe.

*

It can, then, happen that a person who loves someone and wants a genuine observable response does it by inflicting pain. In some people, wires may get crossed: the grimace of pain substitutes for the smile, the blow for the caress. Yet love may be present even though tenderness is missing. The loving sadist's desire is, as it were, to call forth the real person to the surface of the body. Where, by contrast, it is the pain itself that is desired, the other person's body is used simply as an instrument. The sadism exemplified by the Marquis de Sade does not concern itself at all with the partner's wishes. For the hard-line sadist the act of inflicting pain is the denial of the person. The partner is not called forth, but abolished. The loving sadist, however, shares with the more conventional lover the wish to affirm the importance of the person – he or she wants the loved one to desire the pain and to enjoy it.

The sadist may be encouraged by the visual similarity of our response to pain and our response to extreme pleasure. Desmond Morris pointed out in *The Human Zoo* that the 'writhings and facial expressions of pain that he [the sadist] produces in the female are somewhat similar to the writhings and facial expressions of a female experiencing orgasm'. Bearing this in mind, it is interesting to consider Bernini's *The Ecstasy of St Teresa*. Teresa was visited by an angel with a golden spear tipped with flame. 'With this he pierced my heart so that it penetrated my entrails. The pain was so sharp that it made me utter several moans and so excessive was the sweetness that none can ever wish to lose it.' This moment of exquisite agony is the moment Bernini chose to freeze in marble: the angel stands before the saint, his spear pointing down at her body; she writhes on the ground at his feet. It takes little imagination to formulate the symbolic equation – the artist has clearly depicted a moment of spontaneous orgasm. But if one had no knowledge of Teresa's story, what then would one see? Is the woman's head thrown back in pain or pleasure? Is her body writhing in agony or ecstasy? Is she being spitted on the end of that spear – or is it indeed a symbolic sexual coupling?

Pain may also be a means by which people break down the barriers of inhibition. One couple told me that their love-making always started with a certain amount of 'horse-play' – pinches, blows, bites. 'It's as though feeling those sensations brings down the barriers that stop us feeling – or going for – other sensations.' Pain may be the first step in allowing yourself to be overcome by desire. It may, then, be possible to explain the absence of tenderness and, through that explanation, hold on to the idea that the one who inflicts pain nevertheless loves their partner.

Even where there is no hint of de Sade's favoured exploit, tenderness may be absent from sex. It is common to hear women complain that too many men are crude and perfunctory lovers. As one woman described it to me, 'For some men sex is a self-absorbed sprint to ejaculation.' If someone is perfunctory in bed – if he is careless or inattentive to his beloved's needs – then something has gone wrong. Either he does not love her, and his protestations are just so much noise; or else the most natural expression of love has failed: the cogs have jammed and there has been a malfunction.There are, of course, occasions when sex does, quite simply, go wrong. A senior marriage-guidance counsellor told me that a common cause is male anxiety about touching. 'A lot of men have been taught that there's something unmanly – cissy – about touching. The result is that, apart from ritualised touching like hand-shakes, they simply do not do it.' If your man believes that touching is in some way incompatible with his masculinity, he may keep bodily contact to the minimum; you may not get the tender caresses you crave. He may love you all right, but his love has failed to get properly linked to his behaviour.

None of this means that sex without love is never tender. Caresses may be offered out of liking and affection; they may be every bit as tender as those of love. But – unless you have a taste for special forms of fulfilment like bondage – you cannot have love without tenderness. If your partner loves you, you can feel safe in presuming that sex will have its tender moments. If you are not with a lover you cannot make any such presumption.

The most common condemnation of sex without love is that it is selfish; by contrast, sex with love is altruistic: no one is out to grab everything for themselves. Anyone who believes in this dichotomy may very well feel that in sex without love there is a risk of a particularly unpalatable form of exploitation. In surrendering to desire we offer a body to be held, squeezed, stroked; we are already 'overcome' by the other and so we are crucially vulnerable. There are dangers, then, in taking to your bed someone about whom you know nothing and who may entirely disregard your wishes. As one woman wryly advised me, 'If you're going to invite a twelve-stone man to throw himself on top of you you'd better make sure his heart's in the right place. You can worry about other things later!'

In sex, we risk more than physical injury, for we 'become' our bodies; our awareness is reduced to our bodily experiences. To exploit this embodiment by turning another person into a masturbatory machine, or another 'score' to boost the ego, reduces that person to being an object. And to be made less than human is deeply humiliating.

Lust can certainly be selfish, and it can manifest this selfishness in particularly unpleasant ways. Love, on the other hand, in all its forms, implies a desire for the good of the beloved. Erich Fromm believes that, 'Love is the active concern for the life and growth of that which we love.' Aristotle suggested, though, that this benevolence is not limitless. Discussing loving friendship, he said that the friend 'will content himself with wishing for his friends the greatest goods available to a human being'. But he added, 'And perhaps not all of these. For everybody who forms a wish thinks first of himself.' In other words: you will not wish your friends something that will take them away from you. In erotic love there is the same self-interested need to hold on to the beloved. For it is part of love to want to be with the loved one, to be essential to their life. If something that is good for them threatens the relationship, then, as Aristotle pointed out, you will not wish it for them. Indeed, you may fight it, for you will want to resist anything that makes it possible for them to live happily without you and will try to keep them even at their expense. This is why 'I'll never let anyone else have you' is taken as a sign of passionate love. 'I don't mind who you go off with if it makes you happy' is taken, not as a sign of love, but of waning interest or indifference. But the first is selfish; the second is altruistic.

In sex, one who loves must at least be prepared to consider

the beloved's interests, not entirely to disregard them. This does not mean it is necessary to be totally self-abnegating. It means only that the loved one's needs must be weighed in the balance. If the lover will not even do this, then either the love is not genuine – or something has gone amiss. The man who thinks it a sufficient expression of love to take out a mortgage and provide his wife with housekeeping, while feeling free to neglect her sexually, is simply wrongheaded. His perceptions have become distorted; supporting someone is not enough as an expression of love.

Unselfish acts are not restricted to love; after all, some people are innately generous. And even those who are selfish and think only of their own interests will not always – if they are sensible – act selfishly. So long as they need the cooperation of others to achieve their desires they will have to give something. Otherwise, people will soon stop giving to them. Love is on a more elevated plane of unselfishness than egoistic 'altruism' – though Nietzsche argued that even love is really a disguised and selfish attempt to make the loved one dependent. On this view, there is no distinction in terms of selfishness between love and lust: both, he argued, aim at mastery. Even if we disagree and maintain that love is essentially altruistic, we must agree that there is no cut-off point between love and other states. Love may shade into a warm friendship in which there are plenty of loving and unselfish acts. You do not have to love to enjoy a temporary liaison that is not selfish.

Perhaps even more important than the behaviour we display in sex are the attitudes we have to one another. One man told me that, in his experience, 'Lust encourages you to see a woman as an object; love keeps the person there.' It is not obvious that this is necessarily true. You may start off by seeing your sexual partner as the one you love, but as you succumb to desire your perceptions may narrow to seeing the beloved as an object – an object to satisfy your desire. At the moment of coitus the attitudes of lovers and non-lovers may be precisely similar. In both cases the person disappears and the object takes over.

Perhaps this sometimes happens; but it also happens that as you are gripped with desire love leads you to behave in a way that is sensitive to your lover. Suppose you knew, in unheated moments, that your beloved hated you using 'fuck' to describe your love-making. During sex your desire blots this out and you use the word. Later, you realise that what you have done upset your partner and reduced their pleasure. If the person matters to you, then whatever you think of this particular sensibility, you would surely feel it would have been better if you had remembered.

'Love keeps the person there' may simply mean that you are sensitive to your loved one. If you are not – if you do not care – then there has been a breakdown somewhere. For sexual behaviour should surely harmonise with feelings. People in love do not, usually, brutalise or force something unpleasant on their partners.

There is no guarantee of such sensitivity in a relationship motivated solely by lust. If, the next morning, the couple are going to go their own ways and never see each other again, they each may be interested only in their own enjoyment even at the cost of exploiting the other. But lust does not have to be like this; like love, it too can keep the person there. For it is an acknowledgment of the person to be prepared to acknowledge their needs and to be prepared to fulfil them – indeed, to allow them to determine, in fair measure, what form that fulfilment should take. It is not enough to want to give pleasure: you must want to give it in ways the recipient prefers.

Lust need not be depersonalising, but many people argue that it is invariably indiscriminate – that when you feel lustful more or less anyone will do. I suppose the paradigm is the randy sailor leaping off his ship to scour the port for a girl . . . any girl. Certainly Theodore Reik argues that only love is directed at a particular person; sex is a craving – a hunger in the sexual organs that can be eased by activity with some other person, it does not much matter whom.

If Reik means to argue that sexual desire is indiscriminate – it can be satisfied by just anyone – then he is clearly wrong. Everyone, even in the grip of lust, discriminates against some possible sexual partners. Most people would reject members of the family (other than their spouse), animals, and people of their own sex. Even Casanova admitted that his overwhelming desire for the singer Bellino evaporated when he came to believe that Bellino was a man. We may all have stringent limitations on whom we would count suitable to share our bed.

Perhaps Reik is saying that within those limitations lust is indiscriminate; if you go for women, then in the heat of lust any woman will do. (Even this will have to be narrowed down a little; perhaps very young or very old women would not satisfy you.) In line with this view, there is a state of wanting a sexual partner without there being a particular person you want. This is presumably the state of the randy sailor – he is in the grip of general desire. So as he arrives at the brothel he may find that within the range dictated by his own tastes a number of the girls will do for him. This does contrast with the sailor who is in love; as he leaps on shore only one face and one body will satisfy him – no one else could possibly do.

When desire is aroused by a particular person, though, the excitement aroused by this person does not make you want sex with anyone; it makes you want sex with that person. We are not, like the lower birds in Chaucer's Parliament of Fowls, overcome by a desire that will attach itself to anyone. If Jack is swamped by desire for Jill, it is Jill he wants, and no one else will ease the craving. Think how odd it would be to suggest to Jack that if Jill were not interested he should simply switch his desire to Mary. You may, of course, advise him to stop mooning over a woman he cannot have, and he may try to find consolation in Mary's arms. Perhaps, though, the most he can do is use her as a vehicle for fantasies about Jill, for it is Jill he still wants. In time this desire may fade to be replaced by desire for Mary. But the desire cannot be transferred from one woman to another.

The feeling that desires can be transferred is perhaps grounded in the assimilation of sexual desire to appetites like hunger. The eighteenth-century theologian Bishop Butler, for example, put the desire for sex on his list of appetites – though he pointed out that, unlike eating, sexual gratification was not necessary to the individual's survival: the comparative longevity of nuns and priests proved it! Now if the sight of a doughnut in a baker's window impels you to go inside and buy one you will not mind if you are not given the one that originally aroused your taste-buds. All you want is one exactly like it: this will still your appetite. But in desiring a person we do not believe them to be replaceable by a suitable substitute. We do not desire people as we hunger for doughnuts.

Another ground for confusion is the notion that the aim of desire is orgasm, which would imply that the object of desire is not a person but a process, and one that can be accomplished with any number of people. This makes the role of the other person in sex wholly mysterious. If all you want is orgasm, why not masturbate? At least, as Woody Allen remarked, it's sex with someone you love. Or how about an orgasm pill? You took it and POW! I imagine a lot of people would find it fun, less tiring than masturbating and less worrying than the difficult business of trying to form relationships.

In desiring a person, however, we do not desire an orgasm; we desire to have sex – to enjoy a special activity – with that person. We would be very surprised if Jack described his desire for Jill as simply a desire for orgasm, since this is not a thought on which desire is founded. Of course, orgasms are important – so much so that we are disturbed by a report like Kinsey's which recorded that a staggering 56 per cent of women apparently do not achieve orgasm during coitus. There can be huge amounts of tension left over from sex without orgasm, tension which erodes other pleasures, and although an occasional failure may not necessarily leave you tense – you may experience a slow winding down instead of an explosive release – constant failure to reach orgasm is pernicious. No woman suffering in this way is likely to feel consoled by the reflection that in desiring her man she had not desired an orgasm anyway. But saying that once a couple are engaged in sex it is perfectly natural to aim at orgasm as the natural resolution of their activity is not the same as seeing orgasm as what is wanted when you are gripped by desire for someone. In just the same way, the man who yearns for revenge on his enemy may be filled with exultation when he gets it. But it is not the exultation he aims at; he wants the sensation to be attendant on the revenge.

A colleague suggested that this sort of confusion is a product of our living in a goal-orientated society; we need to be able to point to some concrete moment as the achievement of our desire – a moment available to everyone. This explains the countless sex manuals that offer to solve sexual problems by teaching people to achieve orgasm. But this comes dangerously close to treating the other person as an occasion for us to achieve. This must be a mistake. After all, even in masturbation, that self-serving activity, people do not narcissistically think of themselves; they mostly think of some highly desirable other person. For that is what we desire.

The longing for union with another person is never felt more acutely than in sex; yet, ironically, we are never more self-absorbed than during sex. We seem to be caught in the paradox that, even as we join with another, we exclude them. However, what really matters is what happens before and after the moment of self-absorption – and also how both people see what goes on. Imagine, for instance, two trapeze artists involved in giving a big-top performance. The moves they make are not simply for themselves – neither solely for their own safety nor for the displaying of their own skills. They do things for each other's benefit. And even though each artist knows there will be a part of the routine in which they have to concentrate so hard that neither could think about anything else – not even their partner – this self-absorption does not exclude the other because it is within an agreed framework of thinking about one another and acting together. Moments of self-absorption in sex may be similar: they are all part of an agreed joint endeavour. They assume a totally different aspect if they are related to this activity than if there is no cooperative endeavour at all and you are both just in it for yourselves.

This observation will not assuage the feelings of sadness that many report as experiencing after sex. In *Love and Will*, Rollo May describes this sadness as, 'the reminder that we have not succeeded absolutely in losing our separateness'. Sex can be a poignant demonstration that we never overcome our solitariness. As such, it is a demonstration of a necessary truth: it is impossible for one person to become another – to unite with the beloved entirely. We are not two streams of water which flow into each other and, mingling, become one. We are intractably individual. There can, then, be no loss of self, if by that we mean some kind of transcendental fusion with the partner. We may fuse with each other only physically.

There is, of course, a familiar way in which we achieve closeness with another, and that is through empathy. Aristotle suggested that when we feel genuine pity for another we put ourselves into an 'as if it were me' state. A man sees his friend reduced to begging and is able to put himself into his friend's place – to feel what he is feeling as if he were the unfortunate one. People, then, are able to project themselves into another's perspective – to share. When sexual activity is rightly called 'love-making', lovers are able through their gestures to invite this projection, to ask a partner to share the intimacy of identification.

When sex is with a loved one there is a concern for more than the physiological needs of the moment. The lovers' kisses and caresses reflect the wider context of their feelings for each other and about their life together. What they do is not only about sending delicious frissons along a spine – it is also about affirming what they are to each other. They are, as it were, able to move around each other's private landscapes. In the physical union of sex, people can be intimate with what they think of as the other's 'real' self. They can, as it were, lose themselves in the other.

When we love another there is a disposition to be absorbed in the beloved. The world contracts to one person. Perhaps this seems inadequate to love. After all, it is possible to be absorbed in someone you desire very much but do not love. Suppose, though, you were cast away on a desert island. You would rightly see yourself as very badly off. Suppose, then, by some fluke you were joined by an acquaintance who in civilised life was good for an hour's conversation once a month. As he or she came over the horizon you would not feel yourself to be much better off. Now suppose you were castaway with the person you love and who loves you. If you think you are no worse off than if you had not been castaway at all, you may justly say you are totally absorbed in your beloved. It is this level of absorption that feeds the romantic notion that the world is well lost for love. Most people want to be loved in this way, and a slightly smaller 'most' want to love. Love is thought to be the 'ultimate' emotion to communicate, and sex is generally thought to be the most graphic means of its communication.

There are those who think there is an anomaly in the idea of sex communicating love at all. As one woman asked me, 'How's a penis thrusting in and out of a vagina supposed to express

emotion? Are you showing love if you move slowly or something?'

We often use action to convey what we mean: with a loving
glance or gesture we tell the beloved they are loved. But the
movements of sex are involuntary, and nothing can be deliberately conveyed by what is involuntary. A cry of pain may, of
course, tell someone that you are hurt, but it does not deliberately convey that message; it was not what you *meant* when
you cried out. Similarly an erection shows that a man is in a
state of sexual arousal, but since tumescence cannot be willed
it cannot be an expression of love; nor can the gasps of pleasure
or the spasms of orgasm. At its most basic the sex act is a
physical union in which the brute facts may be the same
whether the act is one of love or a casual one-night stand. How,
then, can sex convey love?

The context will make all the difference. From a person's
bodily movements in sex you could not deduce that he or she
loves you. But if you already know the love is there you will see
those movements in a very different light. Suppose you found 'I
love you' written in the sand on a beach, and you knew it had
been written by someone with absolutely no knowledge of
English, simply because the arrangement of letters pleased them
and they thought it would please you. So, by some freak of chance,
they constructed this sentence. Now suppose 'I love you' has
been written by your loved one, as a message to you. You will
view this very differently. The first sentence was just a
delightful – curious – coincidence. The second is a highly
significant communication. But the sentences are typographi-
cally identical.

Present experience, then, combines with knowledge to put a
different perspective on what is happening. In a similar way,
when you see a man or woman you do not know you have a
purely visual experience of them. With love, the sensory input
– the appearance – is the same, but the thought that this is your
beloved will colour your whole perception.

Now apply this to sex. Described purely physically, a stranger's caress may be exactly like that of a lover. But because you
know the one loves you and the other does not, you see each
caress in a very different light.

The involuntariness of sexual acts has been a cause of some

perturbation to those who would like sex to be moral. St Augustine, for example, thought that only acts governed by free will and reason could be moral; since these faculties are clearly vanquished in sex, intercourse is in its very nature immoral. This led him to suppose that before the Fall, when such as there was of mankind was perfect, the sexual organs were completely in the control of the will. Adam could will an erection or will not to have one. The fig leaf with which he covered himself after eating the apple was to cover the shame of being unable to control himself.

More recent thinkers have accepted the involuntariness of sex while trying to give an account of a morally preferable form of it. Thomas Nagel, for example, has argued in 'Sexual Perversion' that there are 'complete' sex acts which are morally superior to other acts. His aim in devising the notion of completeness was to hold a light up to the notion of perversion. Once we know what is complete we will know what is incomplete, and incomplete sex acts are those we should regard as perverted. His project fails, or at least offends common intuitions, for acts in which there is a crucial element of fantasy turn out to be incomplete: I find it hard, however, to see them as perverted. Nevertheless, Nagel's theory does give us a notion of what could constitute ideal sex.

The completeness of a particular sex act depends on the relation the lovers have to their own and the other's desire. In complete sex each partner is taken over by desire. But there is more to this than just wanting the other's body; there is also a wish for the other's desire – I want you and I want you to want me. The first step in getting this chain of desires started is embodiment. Each partner allows desire to take over and direct what is done. Augustinean self-control counts as disembodiment and is thus incomplete. Nagel, by contrast, follows Sartre in requiring that the lover submit entirely to desire; all the impulses of desire are expressed through the body, and consciousness is taken over. As Sartre would have said, consciousness 'becomes flesh'. In complete sex, the other's and one's own desires are wished for, recognised and endorsed. This has the welcome and wholesome consequence that sexual desire becomes desirable, reciprocity is encouraged, and our deepest feelings are both recognised and responded to. In complete sex both partners count.

Incomplete sex is morally inferior to this. The necrophiliac can only have incompleteness since he cannot desire that his partner want him. Similarly, the frigid woman is condemned to incomplete acts because she is not embodied by her own desire. Fantasy makes sex incomplete because the fantasist responds to his own imaginings, not to the partner. For Sartre, masturbation was the archetypal, incomplete act: 'The masturbator is enchanted at never being able to sense himself sufficiently another and at producing for himself alone the diabolic appearance of being a couple that fades away when one touches it.'

The most morally significant aspect of completeness is that it involves respect for persons. Each person stays a 'subject' rather than an object – an object perhaps to be manipulated. No one becomes an instrument to be used by the other because complete sex is mutual and desired by both. It does not follow, of course, that in incomplete sex there is invariably disrespect for the partner; only that in complete sex there can, by definition, be no such feeling. *Pace* the Christian Fathers, then, sex can intimately involve us as moral beings; not in avoiding it or disinfecting it with puritanism but in giving us the opportunity to exercise pre-eminently important virtues.

None of this means that we will prefer abstinence to incomplete sex; pleasure is important and incomplete sex may be very pleasurable. Certainly we are likely to prefer it to celibacy. We can recognise, though, that even if bad sex is better than no sex, the more incomplete a sex act is the more it is likely to be manipulative, unresponsive or even imposed.

Complete sex, on the other hand, does not essentially involve love, though such acts must be conducive to it. Nor does the involuntariness of sex – the person succumbing to the flesh – make sex immoral. As long as there is the necessary hierarchy of desire working, sex involves us as moral agents. St Paul and St Augustine regarded 'the law of sin that is in my member' as a threat to the dominion of the holy will. For Nagel, the immersion in desire does not cancel out humanity; it enhances the lover's sense of himself and his partner.

We have, then, come full circle. From the original supposition that sex must be sanctioned by love we have reached an understanding that desire itself can be a vehicle for morality. Neither the most pleasurable sex nor the morally preferable sex requires love to take it from the province of beasts. We do not have to aspire to the spiritual – deny the animal in us – to be 'good'. On the contrary, we need only allow our own incarnation.

_ 2 _

FLIRTING

I once owned a discursive little handbook on the art of being a lady. I studied it avidly, for at 11 years old I was passionately keen to grow into a Georgette Heyer heroine: men would adore me, put me on a pedestal and count themselves fit only to chew on the hem of my skirt.

Unfortunately, by the time men were interested in me at all, it was the age of the extreme mini-skirt: even the lowest pedestal disclosed a great deal more than my gentility, and access to my hem afforded an intimacy I was not prepared for. I abandoned my perilous enterprise . . . and the handbook. But I still remember some of the coy little directives, for example the condemnation of flirting: 'It is unbecoming in a lady to invite the attentions of gentlemen.'

The handbook had nothing to say on the moral or social probity of men flirting. This was probably because it was aimed at embryonic ladies. Or it might have been that the compilers believed, in common with many others, that flirting was essentially a female pastime. The *Oxford English Dictionary*, for example, says that 'flirt' is usually applied to women, while the Collins dictionary defines a flirt as a 'pert, giddy girl'.

Men do, of course, flirt; indeed, some of the most accomplished flirts you will meet are men. Yet when I asked twenty people to describe what they thought of as a typical flirt, all but three of them described some imaginary woman. What is it, then, about the nature of flirting that encourages the view that it is more a woman's than a man's ploy? To answer this question it will be necessary to establish precisely what flirting is and what dimension it gives to our sex lives.

*

Flirting is a species of attention-getting behaviour. Through words and gestures the flirt impinges on another's consciousness and focuses attention on themselves. We cannot, however, define flirting by its effect because other forms of behaviour may also draw people's attention – hiccuping through a concert or accidentally smashing a coffee cup, for example.

The difference is that flirting is a deliberate action. It is not, like hiccuping or sneezing, an involuntary response to certain stimuli – not even to stimuli like cleavages or broad shoulders. This may seem obvious, but the view that flirting is something one cannot help – for which one is not responsible – was, in fact, put to me with Gallic insouciance by a Frenchman who argued, 'In the presence of a beautiful woman I flirt . . . just as I shiver in a cold wind. It is, you might say, the spiritual equivalent of erection; the soul stirs in response to your sex.' I doubt that this was meant to be taken too seriously; nor should it be. The immediacy of a response does not show it to be involuntary. The glutton may instantly fall upon a cream bun if it is placed before him; but this is something he does, not something that happens to him. In this, flirting is like eating and unlike shivering or sneezing. One does not suffer from flirting in the presence of another's charms as one suffers from sneezing in a high pollen count. Similarly, you cannot flirt by mistake. A hunter may take a pot shot at a pigeon and by mistake shoot off someone's bonnet, but not even the most head-in-the-clouds academic could have a shot at delivering a lecture on Aristotle and find that by mistake he or she had flirted.

Even when deliberate action aims to win attention it may not be flirtation. The woman hailing a taxi is not, of course, flirting; but if she raises her arm 'just so' to show off the trim line of her figure then she may be, for it is her intention that marks off one kind of action from another. The first intends not simply to get attention, but to get sexual attention. It is this that distinguishes flirtation from the rest of the family of attention-getting behaviour.

Nevertheless, not all attempts to arouse sexual interest are flirting. A straight 'Let's make love' may stir your partner, but only the callow would regard it as flirtation. Neither can it be made flirtatious by being veiled. A 'Fed-Up Husband' wrote to

a woman's magazine complaining about his wife's most unromantic method of signalling her desire for sex: when she
wanted him she varied her nightly bathroom routine to include
an audible gargle with Listerine. This is certainly covert
enough. But it is hardly flirtation.

Flirting, then, is something to do with deliberately inviting
sexual attention. Need it have anything to do with consummation? A homosexual I spoke to made it clear it need not. 'I love
to flirt with women . . . it's fun. But not even in the most
hilarious spirit of research would I dream of going to bed with a
woman.' And there are plenty of people devoted to a beloved
partner who enjoy flirting with others as nothing more than
delightful dalliance or an affirmation of appeal.

Since the uninterested and the dedicatedly monogamous
may flirt, it follows that the aim pursued cannot be the aim of
desire. If you desire someone you aim to consummate your
passion in love-making. Whatever the aim of flirting, it is not so
explicitly sexual. This may be why people tend to regard it as
an essentially innocent pastime: it is less about *having* sex than
playing with sex. In *Don Juan*, however, Byron described
flirtation as 'Not quite adultery but adulteration', and the flirt as
'the cold coquette', 'an amphibious sort of harlot'. The implication is clearly that the activity is in some way corrupt. Why
might anyone think this?

One answer might be that people's motives for flirting are
often highly dubious. Admitted flirts acknowledge a variety of
purposes, from the journalist who allowed that he flirts with
his Features Editor 'to get some protection from sub-editors and
their asinine captions', to the woman in her forties who said she
flirted at parties to prove that 'not only teenage anorexics can
strike a spark'. Another woman told me that, for her, flirting is
part of the *realpolitik* of marriage. Married to a constantly and
publicly wandering husband, she flirts with his employees 'to
even the score a little'. Motives for flirting need not always be
dubious: Lady Helen Brook, who established the Brook Advis-
ory Centre, said that she would have 'flirted with a frog' if it
helped the cause of getting contraceptive advice for women.

None of this necessarily justifies flirting, of course. Flirting
with a scabrous office-boy may humiliate a husband; so may

conspicuously failing to laugh at his jokes. And there are other ways than flirting to get changes in the laws that affect women – the suffragettes produced a catalogue of them. Nevertheless, flirting can be an effective and enjoyable means of getting what you want.

What about the pain flirtations can cause? Most people will have felt that miserable sense of exclusion as the loved one happily flirts with another. But to condemn any activity that unwittingly causes pain would be to condemn every human activity, from singing in the bath to eating peas off a knife. The fact that someone is pained by another's action is not, in itself, enough to show that action to be unacceptable. Some people dislike seeing others smoking or holding hands.

If the flirt's motives are unblemished – it was simply an enjoyable way to pass an hour – the activity itself will have to be considered. There is, after all, a distinction between what is morally unacceptable and what is morally neutral but could be a vehicle for wrong-doing. Unfortunately, when sex is involved the lines between these two categories get easily blurred; the widespread suspicion that there is something wrong with sex bleeds into and colours people's attitudes to all sexual activity – even the most innocent. It may, then, be useful to look outside sex to make a vital distinction between the point of an activity and a person's motive in performing it.

The point of a game of chess is to checkmate the opposing player's king. It would not make any sense to talk of this being moral or immoral: it is simply the point of the game. But someone may play chess for motives that seem morally dubious – to win a bet, to humiliate the opponent, or even, as shown in a highly charged scene in The Thomas Crown Affair, to seduce them. In criticising the purpose behind the game one does not criticise the game itself. But compare chess to boxing. In that so-called Noble Art the aim is to hurt the opponent, and there are those who feel, with some justice, that this makes the sport unacceptable – whatever the boxers' motives in fighting each other.

The question, then, is whether flirting is morally like chess or like boxing. Is it an innocent activity that may be exploited? Or is it inherently iniquitous?

In a skilful flirtation there is a certain attractive playfulness

rin argues that a "flirt" who gives every appearance of wanting sex, but who does not actually intend to allow himself to be the other's source of sexual gratification, is nevertheless bound by duty to perform a sex act.' The other has reasonable grounds, it is claimed, to regard flirtation as a sincere offer of sex; simply to walk away after flirting is immoral.

Clearly, it would create havoc if every flirtatious encounter had to end in sex; if the alternative is immoral, however, it seems that flirting has to be given up. It is, after all, more like boxing than chess. But must we accept this conclusion?

The crux of Baumrin's objection is that flirtatious behaviour gives reasonable grounds for thinking sex has been offered. It is immoral, therefore, if the flirt refuses to, as it were, deliver. The emphasis on reasonable grounds is important here. Some rapists and High Court judges have apparently believed that a man's arousal is, in itself, reasonable grounds for thinking an offer of sex has been made. It is not. 'Let's make love' is, however. Baumrin is saying, then, that flirting is as much a commitment as a straight invitation.

Both flirting and the 'come-on' may stir the senses and arouse desire. But the straightforward invitation is unequivocal – there is no doubt where it is heading. Flirting, however, is essentially ambiguous: any behaviour that may be flirtatious – gazing into someone's eyes, touching a hand, leaning close – may in some other context be perfectly innocent. Perhaps she leaned so close because she was deaf, or he held her arm to stop her falling. This ambiguity makes it less than certain what, if anything, is being offered. For example, a friend told me of a dinner party at which, every time he looked up from his plate, his eyes met those of the woman opposite. She was a rather beautiful and very famous actress, so 'The blood stirred, my dear.' Being a modest fellow, he wondered at first if it was coincidence, or if she was transfixed by the obvious signs of dissipation on his face. Or had she realised that if you held his tie horizontal the pattern read 'Bullshit'? 'I couldn't believe she was entranced, so I played it very cool . . . and just as well I did. It turned out she was stoned. High as a kite . . . couldn't see a thing. At the end of the evening she thanked everyone for coming and apologised for the food: the hostess was furious!'

The moral of this tale is that a piece of behaviour can carry a variety of interpretations. In *Moralities of Everyday Life* Maury Sabini and John Silver point out that mutual eye contact can be coincidence (she was looking for Tom and caught Andy's eye instead); or a reaction (a sound made him turn to look at her); or deliberate (he is trying to communicate something). They add, 'What is important to the role of a caught eye in flirtation is that as commonsense actors we know that a caught eye could be any one of these.'

What is said and the way it is said can be just as ambiguous as behaviour. In 'Speaker's Reference and Semantic Reference' Saul Kripke elucidates the distinction between what words mean and what a speaker may mean in using those words. 'For example, one burglar says to another, "The cops are round the corner." What the words meant is clear: the police are around the corner. But the speaker may well have meant, "We can't wait around collecting any more loot. Let's split." That is not the meaning of the words, even on that occasion, though that is what he meant in saying those words.'

Exploiting the ambiguity, the Reverend Sydney Smith observed in his *Memoirs*, 'How can a Bishop marry? How can he flirt? The most he can say is "I will see you in the vestry after service." ' And clearly mean a great deal more. Of course, thinking of all those jokes about slap and tickle in the vestry, common ploys may through over-usage become as explicit as a straight invitation. For example, that hoary old chestnut 'Come up and see my etchings' and the more modern 'Would you like to come in for coffee?'. Not extending this invitation is the flirtatious thing to do; it keeps the issue unsettled.

Flirtation, then, is clouded in ambiguity – an ambiguity that hangs in the gap between what a person means by some word or action, and what that word or action usually means.

Why might anyone generate this ambiguity? Why flirt rather than come straight out with your intentions? Well . . . for one thing there may be good reasons for not declaring intentions. You may not have any beyond the moment: it is very pleasant to be able to strike a spark but you love your spouse and are committed to monogamy. The dalliance is delightful for its own sake, nothing more. Or you may have intentions but you have learned that what seems a very good idea on several gin and tonics can prove a woefully bad idea on tomorrow's hangover.

Flirting can be a very good holding operation, and anyway you need time to rehearse your ad-lib lines.

Of course, the veil of ambiguity in a flirtation may be a mere wisp away from transparency, but it is enough to allow initiatives to be launched and encouragements offered while keeping the lines of retreat wide open. This is the great charm of flirtation: interest is aroused, the sexual waters can be tested but nothing is guaranteed, no one has the right to expect anything. No one is entitled to feel aggrieved. The Baumrin/Vannoy objection to flirtation seems to be grounded in a confusion between flirting and teasing. The tease makes a commitment but has no intention of keeping it. Baumrin cites as an example of this the man who tells a woman he wants to make love to her then, when she takes him home, shakes her hand and leaves. If this was his intention all along – it was not that he simply lost the inclination – then he is a tease. But he is not a flirt, for flirts infuse their behaviour with ambiguity. They cannot reasonably be accused of wanting anything.

Ambiguity, then, is the essence of flirtation, and it is here that the explanation lies for the activity being regarded as more a woman's ploy than a man's. Women have not been encouraged to be 'up front' sexually; frank sexual invitations have been regarded as the privilege of men. Women have had to be oblique. It would be absurdly understated to describe Don Juan as a flirt. He was not. He was a seducer, and the seducer's actions tend towards sex: conquest is the desired culmination of all their efforts. It is possible, however, to flirt with someone in whom you have no sexual interest at all, for the goal of flirtation is not necessarily sex. You do not necessarily want intimacy; all you want is an acknowledgment that intimacy would be desirable.

It is this veiling of intentions that, in the past at least, made flirtation a suitable vehicle for women to use in order to test the sexual waters. Declaring intent would have been far too risky when women were meant to be the docile recipients of men's attentions. Now, of course, women are free to be more open, but it would be a pity if in this openness flirting were abandoned. It does, after all, have its own pleasures. It can be delightful to make just the right move to win recognition of one's charms. Flirting may be covert, but being 'an amphibious sort of harlot' can be fun.

_ 3 _
PROMISCUITY

'Everyone wants to be promiscuous – but no one knows how to justify it at dinner parties.' This comment – made at a dinner party – highlights the extent to which the morality regulating our sex lives can be inimical to our desires. What we want is often what we are not allowed to have. This schism may be due to the fact that our morals have largely been determined by celibate men of God and bachelor philosophers. The former have been dedicated to the world of the spirit, the latter to the pursuit of reason. In both cases the demands of the body tend to be given short shrift.

With the decay of traditional theology there has been a change in our beliefs about what is right and wrong in sex. Very few people would now regard it as a sin if a woman were not a virgin on her wedding night. But not all the old taboos and prohibitions have been abandoned: most of us still think adultery is immoral, and some still believe that only heterosexual sex is acceptable. Promiscuity tends to be thought of as morally on a par with adultery; it is difficult to justify it in moral terms. But how adequate are the reasons given for believing it to be morally unacceptable?

The traditional view was explained to me by a Church of England vicar, who said, 'God tells us we must be chaste before marriage and faithful afterwards. If you were promiscuous you would be disobeying God – and surely no one could be complacent about that.' Any god whom we would regard as worthy of worship is likely to be omniscient, and his judgments unassailable. If, then, He reveals his thoughts through specially privileged people everyone will know how it is morally best to behave. On that basis, we can formulate principles of right conduct which those who are disposed to be good will obey.

Given this, it would be odd, or would at least need explanation, if you failed to do as you knew you should. Of course, moral lapses are a common occurrence, for fallibility is central to human nature; a being immune to error would not be human. Nevertheless, some explanation is needed for moral weakness. Socrates offered an account of it in terms of ignorance. He thought if you did something wrong the error must have been the intellectual one of thinking it was right. If you really knew what you ought to do, could any power, he asked, be greater than knowledge to prevent you doing it?

But as Aristotle pointed out, this does not fit the facts of human experience: people often do what they believe to be wrong. The most common explanation is an inability to control desires. 'I couldn't help myself,' you say. When obligation confronts desire, the latter often triumphs. So any Christian, at least, who is not ignorant of God's will but is promiscuous is guilty of disobeying God because of a serious lack of self-control.

The immediate problem with this conclusion is that of interpreting God's thoughts – of knowing what strictures we ought to obey. Many people we think of as evil – like the Yorkshire Ripper in Britain, or Son of Sam in America – have claimed that God gave them clear instructions to kill their victims. Most of us would reject these claims as madness, and we do so on the basis of an image we have of God as suffused with love and tender concern: there is a *prima facie* case against such a person ordering brutal and bloody murders. One response to such a claim might be that we should not listen to 'voices' inside ourselves but to the voice of authority – the Church. But even within the Church there are disagreements about God's will. The vicar I quoted above, for example, rejects the Roman Catholic embargo on contraception on the grounds that unwanted births are a cause of misery and unhappiness, and not, therefore, something on which God would insist. So he accepts that even 'official' interpretations of God's thoughts may be mistaken. In attempting to distinguish between rival interpretations of God's thought, a sound criterion is our preconception of good and evil: if God is good, He cannot will evil. This allows us to judge right and wrong on our own account without reference to divine commandments. The question then becomes not, What does God think? but, Why should anyone think promiscuity is wrong? And the first stage in answering this is to establish what it means to say someone is promiscuous.

In *The Female Eunuch* Germaine Greer observed: 'nobody feels embarrassed about admitting disgust attendant on promiscuity . . . the kind of depression felt by men forced by circumstances to be more or less promiscuous, like travelling musicians, is really still the same old disgust.'

It is perhaps this sort of observation that led Frederick Elliston, a philosopher at Union College, New York, to wonder if the word 'promiscuity' has 'no descriptive content, but only emotive and/or hortatory force. On this view, to condemn a practice or person as promiscuous is simply to express feelings of disapproval, or to issue a prohibitive "Stop!" '

The theory in which a moral statement is a display of the speaker's feelings, and a recommendation of how to behave, is formally called the emotivist theory of ethics. Less formally, it is called the Boo/Hurrah theory. Words of disapproval are the equivalent of saying 'Boo', and words of approval the equivalent of 'Hurrah'. On this theory, to say that someone is promiscuous is not to give out any information about the person; it is just to say 'Boo' in a rather sophisticated way.

One consequence of this theory is that disagreements about moral judgments could be interminable. We know how to settle a dispute about facts; if one person says there are five birds in the tree and someone else says there are six we can go and count them. But how do we settle a dispute about moral evaluations when there is nothing behind them but a person's own likes and dislikes?

Fortunately, there is no need to grapple with this issue here, for Oxford philosopher, Philippa Foot, has shown that the correct criteria for applying evaluative words like 'promiscuous' are factual. Moral statements do more than just express feelings; they also give you facts – they describe the person or the behaviour being labelled. For example, 'He is rash' may mean 'I don't approve. Don't copy him.' But it also tells you, 'He knowingly takes great risks', and that is certainly factual. So, as Ms Foot argues, when certain facts obtain they are sufficient to show that epithets like 'rash' apply. What, then, are the facts that justify you calling someone promiscuous?

A homosexual I spoke to admitted, 'The homosexual scene is very promiscuous. Gays seem to be into one-night stands and casual relationships much more than straights. When I say I'm promiscuous I mean I have sex with a lot of men.' The first point to make is an obvious one: promiscuity is about having sex. It follows that the flirt and the tease – however many partners they engage with and however much you may disapprove – are not promiscuous, for they withhold themselves from actual consummation. The second point is that you cannot be promiscuous if you have sex only once.

I remember, when I was a teenager, a friend of mine lost her virginity on her first date with the boy she subsequently married. She sobbed all next morning. 'I'll never see him again – he'll never call me – boys don't like girls who are promiscuous.' She was right that in those days a lot of boys despised girls who were 'easy'. But 'easy' and 'promiscuous' are not synonymous, even though in practice they may be applied to the same people. You can be easy just once, but it is impossible to be promiscuous just once.

It is also impossible to be promiscuous with just one person, however often you have sex. If you enjoy daily sexual marathons with a lover there may be many ways to describe you – hyperactive, obsessive or perhaps enviable. But you could not rightly be described as promiscuous. If, however, you have occasional sex with several partners you might justly be called promiscuous.

There is a certain irony in this. 'Promiscuity' as a word smacks of unlimited sexual activity, and Russell Vannoy in *Sex Without Love* makes the extraordinary observation that a promiscuous person seems to be someone 'who is partaking of so much sex that it has become a bore to him; such a person is more like an over-indulgent eater than a sinner'. There is, of course, no reason to suppose that promiscuity is dull; nor that it is an over-indulgence. It is not about the number of sex acts you have, but the number of people you have them with. People who live together and enjoy each other may have more sex than one who is promiscuous. As one free-living man said to me, 'Married couples are supposed to have sex on average 3.4 times a week. I don't get as much as that but people tell me I'm promiscuous.'

What number of sexual partners makes you promiscuous? A friend of mine who is a doctor and worked for a while in a VD clinic said, 'I asked a man who had clap who his contacts were. It turned out that in one week's honeymoon he'd had four women and three men. *That*'s promiscuous.' Seven people in one week does surely qualify as promiscuous. But what about seven people in a lifetime?

Elliston points out that any number you select is bound to be arbitrary, for 'even if a clear line could be drawn the question would immediately arise: Why draw it there, for what is the criterion for assessing the number of liaisons that suffice to justify the judgment "promiscuous"?' It is rather like asking how many grains make a heap of sand. You can recognise a heap when you see one but a single grain is not a heap, and neither are two or three or four grains. At what point, as you add each one, do you agree that *this* number makes it a heap?

Most people I spoke to believed that 'serial monogamy' was not promiscuous even if there had been many partners. As one woman said, 'I wouldn't call Elizabeth Taylor promiscuous just because she's married so often. She may be promiscuous for all I know – but it isn't because of all those husbands. Getting married or living together is a commitment; promiscuity is more hit and run.'

When people talk about 'commitment' in sexual relationships they are invariably referring to a commitment to sexual exclusivity – fidelity. Exclusivity is, of course, incompatible with promiscuity, for all the person's interest is focused on one, and only one, other. This is not to say that an intention to be faithful is a guarantee of fidelity. As Roger Scruton points out in *Sexual Desire*, the habit of fidelity ' . . . is easily broken, and the temptation to break it is contained in desire itself – in the element of generality which tempts us always to experiment, to verify, to detach ourselves from that which is too familiar in the interest of excitement and risk.' Nevertheless, where there is commitment, there is at least the intention to be faithful.

The promiscuous person has no such intention: he or she feels free to seek excitement and risk, to have sex with any other consenting adult no matter what other relationships exist. The extreme case is Don Juan. He puts everything of himself into the process of seduction; but the act itself is both the culmination of this process and the end of desire. He has no further use for his victim, and any further desire will be for her successor. Sex is severed from any idea of long-term attachment; rather, it is a means of attaining novelty. Kierkegaard painted a portrait of an almost psychopathic seducer in the last section of *Either/Or*. This *Diary of a Seducer* is the story of Johannes's carefully planned seduction of the young Cordelia. The process lasts several months and ends on the night of its culmination. It is the essence of Johannes's posture that he remain controlled and uncommitted.

To infer from this, however, that someone who is promiscuous invariably 'hits and runs' is rather like assuming that someone who is not God-fearing is a devil-worshipper. The two extremes – lifelong monogamy and a series of one-off acts of sexual conquest – do not exhaust the possibilities. The most promiscuous man I knew had relationships that lasted for some time. And when they were over it was not always at his instigation. All that promiscuity entails is, in Elliston's words, a 'refusal to issue promissory notes for affection and support throughout an indefinite future'. It follows that promiscuity is logically compatible with having some commitments to a partner. For instance, the promiscuous man may be deeply committed to protecting his partner from risk of pregnancy. Or, if that seems selfish, he may commit himself to making his relationships as mutually pleasurable as possible.

One reason people seem to assume that all commitment is incompatible with promiscuity is that commitment involves self-control – something, it is believed, that promiscuous people most signally lack. Thus Peter Bertocci, author of *The Human Venture in Sex, Love and Marriage*, argues that sex outside marriage is a sure indicator of a lack of self-discipline in people whose desires are running out of control. A similar sentiment was expressed to a promiscuous friend – rather more colourfully. 'I was having a pee – standing next to a mate – contemplating the member as men do in those situations. Bob suddenly said, "The difference between us is that my cock works for me – you have to work for your cock." ' The charge that is being levelled in this unsubtle observation is that the promiscuous person has been in some sense mastered by the body. The injunction that sex is permissible only within a certain framework – marriage or monogamy – is an attempt to reconcile the opposing forces of mind and body. If the body is not disciplined then it has, as it were, won the war. St Augustine saw sexual desire as a witness to our being in thrall to the flesh: to be promiscuous was to be completely vanquished by the flesh.

Clearly, if the promptings of the moment dictate your actions then there can be no commitments from you, for this involves self-restraint for the sake of projects that go beyond the moment. Suppose you commit yourself to an exclusive rela-tionship with someone. In making that commitment you have taken on an obligation that whatever desires you may have tomorrow or the next day will be restrained if satisfying them would conflict with exclusivity. But if your desires invariably trump your obligations – rather than, as with most of us, occasionally trump them – then you cannot sincerely make commitments for you are not able to control your wants. You have, as they say, no self-control; you always give in to the desire of the moment. It is interesting that Kierkegaard described Don Juan as living solely in the present, in a series of disconnected moments ' . . . in that he constantly finishes, and constantly begins again from the beginning, for his life is the sum of repellent moments which have no coherence'. Because Don Juan focuses his energies on sexual conquest he immerses himself in the present moment, disregarding both past and future. There is no commitment beyond what is necessary to win the present object of desire. This is Bertocci's model of the promiscuous person: confronted by desire, he or she must always act for the present, never for the future; thus there is no commitment to any project beyond the here and now, and so no self-restraint.

But is promiscuity really like that? If you are not on a diet, then there is nothing uncontrolled in eating cream buns, for lack of control crucially involves an inability to do what you believe you ought to do. This is weakness of will, what the

Ancient Greeks called 'akrasia', literally 'not being strong enough – to control yourself'. A friend described it as 'lots of will power; no won't power'. We all display it sometimes, for our everyday moral code is packed with principles and ideals we do not always succeed in fulfilling. As Hume wryly observed, ' 'tis one thing to know virtue and another to conform the will to it'. But suppose you find yourself in a situation in which there is no particular thing you believe you ought to do – nothing you believe you should conform your will to. Then failing to do so is not lack of self-control.

Don Juan was not fleeing, out of control, from a set of principles he believed he should – if only he could – uphold; he had no principles. Indeed, Mozart's Don Giovanni never addressed himself to the issue at all until the Commendatore's statute forced it on him. Similarly, Kierkegaard's seducer Johannes has only one obvious aim, which is the pursuit of 'the perfect moment'. He is capable of planning and self-control to achieve that moment, but he has no sense at all of moral principles to which he should conform. As with Don Juan, the notion of his displaying lack of control is inapposite. It is just a mistake to blame people for not displaying self-restraint because they fail to act according to principles they reject.

I find it interesting that, against a background of constant exhortations to display sexual control, popular culture tells us *lack* of control can be an indication that you have found your ideal mate. Bodice-ripper romances are full of men and women battling unsuccessfully with the passion of the moment. The 'Mills and Boon' hero groans: 'You drove me to a pitch no woman has ever done before. I've always prided myself on my self-control – I can't trust myself where you're concerned.' When the heroine stops preening herself on the devastation wrought by her sexual powers, she too finds all resolve turned to water. 'She arched her body to press against him – all control gone she was aware of nothing but his hands caressing the contours of her bare body.'

However disinclined you may be to sink into the state of feverish passion encouraged by this titillating mush, it is obvious that self-control in sex may be self-defeating both physically and emotionally. As a sex therapist explained to me:

'Some people are determined to be in control at all costs, and that can be terribly damaging in sex. We see men who cannot reach climax because they cannot risk being out of control. And this has its emotional counterpart – people stay locked up because they're terrified of emotional abandonment.'

As Bertrand Russell pointed out, self-control is not in itself desirable. In *Marriage and Morals* he argued for our institutions and moral conventions 'to be such as to make the need for self-control a minimum rather than a maximum. The use of self-control is like the use of brakes on a train. It is useful when you find yourself going in the wrong direction, but merely harmful when the direction is right.' If, then, you have done your moral groundwork properly and established a set of principles to act by, self-control will help you to keep to them. So anyone who thinks that morality demands monogamy will also demand that control is exercised in deciding when and with whom to have sex. Only within the appropriate relationship may restraints be loosened. There is no reason to suppose that the promiscuous person is incapable of this first stage of control. Given good reason he or she might be as controlled as any could wish. The point is that monogamy is not regarded by the promiscuous as good reason.

Closely allied to the view that promiscuity entails lack of self-control is the idea that promiscuous behaviour is essentially indiscriminate. Webster's dictionary defines promiscuity as 'engaging in sexual intercourse indiscriminately'. Clearly, if you are indiscriminate and say yes to everything on offer, you are not exercising self-control. But does promiscuity entail lack of discrimination?

Even someone we would unhesitatingly describe as promiscuous may discriminate against animals, members of the family other than the spouse, the very young and the very old. In Mozart's opera, Don Giovanni fails to recognise Donna Elvira, whom he has seduced, and desires her again. When he realises who she is, he flees the scene. So even he discriminates against those he has already enjoyed. It makes no sense to accuse the promiscuous of not discriminating at all.

In *Sexual Morality*, Ronald Atkinson describes what he calls the 'Western norm': 'Sexual relations shall be exclusively heterosexual and . . . no sexual activity shall take place outside

monogamous unions which are, intentionally at least, life-
long.' The charge, then, may be that one who is promiscuous
fails to discriminate according to this norm. And this is
certainly true; there is nevertheless no valid inference from 'He
has sex with many others' to 'He has sex with any others'. The
truth that promiscuous people do not apply a certain rule is
stretched into the falsehood that they apply no rules.

Discrimination need not be just an accident of taste – like
preferring blondes to brunettes. It may be moral discrimination.
One woman told me, 'I never get involved with married men or
those who have steady relationships. I'm not interested in
making commitments myself but I think if you do you should
stick to them. So I'm not going to be part of breaking them.'

Promiscuous people are as likely as any others to operate
moral restraints and to be discriminate. Anyone who thinks
that promiscuity entails satisfying sexual desire with anyone –
whatever age, sex or type, without regard to any morality at all
– is guilty of the same kind of hysterical overstatement as those
Victorians who seriously suggested that if you masturbated you
showed yourself to be prepared to indulge in any kind of
physical or mental debauchery.

This point about moral restraints is important, for some
people think if there are no restraints on numbers there are no
restraints at all. One woman, for example, argued, 'Isn't the
thing about promiscuity that people don't abide by ordinary
sexual taboos?' This is making too much out of too little;
someone who is promiscuous may abide by many taboos –
against rape, incest, paedophilia, adultery or bisexuality.
The only taboo he or she necessarily disregards is the taboo
against plurality. To call someone promiscuous, then, does not
mean that they are uncontrolled, indiscriminate or amoral
about sex. It simply means that in sexual relationships the
person offers no guarantee of exclusivity and so may have any
number of lovers. There is no intention to establish a single,
life-long relationship.

In *The Wanderer and His Shadow* Nietzsche asks why a girl
who has surrendered her virginity to a man before marriage
should be considered immoral. He argues: 'the reproach is
really directed against disobedience: it is this that is immoral

. . . One says of her: she could not control herself, that is why she was disobedient against the mores . . . The mores are then seen to demand that one bear the displeasure of unsatisfied desire, that the desire be able to wait.'

The person who is promiscuous is one who wants the pleasure of sex without having to abide by the rule that sex is appropriate only within a monogamous relationship: he or she disregards the 'Western norm'. Is Nietzsche right to state that it is this disobedience which earns reproach – that strong reactions to promiscuity are simply reactions to the violation of the code?

This is important, for it has been argued – by Kant, for example – that an unqualified commitment to obey commands is not appropriate for a truly moral agent. James Rachels has even argued, in the paper 'God and Human Attitudes', that obedience to God is inappropriate, for 'to be a moral agent is to be an autonomous or self-directed agent'. It follows that no system of moral conventions can demand the right of obedience; if disobedience is the reproach levelled at one who is promiscuous, the reproach is wrong-headed.

Russell pointed out that those of us who have been encouraged to believe that we have a right to veto the action of others in the name of virtue will 'undoubtedly find it difficult to forgo the exercise of this agreeable form of persecution. It may even be impossible.' Nevertheless, he urged us all to abstain from interfering in the way others lead their lives, out of respect for their personality and freedom. The one proviso is that what is done does not hurt others.

The familiar image of the promiscuous person, however, is of someone who does hurt others – who is feckless, unreliable and deceitful. Promises are made and never kept; love is avowed and never meant. It is lies, lies, all the way. If there were a logical tie between promiscuity and violating the rights of others to respect and consideration, there would be a *prima facie* case against it. But does promiscuity necessarily involve such behaviour?

One woman I spoke to thought it did – because of the pressures involved. 'The woman who screws around is still thought of as – well – sinful, I suppose; that's bound to predispose you to lie.' There are still people ready to condemn the sexually free woman, even though they applaud Don Juan. What woman is going to risk being honest about what she wants if people will think she is a tart? The psychologist John Nicholson agrees: 'As long as sex was thought of as an essentially masculine preoccupation, each act of sexual intercourse could be regarded as a small victory for the male partner, since he had "persuaded" the woman to cooperate in a venture likely to bring him more pleasure than her.' If the prevailing ethos dictates that women should *not* have free sex while men *should*, then there is bound to be subterfuge, for the woman who admits she wants sex without strings risks social opprobrium; the man who admits he wants the same risks not getting the sex.

Circumstances, then, may encourage underhand dealings. If you read in the standard rule book that promiscuous people are defiled by their activities, or that it is diminishing to be one of several rather than a chosen one, those who are promiscuous and so need the cooperation of others may dissemble. If you want something badly and it is on the black market then you are likely to break the law to get it. But this is no ground for inferring that promiscuity *necessarily* involves such behaviour. Some people, after all, are honest whatever the cost in social condemnation. Socrates gave his life rather than be false to himself.

Suppose though that, for those of us who are not morally heroic, the cost is so great that we feel unable to be open about promiscuity. These lies are not the fault of the activity; they are the fault of the repression. If you are confronted with the equation 'promiscuity + the prevailing moral code = deception' you have the option of changing *either* side of the equation. That is to say, to do away with deceptions you may choose to eradicate promiscuity or you may loosen up the code. And it would need further argument to determine which you should choose; the argument from deception is not in itself sufficient.

Of course, even in an atmosphere of freedom promiscuous people may lie: some people just do. But this will not give you an argument against promiscuity itself. Just about every human activity has been the vehicle of lies for some people – marriage, religion, politics, parenthood. If you insist that because some people lie the activity they engage in must be eradicated, all human life would grind to a halt. And that is as absurd as supposing that because deception is immoral any activity in which deception has been practised is immoral.

Even if lying is not necessarily a part of promiscuity, some people believe that exploitation is. L.M. Starkey, author of *James Bond's World of Values*, has argued that promiscuity entails treating people as 'a thing', a sexual organ or function to be used quite separately from the rest of their personality. He goes on, 'Every individual must be treated as an end rather than as a means or an accessory to an end.'

Starkey's maxim is similar to that formulated by Kant: 'Act in such a way that you never treat humanity, either in your own person or in the person of others, as a means only, but always equally as an end.' For Kant, a person is a means or an end only in relation to some plan that has been put into practice. To be a means is to be used as a tool to achieve the aims of the plan; to be an end is to be one who cannot be used only as a link in the chain of another's desires. For everyone has his own plan, and so has a claim not be treated merely as a tool. To treat someone only as a means to an end is therefore morally unacceptable. 'Man and every rational being exists as an end in itself, not merely as means for arbitrary use by this will or that.'

It is interesting to note a crucial difference between Kant's formulation of the maxim and Starkey's. Kant insists that we must never treat a person *only* as a means to an end. 'Only' is the vital word here – one that Starkey misses out. If you could never treat a person as a means to satisfy some desire of yours then you could never order food from a waiter, ask for treatment from a doctor or indeed procure any service at all. But Kant was not postulating anything so stringent; he was simply insisting that when you do use a person as a means you also recognise that they are a person. You must recognise, for example, that the waiter has his own hopes and desires and that these must be respected; it is only if you treat him as nothing more than your instrument that you have violated Kant's principle – and only then are you exploiting him.

Does it follow from someone wanting uncommitted sex that they are bound to use the other person only as a means to satisfy those desires? Surely not. It is perfectly possible to respect your partner, to take account of their needs and wants, and not wilfully to interfere with their way of life. You do not have to be committed to lifetime exclusivity to treat your lover as a person. One woman agreed and offered me her own account of what it is to be treated as a person. 'My husband was not promiscuous – but he exploited me in bed. He never gave a damn about my pleasure. All he wanted was to get his leg over – his phrase, not mine – when it suited him. Now Tim, who's as promiscuous as they come, does think about me. Hell – I'm not exploited – he's the only man I've ever known who will suck my nipples till I come . . . it takes about twenty minutes!'

If any relationship between the sexes has been exploitative it has been marriage. Emile Durkheim's conclusion that women lose more and gain less from the institution than men has been shored up by a substantial body of research. Yet despite the obvious and by now well chronicled horrors that can deform a marriage, people do not make the same kinds of mistake in arguing about this institution as they do in arguing about activities like promiscuity. If promiscuous people do inconsiderate or callous things people enthusiastically leap to the conclusion that promiscuity is immoral. But from the equally true observation that married people perpetrate horrors on each other they do not infer that marriage is immoral. Nor should they, for the inference would be illegitimate. It seems that fears about sexual freedom oil the wheels of bad reasoning and encourage prejudice.

One particular piece of prejudice was exposed by a woman who asked me: 'How can you trust someone who is not committed to you? And if you can't trust him – how do you have a relationship?' If you are asked to give your reasons for trusting someone you may say your trust is blind. In which case it is irrational and you may be able to trust someone whatever they are like. Or you may point to certain qualities the person has that make for trustworthiness. A general may say he trusts his soldiers because they are loyal; an employer may say he trusts his staff because they are honest. People, then, may be trustworthy for different reasons. Also, because everyone is such a complicated mixture of qualities you may trust a person in one direction but not in another. A friend of mine says she would trust her husband in a brothel – he would never be unfaithful to her – but she would not trust him in a betting-shop; he can never resist blowing every penny he has on a good tip.

To say that a promiscuous person is not to be trusted is to say that they have none of the qualities that make for trustworthiness. This has to be a mistake; a promiscuous person may be perfectly honest about what they want, and since being honest is a good reason to be trusted, such a person merits trust. Promiscuous lovers may phone when they say they will, always turn up on time and never abandon you at parties for fresh fields. They may, in short, be trustworthy. Of course, you cannot trust them not to take another to bed; but then, if they have been honest they never said you could. In which case, to say you cannot trust your promiscuous lover because of their refusal to guarantee fidelity to you is as daft as saying you cannot trust someone because they emphatically and sincerely insisted they were going to Liverpool when you wanted them to go to Manchester. Of course, the person who is promiscuous may not be honest. If they swear eternal fidelity to you – and all their other lovers – then you cannot trust what they say. But that is because of dishonesty, not because of promiscuity.

John Stuart Mill set out this principle of liberty: 'the only purpose for which power can be rightfully exercised over any member of a civilised community against his will, is to prevent harm to others.' Mill was arguing that as long as people observe basic moral rules against deliberately harming others they should be left free to live according to their own individual plan of life. Since promiscuous people may very well obey such rules, there seems no reason at all to condemn them.

Mill also argued that a person should aim for the 'highest and most harmonious development of his powers to a complete and consistent whole'. In all sorts of areas – clothes, work, leisure – diversity and the freedom to experiment are recognised as vital to this development. Now a promiscuous person is one who grasps the freedom to enjoy a wide range of sexual partners, and this encourages Elliston to suggest that, from the standpoint of Mill's liberalism, 'promiscuity may increase the pleasures of individuals, enhance the cultivation of their higher faculties and enrich society with the ensuing institution'. In an area as crucial as sex, should we not be allowed the same scope for development as in other areas?

AIDS immediately gives a reason for saying 'no'. There have always been health risks attached to promiscuity, but this new and deadly virus is a risk to life: unless there is some dramatic – and unexpected – medical breakthrough, no one who contracts AIDS will survive.

It would be less than convincing to argue, however, that promiscuity is immoral *because* it is dangerous. Bomb disposal is also dangerous, but who would insist that this makes it morally unacceptable? Of course, bravely taking risks for the safety of others might be said to be morally different from taking risks for the sake of self-regarding pleasure. Yet anyone who adopts this line must in consistency be prepared to consider that other dangerous activities such as mountaineering and racing driving – which are also indulged in for pleasure – are morally indistinguishable from promiscuity. Few people are likely to accept that.

The risks in promiscuous behaviour can be reduced. Dr John Oates, Senior Consultant at Westminster Hospital, told me that, 'AIDS is transmitted by the virus being introduced into the blood-stream. In sex that most usually happens through infected semen being transferred to a partner who has abrasions – most commonly in the anal passage but also in the vagina, for example, at the neck of the womb. Once the virus is in contact with damaged areas it gets into the blood-stream and the partner is infected. The risk is obviously going to be reduced if the active partner uses a condom to prevent the semen getting into his partner.'

Of course, those who are promiscuous are a risk, not only to themselves, but to others. It would certainly be quite immoral for those who have many partners to hide their promiscuity. It is one thing to take risks yourself – another to impose them on others. If someone chooses to be promiscuous and is honest with prospective partners, we may certainly point out that he or she is greatly imprudent. It would need considerably more argument, however, to show that what was unsafe was immoral.

Even if there were no risks in promiscuity it would not follow that it is advisable for us all of the time. Temporary, uncommitted relationships may have their value, but I believe that in the end commitment may have more to offer. As one friend said, 'I went through a phase of being promiscuous – and I loved every minute of it. But in the end I wanted something with more depth – it's lovely to keep travelling but in the end you want to arrive somewhere.'

_4_

ADULTERY

God had no doubts about adultery. 'Thou shalt not,' He said. For those who have no doubts about God there is an end to the matter; adultery is wrong. Hence, Thomas Aquinas argued, 'Matrimony is natural for man and promiscuous performance of the sexual act, outside matrimony, is contrary to man's good. For this reason it must be a sin.' St Augustine concurred, sternly observing, 'For adultery and fornication are evils.'

This is not a uniquely Christian morality. In traditional Jewish law adultery was a crime punishable by death, while three centuries before Christ Aristotle pointed out that if you describe an act as a sex act your description is morally neutral, but if you describe the same act as adultery you have condemned it. Adultery is morally like murder: in Aristotle's words, 'such things imply by their names that they are themselves evil. It is not possible ever to be right with regard to them; one must always be wrong.'

This general conviction has so permeated our thinking that many people consider it pointless to discuss the issue. It is noticeable that in recent discussions about the legal enforcement of morals the focus has been on whether adultery should be illegal – as it is in some states of America – not on whether it is immoral. Adultery carries its immorality in its name. Bertrand Russell suggested that the immense weight of moral reprobation carried by the word made it impossible for people to think clearly on the subject. He advised sacrificing colour for clarity and employing 'dull, neutral phrases, such as "extra-marital sexual relations" '. The question then is, do we really have good reason to believe that if a married person voluntarily has extra-marital sexual relations a crime has been committed?

One strong argument for adultery being immoral is that it involves deception, and deception is *prima facie* wrong. As one woman told me, 'The only way you can have an affair and stay married is if you deceive your partner. That's a pretty nasty way to treat someone who's given you trust and love.' Most people will accept that lying is immoral, yet few of those same people would have the nerve to be honest about any extra-marital shenanigans. So, like a warped shadow of love and marriage, adultery and duplicity seem inevitably to go together. Indeed, the eighteenth-century deist William Wollaston thought this sour duo were inseparable. He insisted that sexual coupling graphically represents the protagonists as man and wife; if either is married to someone else this is equivalent to telling a lie. Lies are immoral, *ergo* adultery is immoral.

In the 'old days' of course, a couple wishing to share a room had to register at hotels as 'Mr and Mrs', so they were indeed representing themselves as married. But the act of adultery itself is not obviously this sort of lie. Wollaston's contemporary, the philosopher David Hume, pointed out that if the immorality of adultery consisted in lying about marital relations, then adultery kept under wraps would not be immoral. An untruth uttered in an empty room, with no intention to deceive anyone, is not, after all, a lie. Sexual activity would become a lie only if the lovers invited spectators to view the consummation. Hume might have added – if he had known about such things – that if any couple did this it would be more rational to regard them as actors in a pornographic movie than as husband and wife.

Most of us will gag on a further consequence of Wollaston's theory: all sex outside marriage is on a moral par with adultery. Unmarried men and women openly and honestly enjoying their sexual freedom would be 'representing' themselves as married to their partners; they would be committing a sin as heinous as adulterous spouses covertly slipping into their lovers' beds. Wollaston must surely have it wrong; if adultery is immoral it is not because of some theory about misrepresentation.

Wollaston's story is ingenious, but no more so than those told by the average adulterer trying to keep peccadillos hidden. So much more brilliance has gone into the the web of evasion than into any other sexual activity that it is sometimes hard not to be impressed by tactics – and harder not to sound pompous moralising about them. Nevertheless, deceptions are wrong; like physical violence, they are quite incompatible with a loving relationship.

Of course, however shoddy it may seem, errant spouses may justify a deception as the lesser of two evils. Telling lies is certainly an evil, but telling the truth may have unacceptable consequences: the deceived spouse would be badly hurt. As one man I spoke to observed, 'Lies are demoralising for everyone. But honesty can sometimes be worse.' Kant argued, however, that even a benevolent lie is wrong, for we have a duty to tell the truth quite irrespective of the consequences.

For most of us, Kant's rigorous approach may seem unappealing. Once someone is embroiled in an affair there may be no easy answers about whether or not to be honest. Lies can be looked at from two perspectives – from that of the deceiver and from that of the victim. From the perspective of the victim the 'humane fiction' may seem like a form of coercion, for a lie makes someone believe what is false and so encourages the dupe to act in other ways than if the truth had been known. When this happens it makes the case against adultery an easy one.

Are lying and adultery necessarily linked, even if, typically, they go together? Ideally, marriage combines a number of features – openness, trust and a wide range of reciprocal obligations – and adultery does tend to be inconsistent with at least the first two of these. You cannot be completely open with your spouse if what you have described as vital negotiations in the corridors of power are scurrilous goings-on in the corridors of discreet hotels.

Suppose, however, that a husband and wife have agreed that in certain circumstances extra-marital sex is acceptable. Bertrand Russell considered a situation in which a man had to be away on business for a number of months on end. Both he and his wife, Russell suggested, would find it hard to remain faithful throughout this time; yet, he argued, this should be no barrier to their happiness and no grounds for deception. 'Each party should be able to put up with such temporary fancies as are always liable to occur, provided the underlying affection remains intact.' A businessman told me that he has precisely this agreement with his wife. 'I travel on business a great deal – and of course I have affairs. But I don't lie to my wife about them – that would be sordid. She knows what I do and it doesn't fuss her.'

Since it is possible for adultery to happen with the full knowledge of a complaisant partner, it does not necessarily involve deception and therefore cannot be condemned on these grounds. It might be argued, however, that even if there is no crude deception about the actual occurrence of adultery there is a more subtle and pervasive kind of lie that is a feature of extra-marital sex. In 'Is Adultery Immoral?' Richard Wasserstrom observes that for the culture in which he grew up there was an important correlation between sexual intimacy and feelings of love and affection. Sexual behaviour 'meant a great deal concerning one's feelings for persons of the opposite sex in whom one was most interested and with whom one was most involved'. It was, he adds, 'among the most authoritative ways in which one could communicate to another the nature and degree of one's affections'. If, as he says, 'this sketch is even roughly right', sex is a way of telling someone that you care. It would follow that, in adultery, 'Deception is inevitable ... because the feelings of affection that ought to accompany any act of sexual intercourse can only be held toward one other person at any given time in one's life.'

Wasserstrom has highlighted a conviction that surprisingly many people share, the conviction that sex means love. Taking someone to bed is more than a sign of physical attraction; it is a sign of deep emotion. A friend of mine, for example, once had an affair with a truck driver whose taciturnity about his emotions drove her to the folly of asking if he loved her. He replied, 'Course I love you. Fuck you, don't I?' On this assumption adultery must either be loveless, in which case it is an ugly deception for the 'other' man or woman – an implicit declaration of a love that is not there; or, if it is loving, an indication that there is no love left in the marriage. Either way, the adulterer is deceiving someone and so what is done is immoral.

There are two weak seams in the fabric of this argument. First, it must be obvious that sex is not necessarily a declaration of love. How could any but the deeply perverse see love in a rape, for example? Admittedly, there are people for whom sex does carry a special message, but this is a matter of individual psychology, not a fact about sex. It is perfectly possible to desire someone you do not even like. Adultery, then, would not be a deception if the partners saw sex as, for example, a way of assuaging need.

But maybe morality demands that sex should be kept for the one you love, that loveless sex is immoral. Even if this were true – and heaven knows why anyone should think so – this does not make adultery immoral. A woman may fall out of love with her husband and in love with another man. Sex with her lover would not be wrong; but sex with her husband would be, which seems absurd.

The second weakness is that even if sex were seen as the expression of love there need be no deception in adultery. For it must be a mistake to think that love is necessarily exclusive. It is possible – indeed it happens – that a person may have feelings of love and affection for more than one other. With both the spouse and the adulterous partner sex will be a genuine expression of those feelings.

Some people I spoke to think the immorality of adultery consists less in the lies and more in the breaking of a very important promise: the promise of sexual exclusivity. Lies are simply an excrescence on the basic offence. As one woman said, 'The vows you make in the marriage ceremony are the most important promises you can ever make. It's dreadful to think of them being broken.'

A promise is the strongest form of commitment there is. It is so strong, indeed, that we use the word 'promise' in threats: 'If you don't do this I promise you'll be sorry.' Promises bind our future behaviour and so generate expectations in others.

A promise is also one way we have of making people act as we want them to. If someone says, 'I promise', then you are entitled to say, 'You must do it . . . you promised.' Promises made in the marriage ceremony are particularly poignant because they are typically made out of love and need. Because the lovers command each other's affections they want exclusivity, and they may ask and be given the promise of it. There are, of course, promises from which even a small amount of inconvenience may exempt you – solemn commitments are comparatively rare. But this is one reason why when they are made, as in marriage, they achieve a certain prominence. Anyone who wilfully breaks a promise simply through expedience deserves reproach, and the more solemn the commitment the greater the reproach.

Human ingenuity is, of course, adept at producing excuses for such backsliding. One friend was assured by an errant husband, 'I would never have touched her if she hadn't reminded me so much of you.' Sometimes the excuse even carries conviction. One man told me, 'When we'd had the children my wife seemed to think I should put my penis away with my cricket bat – toys I was too grown up to go on playing with.' Fidelity to a spouse who never wanted sex with you would be a degree of moral heroism beyond most of us. But the typical case of adultery is not a response to such deprivation. It is usually that familiarity has dulled, if not entirely obliterated, the thrills of marital sex.

But even though people do have affairs it does not necessarily mean that they have utterly abandoned their promise of sexual exclusivity – that it is, for them, quite empty. In typical adultery the promise is still thought of as being in force; the adulterous spouse is bound by the promise even if they are breaking it. This is one reason why adultery is so strenuously kept from the partner: few adulterers would respond with 'So what?' when found out. Usually they acknowledge that they have acted wrongly, and are committed not to do it again. The situation is similar to that of the priest who breaks his vow of celibacy. He does not see himself as no longer bound by his promise to God; he was tempted beyond his power to resist, and must now begin to live by his promise again.

If a married couple released each other from the promise of exclusivity – they neither gave nor expected it – then there would be no broken promises and no need for lies; adultery would be stripped clean of its unsavoury trappings. By the above arguments it would follow that there was nothing wrong with it: extra-marital sexual relations would be morally neutral.

Many people believe, however, that adultery constitutes a threat to marriage, and that this is what makes it morally unacceptable. As one woman explained to me, 'If you can get sex outside marriage, it's bound to undermine it. And anything that undermines something as valuable as marriage must be immoral.'

The Christian attitude to marriage is grounded in St Paul's dislike of the institution as anything other than an expedient. For him, the satisfaction of sexual desire was likely to reduce one's chances of reaping heavenly rewards. Anyone who burned with desire, however, could marry. Marriage, then, was a way of controlling anarchic desires, and this made it a very powerful institution, for it became the only sanctioned pathway to the intense gratification that sex affords. If you may have sex only with a spouse, then marriage becomes highly desirable. Further, you are likely to be dependent on your spouse, who provides a delicious pleasure that cannot legitimately be taken elsewhere.

Like St Paul, Kant allowed only one condition under which sex was acceptable, and that was within non-adulterous marriage. For him, sex was essentially manipulative, and could be transformed into a morally acceptable union only by marriage. 'Matrimony is the only condition in which use can be made of one's sexuality.' Marriage begins to look rather as the sole supply of alcohol must look to an ardent drinker. Clearly, if other sources of supply open up, then the importance of marriage will be diminished and marital bonds loosened.

But even if marriage is desirable it does not follow that what threatens it is immoral. It is often said, for example, that a woman's career threatens marriage, but no one could seriously argue that it is immoral for a woman to have a career. Similarly, a recent survey of divorce claimed that there was a high failure rate in marriages where the wife is better educated than the husband. But no one would think that because a woman's education can undermine marriage it is immoral. It may even be better for a woman to be educated – with a smaller chance of finding a suitable mate – than to be kept 'unlettered and unlearned' simply in order to have a better chance. Similarly, it may be better for people to be open to a wide variety of sexual partners and not marry than to marry and be deprived of delightful opportunities. As far as logic goes, the options are wide open!

*

Logic, however, is not all there is to it. There is also a widespread and pervasive view that monogamous marriage is essential to the well-being of the next generation. An impressive array of thinkers have upheld and propounded this view. John Locke, for instance, criticised Rousseau's vision of the state of nature with the reflection that marriage is necessary for the survival of the species; accordingly, no state of nature can reasonably be envisaged that does not suppose the existence of the nuclear family. Schopenhauer argued that love and marriage were the means by which the species chose to manipulate the individual for its own survival. He observed, 'Happy marriages are known to be rare just because it lies in the nature of marriage that its chief end is not the present but the coming generation.' And Spinoza, in the seventeenth century, concurred with the view that it is 'a love of begetting children and wisely educating them' that makes marriage a rational choice.

It is hardly surprising that the picture of Daddy Bear, Mummy Bear and the 2·4 Baby Bears is so much a part of our culture that few of us can imagine any other way of begetting and raising children. It also seems to be unassailably true that if children are to be well adjusted they need two parents and the security of a settled environment. And it must surely be of benefit to children to be brought up in a happy atmosphere at home. This is not likely to happen if, however officially together the parents may be, one sleeps somewhere else most nights. Adultery in this form is a recipe for misery – for everyone. By fiat, then, it may seem that monogamous marriage is the best way to raise children – to look after the future generation – so that whatever undermines this is immoral.

The utopian views of philosophers, who were usually bachelors, tend not to capture the reality of marriage and family. Some of the most neurotic, disturbed people one can meet are the product of the respectably married. Indeed, the prevalence of child-abuse by parents shows that even if family life has a potential for great good it also has the potential to be very damaging. No one could intelligibly claim, then, that monogamous marriage is a sufficient condition of happy, healthy children.

These sorts of consideration have led people to suggest that, as small, self-contained nuclear families are so adept at breeding hang-ups, repressions and complexes, they should be replaced by extended families. In The Female Eunuch, for example, Germaine Greer savaged the small family as the spawning ground for obsessive dependencies. This was not an attack on monogamy itself so much as on one undesirable setting for it. But the distinction is sometimes obscured, and a successful attack on the nuclear family is assumed also to tell against monogamous marriage.

The Canadian philosopher John McMurty insists that the nuclear family 'actually inhibits the achievement' of 'a loving context for child-upbringing'. He believes that this loving context can be achieved only within some kind of commune – and that communes are incompatible with monogamy. They are not, of course: the kibbutz in Israel and the extended families of London's East End both satisfy the requirements for communal life, yet both are compatible with monogamy.

It is difficult to tell whether monogamous marriage is or is not the best setting in which to rear children, because the issue is muddied by the way people live family life. A couple living in a little box in a crowded city may be bound to produce maladjusted children. But even in an extended family it may be much better for a child to have the security of parents who are committed to each other to the exclusion of others.

Suppose, though, that the results of social experiment proved that it is psychologically possible for us to live in a society in which there was no sexual exclusivity . . . and that we would all be much happier. Marriage as it now is, the report would say, is not the best rearing ground for children. It is preferable that the young are taught to be warm and expansive to as many people as possible; monogamy is too cramping. There is, then, nothing wrong with adultery – indeed, it is desirable.

I suppose this must be at least theoretically possible. But what are we, here and now, supposed to do with this information? Liberate ourselves? How? I am certain that people who were brought up as I was would find it culturally impossible to launch into some large, open marriage set-up. I simply could not do it. Even if it were proved to me that everyone would be better off this way, I still believe I could not do it. If you think I am being feeble, showing myself to be a prisoner of petty bourgeois restrictions, you are probably right. But consider this. Suppose the experiment found that happiness depended on abandoning the taboo on incest. You were suddenly free, even encouraged, to have sex with any member of your family you might choose. Could you, the person you *now* are, do it? The point is that we might all be better off in a radically different society, one in which we could be sexually available to many. But it is not clear what force this could have in guiding our actions now. At an individual level, probably very few people could make the adjustment.

Of course, in the long term, education could change people. But this does not address the question of how things are for us, *now*. It is a mistake to infer that because people can be re-educated, what might be acceptable to them then should be acceptable now. We cannot simply ignore our own culture; and in this culture many of us have been conditioned to find only a certain kind of marriage relationship tolerable – one in which we are sexually exclusive. In a different society, after all, we might have been educated to find cannibalism tolerable.

A similar line of argument – we can be changed and would be better off if we were – is often launched against the pain felt at adultery, which is seen as out of proportion to the injury. One woman told me she could see no reason why people should suffer so much at their spouses' infidelities. 'It's not likely that in a lifetime a person is going to want only the one they're married to. It doesn't mean the marriage is over if you have sex with someone else – it doesn't even mean you love someone else more. It's just normal to be attracted to others and rather stupid to make such a fuss about it. It would be so much better if we all learned to accept that we are naturally polygamous.'

The desire of two people to commit themselves in marriage is a unique affirmation of each other's worth. We do not typically marry someone who could have been replaced by another; we marry 'the only one for me'. Adultery, by contrast, is proof that in a very important way one is not unique. The beloved spouse has found someone else who, sexually at least, can replace you. Hence for most of us adultery is a dreadful betrayal, a rejection, and a loss of a precious perception of ourselves. The perfectly rational and understandable response to this is a feeling of pain and misery.

In our acknowledgment of this pain as appropriate we

separate erotic love from all other forms of love. The love of parents, children and friends is not thought of as exclusive, so jealousy is not deemed appropriate. No one expects you to love only one friend, one parent or one child. Of course, friends, children and parents do suffer from jealousy sometimes, but we feel this pain is something they must overcome. For as things are, we see it as a hang-up, something that may rightly be discounted.

You might now be tempted to suggest that erotic love is, in fact, no different from other forms of love, and that it is absurd to demand that a person should feel it for only one other. If we easily understand parents loving any number of children, then it should not be impossible to understand that adults may feel sexual love for more than one person. It is, you might continue, absurd that we should find this so offensive. From this you infer that we need a programme of social and educational reform to make us feel blithe about our mates mating with other people. Perhaps we should. We might, for instance, be taught to think of sex as being like friendship; you can have it with more than one person without any lessening of love and affection. If we did think like this, life would probably be easier; we would at least feel no pain if our lovers had sex with others. But it would be quite wrong to conclude from this that the pain actually caused now – as things are – can be discounted. The fact that if a man had been educated differently he would not give a damn about his wife's adultery does not mean that anyone may lightly disregard the pain he does suffer.

Nor does it follow from the fact that we can be educated to find a certain way of life valuable that our present way of life is worthless. It is easy to imagine a cynical government spiking our water to prevent us feeling pain at the increasing encroachments on our liberty. We would all be contented puppets. No one would think, however, that the pain we do now feel at such erosion is something to be eradicated. To the contrary, many people would say it is vital that we should feel it. Those who value personal freedom do not want to end up as white mice in the social equivalent of a government laboratory. Pain at the loss of freedom will encourage us to fight to preserve it. Similarly, people who think marriage is valuable may find it valuable to feel pain at adultery: it encourages us to battle for our ideal of sexual exclusivity. The point is that before the programme of re-education is implemented you must already be happy about the direction it will take.

Attacks on the exclusivity of marriage are often based on a certain view of human nature. One man I spoke to argued, 'We're all multi-faceted but monogamy restricts us to the smallest possible number of partners – one! It is bound to be inadequate for us.' The nineteenth-century utopian Charles Fourier held a similar view. He thought that a person consisted of more than body alone; there was also the soul, or the 'passional' person. Two bodies could make one complete physical person, but it needed a staggering 810 distinct character types to make one complete passional person. Clearly anyone holding this metaphysical view of human nature is bound to find that monogamy falls short of the ideal; no two people can satisfy each other's needs. But even a less extreme view of human make-up may see the exclusivity of marriage as potentially limiting. Bertrand Russell complained, 'To close one's mind on marriage against all approaches of love from elsewhere is to diminish receptivity and sympathy and the opportunity of valuable human contact.'

How restrictive is marriage? None of us is married for the whole of our lives; we may enjoy any amount of freedom before, between or after marriage. And when we are married there is no requirement that we reject the love of friends – all that is demanded is that we do not respond to the 'glad eye'. We are still perfectly free to be receptive in all sorts of other ways. One woman's response to this was, 'We've always in the past been forced to put restraints on our sexuality – now we think that's bad. So why should we be doing it in marriage?'

This is ill thought-out. It is not 'bad' to put restraints on rapists, nor, many would say, on those who want sex with children, animals or members of their family, other than the spouse. Nor, indeed, is it bad to put restraints on your desire if your partner happens not to want sex at a certain time. And, of course, within marriage you can be as unrestrained as you both may wish. More important, there are two sides to this. Your sexual activities may be restricted to your spouse, but you are rewarded for this by their restraint. And this may be a great relief – the end of a worry. You may sacrifice the freedom to pursue new relationships, but you are recompensed by the serenity of a day-to-day assurance of your beloved's commitment to you. Of course, nothing can ever be an absolute guarantee, but this reciprocity can give a sense of security and comfort that may be considerably more valuable than the excitement of sex outside marriage.

A powerful criticism of marriage was made at a woman's group I attended. 'Marriage,' one woman argued, 'is a form of property. It isn't grounded in love but in ownership. You've only got to think of the words people use: "to have and to hold", "he's mine", "you've taken her from me", "husband-stealer". It's not very far removed from slavery. Anything that undermines it and puts relationships on a basis of love must be good.'

The tone of this objection to marriage reflects comments from John Stuart Mill that marriage is a form of bondage. 'Marriage is the only actual bondage known to our law; there remain no legal slaves, except the mistress of every house.' The assimilation of a wife to a slave will not, in fact, work. For man has none of the rights over a wife that he would have over a slave. He cannot, for example, sell her sexual favours simply because she is his wife. Nevertheless, marriage has in the past been seen as a form of ownership – so much so that, when in his Utopia Plato abandoned ownership of property, he found he had dispensed with marriage too. Rousseau rather waspishly remarked that this left Plato uncertain what to do with women, with the result that he tried to turn them into men. The objection is hardly fair; nevertheless, it does show a clear causal link between the abolition of marriage and the freedom of women.

For all this, the conception of marriage as property ownership is not the only one that is possible. There is a perfectly good conception of the institution that does not involve a husband owning his wife.

Bertrand Russell – who, being much married, should have known – argued that marriage could be 'the best and most important relationship that can exist between human beings', provided there is 'a feeling of complete equality on both sides; there must be no interference with mutual freedom; there must be the most complete physical and mental intimacy and there must be a certain similarity in regard to the standards of value'.

You may think he was whistling for the moon, but at least this shows that there is more than one vision of what marriage may be.

Ownership is not an essential feature of marriage; the vision of a slave-owning husband is not universally applicable. This is especially true now, when a couple may decide what rights and duties their own marriage will incorporate, and what each person's role will be. There is a chance for each to shape the marriage in a way which allows individual potential to flower: both may bring their own vision to bear and mould their marriage accordingly. Sometimes these visions may be given a concrete form in supplementary marriage contracts. The details of these contracts are sometimes absurd, but the idea itself is proof that there is more than one conception of what marriage may be.

It might be objected, however, that this has failed to take account of a crucial element in the property argument. As one woman in the group argued, 'Okay. So there's no legal ownership now – but I certainly felt, and other women have too, that my husband did want to own me. Lock, stock and barrel.'

This woman is suggesting that there are two possible levels of ownership in marriage – the legal level and the psychological level. At the legal level it is arguable that not all the ingredients of chattel ownership blight the marriage contract; it really is a contract which a man and a woman enter as a reciprocal agreement that benefits both of them. But there is something like the desire to own a person which, at a psychological level, is part of many people's monogamous pairings. It is perhaps not a very worthy desire – but it seems to be a fact. There is no obvious necessity in this, however. Another woman told me, 'My first husband was as territorial as the Silver Backed Gorilla. I was *his* and God help anyone who took liberties. The man I'm with now isn't like that at all though. I go out with friends – even other men if I feel like it. He doesn't think he owns me.' Clearly, it is possible to find a spouse who is not proprietorial. The psychology of any two people launched into conjugal intimacy is a purely contingent matter.

Discussing the benefits and disadvantages of marriage, two separate questions are often run together. The first is whether marriage as a monogamous relationship enshrined in law is desirable; the second is whether marriage encrusted with the barnacles of law, social mores and individual psychologies is desirable. Marx, more clearly than most, distinguished monogamy from the practices that surround it. He approved of monogamous marriage, describing it as 'the sanctification of the sex drive through exclusiveness, the restraint of the drive through law, the ethical beauty which turns nature's command into an ideal moment of spiritual vision – the spiritual essence of marriage'. His later attacks on marriage were a recognition that the institution had become grounded in property, not in love. Monogamy itself, however, he continued to see as desirable.

You may have no stomach for the grim workings of a Victorian marriage; you may baulk at marrying in a country where there is no divorce; and you may never consider marrying someone wildly possessive. It does not follow from any of this that legally recognised monogamy must be decried. Indeed, Aristotle described the good marriage as profoundly beneficial because the couple 'help each other by throwing their unique gifts into the common stock'.

There is a commonly held view that any value in monogamy comes from its being a personal choice based on love, that to intrude the law into such a relationship is in some way to sully it. Monogamy should not be sanctified, goes this view, because this tries to hold in place by law what ought to be held in place by the feelings of the couple.

It is not obvious that the law does shore up what should be an emotional tie. There are surely two components to marriage: one is the pairing of two people, which can in theory be held together by their feelings; the second comprises the legal bonds that apply to such matters as finances and children. Marriage laws do not necessarily usurp the cementing properties of love, thereby outraging all our romantic notions. Rather, they give a set of rules for what happens when love evaporates and the relationship collapses. Rousseau pointed out that marriage is essentially a social institution. The feelings on which it is based are, of course, personal – tenderness, trust, esteem – and they are strengthened by the bonds that children form. But children bring with them responsibilities and obligations, and the point of the legal form of marriage is to ensure recognition of those obligations.

Bertrand Russell argued that there must be a social ethic that protects children and that may override the claims of love, which are, he said, anarchic. Marriage has always been part of such an ethic, and so there is a certain impersonal element in the institution: its obligations are not altogether chosen; they are imposed. Further, people marry for all sorts of reasons that have nothing much to do with love – money, social status or, of course, children. Love, however, is never a means to something else, but is desired and valued for its own sake. In the Middle Ages, when marriage was little more than an economic and procreative contract – a match of interests – love was sought outside. And because that love had no other purpose but itself, it was seen as pure and untainted by any external morality. Adultery created its own obligations, out of love, and this, for the courtly lover, was the means to achieve purity and virtue. Rousseau went a step further, believing that romantic love was essentially exclusive: it shut other people out. Marriage, being essentially social, was therefore incompatible with passion.

This sort of conviction is still common. Marriage is seen as a rather drab, respectable relationship which is bound to oversee the decaying of the passionate feelings that prompted lovers to marry. Adultery, by contrast, seems exciting and, because it is personal not social, somehow more pure. As one man told me, 'My affair somehow felt much more "me" than my marriage. That seemed more about doing what everyone else did – what was expected of me – settling down and taking on responsibility. What I had with the affair was, well . . . love. It seemed so much more honest somehow – less cluttered with things that had nothing to do with me.'

Adultery, by definition, demands a background of marriage. Its pleasures, on a general acceptance that marriage legitimately excludes others, are parasitic, the pleasures of forbidden fruit. Even the most irreverent adulterer, then, does not challenge the basic institution. But what of the people who reject the public form of marriage and live together 'without benefit of clergy'? In practice, they tend simply to mimic the basic structure and form of marriage. The man who found love in his adulterous affair eventually left his wife. But in his new relationship he could not countenance the possibility of his lover having anyone else, and he longed, he said, to have children by her. So all the habits and taboos have their hold, albeit without the public recognition.

Kant had a contrasting view of what monogamous marriage could be. He regarded sex in the unromantic light of a means to enjoy your own orgasms. Each partner was simply the other's instrument in an essentially manipulative, masturbatory relationship. In marriage, however, this is transformed into an authentic, sublime unity. Two people transcend their separateness and become one, 'complete'; they find, as we might say, their 'other half'. Of course, no one could seriously claim that marriage is a sufficient condition of such blissful completion. As your neighbours give their daily brawl a public airing you will be aware that marriage can be a profound disunity, a horrible clash of self-contained and separate egos, and you may come to see as an absurd sentimentality – a cliché for the penny romance – the idea of marriage as fusion.

I do find it tenable, though, that only in marriage can you achieve a certain kind of relationship. Marriage, after all, combines two seemingly disparate elements: sex, which in itself may have little value, plus the psychological bonds – trust, esteem, need, love – which are the basis for a special reciprocal relationship. When these two elements are joined you get a whole that is greater than its parts. This is, of course, the standard romantic conception of marriage yearned after by all those Mills and Boon heroines – and it is not all stuff and nonsense. No one could claim, though, that such bliss needed marriage in the legal sense; homosexuals must be as capable of achieving it as heterosexuals, after all. This kind of marriage would be marriage in the sense, for instance, of making vows before God, or simply to each other.

When people talk about 'the institution of marriage' they usually mean more than whatever makes it formally true that a couple are married. They think of a relationship where the legal ties are supplemented by the desire for children, by expectations of love and support, and where there is a guarantee of sexual exclusivity. If people marry simply to give one partner citizenship in another country it is said the marriage is in name only. If all the ingredients are there but law the relationship is a common-law marriage. And if there is no promise of exclusivity there is open marriage. All these bear a family resemblance to the central type of marriage, but they are deviations from it.

It may be better, though, to recognise less than full marriage rather than to force people to make vows it is unrealistic to expect them to keep. One man said to me, 'I believe that monogamy is ideal, but in the kind of society we live in a vow of perpetual fidelity may be impossible to keep. And perhaps it makes for anxiety and insecurity.' In this sexually unstable society it may indeed be irrational to expect one person to be faithful to another through what could amount to several decades of marriage. Perhaps, then, it would be better for some people to make a smaller, more rational commitment than one that will certainly end in disappointment: the person who can scramble up Snowdon may not want to try battling up the side of the Eiger.

In recognition of this, John Stuart Mill proposed a free contract, one that could be dissolved at the wish of the contracting parties provided children were well cared-for. 'Surely it is wrong, wrong in every way, that there should exist any motives to marriage except the happiness which two persons who love each other feel in associating their existence.' Many people I spoke to thought this sort of contract would encourage married couples to give up on relationships too easily. They felt that the difficulties of divorce made a couple attempt to stick at a relationship, to try and make it work.

I suppose that if you find yourself in the ranks of the miserably married and cannot extricate yourself, you may work hard at making something of what you have. There is little alternative. But the fact that you may achieve some happiness if you are forced to stick at something is a wretched reason for keeping people locked within a relationship. This kind of view seems grounded in an assumption that because on the whole marriage is desirable, every instance of marriage is desirable.

To a good marriage – one where there is trust, openness and expectations of exclusivity – adultery is a kick in the teeth. So if you think well of marriage, and if you think monogamy is desirable, you cannot also believe there is never anything wrong with adultery: it would be inconsistent. Nevertheless, while insisting that typically adultery is unacceptable you can allow that there may be cases where it is not. Some marriages may be so bloody it would be better if something came along to end them.

Observations, then, seem to show that monogamy for some people is the opportunity for the profoundest affection and intimacy. The law even recognises and safeguards this intimacy by not requiring a spouse to testify against the partner. But for other people marriage is stifling and demoralising. Attitudes vary quite a lot in our culture, and infinitely across all the cultures. A rational society would surely accommodate, not ignore, such human differences. It would perhaps offer not just one marriage contract, but a variety of contractual relationships, between which you could choose according to the needs and psychologies of both you and your partner: you may contract for monogamy or for sexual freedom. (Presumably if you changed your mind you could be sued for breach of contract.) There would need to be quite general laws about children and means of support – simply because it would be safer and easier all round if there were clearly defined procedures with regard to them. But within this very general framework you could choose what is best for both of you. St Paul grudgingly allowed, 'It is better to marry than to burn.' And the evidence is that most of us agree with him: we prefer to be married than to stay single. But not everyone has a preference for one particular type of pairing – given that people are so different it would be surprising if they did. It must be better to recognise this, and make room for it, than to pretend that we are all uniform.

_ 5 _

CONTRACEPTION

Pills, coils, caps, jellies, pessaries, *coitus interruptus*, fertility charts, the rhythm method – all the sticky, tricky and sometimes hazardous paraphernalia of contraception are products of the desire to have the pleasures of sex without its demanding fruits.

For many, contraceptive devices are the hope of the future. As an ecologist explained to me, 'In their present numbers people are a pollution – there's just too many of us for the earth to support. We must control the population growth, and the best way of doing that is contraception. Everyone must come to realise that it is morally necessary that we control the numbers of people born.' This necessity is not apparent to everyone. The Roman Catholic Church, for example, has argued that a family which raises many children in an area of over-population is especially deserving of praise. As one priest said, 'We value obedience to God's will . . . it is best to leave the Almighty to deal with such problems as numbers.'

The ecologist I had spoken to was aware of the dissenters to his view: 'You sometimes get an alliance between the Church and the Marxists. The Church thinks contraception offends God: Marxists think it's a ploy of the rich to slow down the revolution. The result is that in many poor countries the people are told that it's a device to take their children away from them.'

The problems of the world and its diminishing resources are immense, and not even the experts agree on their solution. In *Man's Responsibility for Nature,* for example, John Passmore concluded, ' . . . we encounter a head-on collision between experts, on which we cannot hope to arbitrate'. He adds, however, that we are entitled to venture this modest conclusion: 'A decline in the rate of population growth would not necessarily ease the problems . . . but a high rate of growth accentuates them.' It is rational, then, to encourage population control. The question is what constitutes a morally acceptable form of that control. Many feel, with some justice, that however parlous the state of the world, infanticide or euthanasia would be morally unacceptable solutions. Other people would add abortion to the list. What, then, of contraception?

Contraception is not simply the process of ensuring that a woman does not give birth; abortion does that. Rather, a contraceptive device prevents the male sperm from fertilising the live egg: it prevents conception.

However, some devices which are categorised as contraceptives do not, in fact, prevent conception. Intra-uterine devices, for example, while being an effective form of birth control, do not aim to stop an egg from being fertilised. Instead they prevent any egg that *has* been fertilised from implanting itself in the lining of the womb; they achieve this by turning what should be a sustaining environment into a toxic sink. Certain contraceptive pills act in a similar way, causing unwelcome changes in the lining of the womb – essentially by making it poisonous to the egg. Because such devices allow conception to take place but disallow the pregnancy, many people regard them as early abortion techniques, not contraceptives at all. A medical scientist at a London college pointed out: 'If you look up the definition of abortion in the "Offence against Persons Act" it's quite clear that things like the coil and mini-pill are simply a means of inducing an early abortion. Just think that in theory a woman fitted with a coil could be undergoing several abortions a year.'

This is certainly a startling thought, and you might have expected it to put such devices right in the middle of the inflammatory debates about abortion. However, 'Some people do say,' the scientist continued, 'that you can't induce a miscarriage if there's nothing being carried. So preventing implantation is not abortion.' It seems then that there is a gap between contraception and abortion, with fine jesuitical points being made to determine the morality of what goes within it.

The issue is further muddled by the law. If a woman has unprotected sex, the law allows her to have an intra-uterine device fitted up to seventy-two hours after the act to prevent pregnancy. The idea seems to be that the egg will not by then be implanted in the womb, and therefore the effect of the device is morally unproblematical. However, an egg may in fact implant itself within two days; in such an event, the device would act as an abortionist's tool. The law's deadline is purely arbitrary.

Further, the manufacturers of intra-uterine devices admit that there 'have been reports of an increased incidence of septic abortions in women who become pregnant with an IUD in situ'. A research chemist told me, 'If you fit a woman with an IUD you're putting a foreign body in the womb. It isn't clear that this inevitably discourages the egg from implantation. It may allow it and then disturb – abort – it. The point is that with IUDs and mini-pills there are a number of factors that may prevent pregnancy and no one is sure how they work – or how relevant each is.' If you believe that life begins at conception, you must allow that preventing the implantation of the fertilised egg causes death. Further, there can be no denying that an intra-uterine device, or mini-pill, may work by causing early abortions. They are not unequivocally contraceptives, for contraceptives work by preventing life.

There is, then, a significant and morally relevant difference between the methods of birth control that prevent conception and those that allow it but dislodge the fertilised egg. This difference will not, of course, perturb those who have no qualms about abortion at all. Indeed, to them, the ease, the privacy and the fact that it all happens so early that the woman will not even know if she has conceived will seem to be bonuses. But other women do have qualms about abortion, and for them these devices will be perplexing: are they abortion techniques or are they not?

The problem is not eased by the hypocrisy that surrounds the issue. I find the idea of a womb permanently set up as a slaughter-house quite disgusting, though my distaste is partly aesthetic. As a friend said, 'I looked at this thing they were going to fit me with – and it looked just like the worst kind of fish-hook. So I changed my mind.' But there is also a moral point. If it is acceptable to abort a fertilised egg very early, all a woman needs is a pill to take if her period is late and she believes she may be pregnant. Anything that poisons the system must be better used only when it is needed. No one could be happy about using it all the time whether it is needed or not. If it is morally acceptable to have a coil permanently *in situ*, or to consume mini-pills every day, then they are all redundant. Let us have an abortion pill, and if that sounds too brutal, let us call it a menstrual regulation pill, or a morning-after pill. If, however, such a pill by any name would be unacceptable because a woman taking it *may* be disposing of a fertilised egg, then IUDs and mini-pills, on the same grounds, are unacceptable. Of course, we may prefer not deliberately to do what we would be happy to let happen. It is easier, perhaps, not to care about installing a device which undetected may abort a fertilised egg than deliberately to abort it. But we should not try to convince ourselves that what we are unmoved by is morally acceptable. Our not caring may be a human limitation.

It is obvious that if a woman does not want a child it is better that she does not become pregnant, and thus that any effective birth-control device has its advantages. But it is not obvious that it is desirable to turn the womb into a poisonous trap. The ideal must surely be to control fertility without destroying life, and the most common way of doing this is to place some kind of barrier between the sperm and the cervix, such as a diaphragm or a condom. Unlike the coil, these devices will be morally unproblematical, to anyone who thinks that contraception is unobjectionable. Diaphragms and condoms aim to stop conception, but if they fail they have no power to dislodge the fertilised egg.

Some men I have talked to complain, however, that the whole point of using contraceptives was defeated by their having to use a condom. As one said, 'Contraceptives are supposed to make sex more pleasurable by taking the worry out of it. But using a condom is like having a bath with your socks on. Horrible!' Clearly, if some device significantly decreases sexual pleasure then it is not ideal – though some small diminution of immediate delight may be a reasonable cost for the removal of overall worry. It seems, though, that there is no necessary connection between loss of pleasure and condoms, and another man I interviewed dismissed this complaint out of hand: 'Most French letters nowadays set out to make the whole thing feel even better. I mean – there are these ripple-banded ones that guarantee extra sensation.'

Still, there is a substantial complaint to be made about some contraceptives. Most of us want more than safe sex; we want aesthetically pleasing sex, too. And that can be difficult. Every summer the local common is garlanded with the pendulous fruits of the previous night's protected sex. It is easy to imagine that disposing of these used condoms may offend romantic sensibilities. This aesthetic problem is even worse with the diaphragm. There is no doubt that, properly used, it is a highly effective contraceptive, acting as a rubber barricade from which spermicides can repel sperm from the cervix. But doused in its spermicidal jelly it is as slippery as a blob of mercury. Beautiful sex is not easy when you must first overcome the malevolence of sticky, inanimate objects. It is not surprising that those of us who had fought our diaphragms in assorted bathrooms should have greeted the pill with something akin to religious fervour. The pill works by suppressing ovulation; simply by swallowing a pill every day you can ensure that you do not produce live eggs for the sperm to fertilise. In terms of sex it has obvious advantages. As a friend remarked, 'I realised the sheer wonder of the pill when my boyfriend wanted to make love in the woods. I didn't have to whip out my Dutch cap and disappear behind a bush squirting jelly.'

Our extreme pleasure was dimmed, however, by some of the pill's side effects. Cancer scares, for example, led many people to see pill *aficionados* as hurtling on a glorious wave of free sex to an early death. And so paternalism reared its head. A woman who admits that her own sex life has always resembled some kind of Russian roulette nevertheless insisted, 'It's mad to take the risk of the pill – just for sex. Would you let your daughter take it? I wouldn't.' Put in these terms the argument is ill thought-out. Statistically, taking the pill every day is about as dangerous as driving a car every day: that is to say, minimally dangerous. Also, it is part of life that certain activities carry risks: sports, smoking, even having a baby. For those who want to do these things the risks are accepted because of the pleasure the activity brings.

It is common, however, to hear complaints that even if the long-term risks are small the short-term side-effects can be highly unpleasant. As one woman told me, 'I was so depressed on the pill. It completely killed my libido as well, so I wasn't even having sex. There didn't seem any point taking it.' If all a woman wants is to have sex while being absolutely certain of avoiding pregnancy, then even if the pill makes her miserable she may go on dutifully swallowing it. But if the misery is so acute that it destroys any inclination for sex, then the rational thing to do – if pregnancy must be avoided and there are no reasonable alternatives – is to embrace celibacy. At least the body is not then being filled with chemicals. This is, of course, a dreary conclusion, one that hardly anyone will find palatable. Those of us who clamoured for the pill wanted freedom from pregnancy along with good sex – not migraines, chubby ankles and dulled libidos.

The fact that this is the experience of some women, however, does not, as has been suggested, make a case for withdrawing the pill. Further, the discomfort that may be experienced by certain people in using a device does not justify taking that device away from those who undeniably benefit from it. It would be analogous to arguing that because certain people are allergic to cheese the product must be removed from general consumption. Further, if a woman chooses to take a relatively minor risk – even chooses to be miserable – that is her business. The only obligation on other people is to ensure that she knows what the risks are: that the pill is a powerful medicant which may have undesirable side-effects.

All these practical conundrums may be sidestepped by undergoing sterilisation. In the USA more than 600,000 operations are performed a year – a sure testament to its popularity. And it is easy to see why it is appealing; your sex life no longer contributes to the profits of the pharmacological giants, you are free of copper coils and bits of rubber, there should be no side-effects and you are absolutely sure of being protected from unwanted pregnancy. One man told me, though, that he believed sterilisation was immoral because 'it alters the proper workings of the body'. A body worked properly, he explained, when there was no interference with natural processes. All that needs to be said to this is that it would count the ravages of cancer as a natural process with which it would be immoral to interfere. Any argument about the immorality of a contraceptive device that has as a consequence that it is wrong to use other devices to save life must be absurd.

There is, however, a heavy demand for the reversal of the operation, and this highlights the disadvantages of limiting your choices for the future in circumstances that may radically change. Existing children may die or, more common in this sexually unstable society, you may change partners. A woman I spoke to had four children by her first marriage and was then sterilised. 'We didn't want any more and I didn't want the hassle of pills or coils. The operation seemed obvious. Then my marriage broke up and I married again. And of course John wanted children of his own. I've been everywhere but there seems no hope of getting it reversed. Now it seems so stupid to have done it at all.'

In terms of benefit to the species, sterilisation seems to many an ideal form of contraceptive. As a doctor put it, 'There's no doubt that it is the most trouble-free way of limiting the size of a family. And if there was some natural disaster that reduced human numbers drastically there would always be people who had not been sterilised to go on reproducing.' Such a sentiment seems a little chilling, for children are not simply of benefit to the species: they are of huge benefit to the individual. Permanent sterility is not, then, ideal. What is needed is a process that is reversible.

These are just some of the technical problems of contraception, but more important, for some people, are the moral problems. An accountant with four daughters argued in a letter to a local newspaper: 'Morality today is at an all-time low. People have no sense of responsibility – of right or wrong. And the pill is just a charter for free sex without moral considerations at all. I don't believe it should be readily available.'

This is a not uncommon refrain: contraception as the devil's aid to a steadily declining morality. And it is certainly true that separating sex from reproduction will change moral attitudes. If you engage in an act which you know may produce a child, giving you a whole new range of responsibilities and obligations, you are bound to feel differently about it than if the act had no such consequences. But does it follow from this that we will all be plunged into moral laxity? I cannot see why it should. There are still two people involved in the sex act, and thus it carries all the moral obligations of any interpersonal relationship. These obligations may be met as fully as anyone could wish. Not everyone who wants sex without children can be accused of avoiding all moral responsibility. I suspect, though, that the real core of this view is that untrammelled sex is morally unacceptable, and that anything that facilitates it must therefore be wrong; in other words, we should discourage people from having 'free sex' by threatening them with the Damoclean sword of pregnancy.

In the past it would not have been prudent for an unmarried woman to have a child. This is presumably why women were encouraged to save their virginity for the 'someone special' they would marry. But clearly fear did not override all desire: there were illegitimate births. Further, though fear may stop a penis ejaculating into a vagina, it needs only a little ingenuity and good will to find other forms of sexual activity – mutual masturbation or anal sex, for example – that can be enjoyed without the fear of pregnancy. Anyway, before the pill there was the condom. Preventing women from having the pill will not stop sexual activity, though it will perhaps increase the anxiety that goes with it. And it may be that this is what is really thought desirable: sex without the possibility of children should not be pleasurable. Or, worse, the fear of pregnancy is regarded as the appropriate punishment for the pleasure the act gives.

Janet Radcliffe Richards thought some such desire to punish those who want only the pleasures of sex may be behind the refusal of certain people to countenance women having abortion on demand. In *The Sceptical Feminist* she asks, 'Can it be that you are morally all right if you put up with sex if you see it as a means to an acceptable end (having a child) . . . but not if you actually want it? It may sound incredible but there seems to be nothing else which fits the facts.' The attitude she describes, whether with regard to contraception or to abortion, is not one that most of us will find tenable.

If people think the bogeyman of pregnancy prevents us all from behaving immorally, then I suppose they would be sorry

to see it wafted away on a tide of medical advances. If, on the
other hand, they think it is just getting in the way of our
enjoying perfectly acceptable pleasures, they will be glad to see
the back of it. I find it quite mysterious that anyone should
think the sex act in itself either right or wrong. Of course, all
sorts of unacceptable behaviour may go along with it, from
lying to rape – but sex itself is morally neutral. If people want it
and can find willing partners, that is no one's business but their
own. If they do not want to be saddled with children, that is
their business too.

A rather dour attitude to contraception was put forward by a
woman who said, 'A huge amount of money goes towards
research into contraceptives – ratepayers' money. Why should
we pay for other people's pleasures. It makes me furious when I
hear people saying they want free contraceptives. If they don't
want children why shouldn't they do without sex?' It is also
true, of course, that through her rates this woman pays for the
education of other people's children. Did she think this was
also unacceptable? 'Education is a serious, important matter,'
she replied. 'Sex, on the other hand, is somewhat frivolous.'
Those who think that sex has obvious and important benefits –
who think that there is even a place for frivolity – will find this
rather unsympathetic, and perhaps sad. It is also unlikely to
reduce the rates bill, for people are going to take their pleasures
anyway, as they always have. Without effective, readily available contraceptives, they will simply trust to luck or quackery;
what they will certainly not do is abstain. So all of us will be
landed with batches of children that no one wants, children
who will be a drain on our resources just as contraceptives are.
We will not enjoy much of a financial saving if we abandon
contraception, and we will suffer an increase in unhappy
people – unwillingly pregnant women, unwanted children and
anxious families.

Victoria Gillick, doom-laden speaker for the anti-contraception
movement, has argued that a doctor's right to prescribe contraceptives to under-age girls without informing the parents is
'a male charter to abuse and harm the young female population'. Ms Gillick is a devout Roman Catholic, so it is no surprise
that her diatribe reflects a passage from Pope Paul VI's encyc-

lical on birth control. 'It is also feared that the man growing used to the employment of anti-conception practices may finally lose respect for the woman and no longer caring for her physical and psychological equilibrium may come to the point of considering her as a mere instrument of selfish enjoyment.'

I am shocked by the picture of sexual relationships envisaged by these people. Are we really to suppose that men – their rapacity freed by effective birth control – crouch waiting to pounce on frail little creatures nibbling their pills? Are we to believe, despite all evidence to the contrary, that sex is a one-sided demand made by men on women, that women do not really want it, yet mindlessly trot along to their doctors to fit themselves up to be vessels for the pleasures of exploitative men? It is a sick vision. It is also confused. Men who do not give a damn about women, who use them and cast them aside when they are done, are not going to be restrained by reflections that their pleasures may result in their victim being made pregnant. Clearly, no such anxieties inhibited the traditional roué Casanova as he launched himself over the nunnery wall in Venice. Men, after all, have *always* been able to have sex without the necessary encumbrance of children. Effective birth control simply allows women the same privilege. To deny it to women is not to protect them from men; to the contrary, it is to put them at the mercy of men's altruism or foresightedness. Women want sex just as men do. Rather than have to rely on lovers turning up with a packet of condoms, it is far, far better that they should have the freedom to take responsibility for themselves. The American philosopher Carl Cohen said of the Pope's encyclical (and we may apply this also to Ms Gillick):

> the implicit distorted picture of what sexual intercourse for its own sake may be, reveals enough about the authors of this document to put their competence in this entire sphere, not to speak of their authority, in gravest doubt.

Pope Paul's apocalyptic vision was an attempt to give us the very best of reasons for rejecting birth control. Earlier in the document he had proclaimed the view that birth control was anathema to God. Perhaps reflections on the Fall made him feel this might be insufficient to keep the daughters of Eve virtuous,

leading him to back up this argument with the threat that if
women go on the pill their menfolk will abuse them. To any
woman bearing her umpteenth child because her church for-
bids her to regulate her fertility, this must seem the sourest
kind of joke. Still, there is another spectre to be pulled out of
the papal hat: acceptance of contraception will lead to a
chilling state control of human fertility.

> Who could blame a government for applying to the solution
> of the problems of the community the means acknowledged
> to be licit for married couples in the solution of family
> problems? Who will stop rulers from favouring, from even
> imposing upon their peoples, the method of contraception
> which they judge to be most efficacious?

The idea that population control will be imposed by iniquitous
governments is not unique to the Church. The 1967 Black
Panther manifesto described laws liberalising abortion and
contraception as an attempt to exterminate its people.

No one could blame a government for encouraging their
populace to take responsibility for keeping numbers within
reasonable limits. We know that over-population causes pover-
ty, starvation, misery. If individuals may use birth control to
keep their numbers down, why should governments not encourage them to do so? This is not to say that anyone would
want to witness the scenes that took place in the Emergency
under Mrs Gandhi's government; people dragged off forcibly to
be sterilised. But not all governments are tyrannies; some
understand individual freedom and recognise the difference
between choice and force. There is no way, then, of deducing
that as a result of contraception being regarded as 'licit' it will
be forced on us by governments. After all, many governments
regard homosexuality as licit, but we would be very surprised
indeed if it were made compulsory as a means of controlling
the population boom.

The central point of the encyclical, however, was to argue for
the Roman Catholic Church's conviction that contraception is a
sin. It insists that only sex for the sake of procreation answers to
the will of God. As a priest explained to me, 'God has revealed
that sex is a special pleasure reserved for those men and

women who have a general intention to produce children . . .'
(which seems to make the whole business of sex rather like
giving sweets to the kids to encourage them to do the washing-
up).

Those who defend this view often point to God's injunction
to mankind to be fruitful and multiply. I find no reason to see
this as a requirement that people should produce as many
children as they possibly can. Perhaps God would count you as
having multiplied if you had two or three. And why should the
laity regard it as binding on them alone? If it is God's command,
why, in their avowed celibacy, are the Christian Fathers, popes
and priests disregarding it? St Augustine went so far as to say,
'In these days no one perfect in piety seeks to have children
except spiritually.' St Thomas Aquinas adopted a less stringent
position, but one that nevertheless released some people, at
least, from child-bearing. 'Sufficient provision is made for the
human multitude if some undertake the task of carnal generation.' Given all this, why should not an already over-burdened
family opt out of multiplying and leave having children to
others?

The answer was given me by a Catholic priest, who said, 'We
believe that children are the natural and proper result of the
conjugal life, but it is a great gift to give one's sexuality to God.'
The idea seems to be that the willingness to give up sex
altogether is a good that releases one from the burden of being
fruitful. If, however, you choose to have a sex life then it must
be part of that life that conception is not hindered. Obviously
not every sexual act will culminate in a child, but each one
must be performed within this intention. It follows that anyone
having sex without such an intention (most of us in fact) are
committing an offence. Nothing could be clearer proof that no
such intention exists than regularly taking contraceptive pills.

This view – when it comes down to a practical choice of
children or contraception – leaves many women unmoved.
According to a Roman Catholic friend of mine in New Zealand,
'Every Sunday there's a row of women sitting at the back of the
church not able to go to confession or take the sacrament.
They're the ones on the pill.' But other women take the risk of
pregnancy rather than disobey. A 16-year-old from Lisbon
admitted having sex since she was 14 (which is, of course, a sin

in the eyes of her Church), but added, 'I would never dream of using contraceptives. It is God's will if I become pregnant.'

Anyone whose sexual preferences are such that there could be no intention to conceive – homosexuals for example – are condemned by the Roman Catholic Church to celibacy. But what of the woman for whom a pregnancy would be fatal? May she protect herself by contraceptive devices?

The encyclical is unequivocal:

> It is not licit to make into the object of a positive act of the will something which is intrinsically disordered and hence unworthy of the human person even when the intention is to safeguard or promote individual, family or social well-being.

Most reasonable people think that if a small evil is the price of a greater good, then it must be acceptable to do it. Telling lies is an evil, but generally if it will save someone from harm most of us would consider this justified. You can see, though, why this reasonable view needs to be excluded by the Pope. If you may do evil for the sake of a good, then for the sake of a family's well-being a couple would be entitled to avoid further births; limiting a family can easily be justified as being for a greater good. If the Roman Catholic Church were to allow this small concession, the whole official position would be blown apart.

Ironically, the Church has done just this. The argument that contraception is immoral because it impedes God's plan is, as stated, unassailable. But the encyclical undermines its own central position by conceding that you may use the rhythm method to avoid pregnancy. You may, that is, without committing a sin, deliberately limit your sexual activity to those times when the woman is not fertile.

This flatly contradicts the original position that it is heinous to thwart God's will. If God's plan involves an indissoluble bond between sex and procreation, then having sex with no intention to make a baby must be a sin: the means used to avoid pregnancy are irrelevant. Indeed, the divinely revealed will is presumably most strongly present at the woman's fertile period. Deliberately to abstain at this time shows a blatant determination to act against God's plan. If using a diaphragm is a sin, using the rhythm method has to be a sin too. *Both* are the calculated avoidance of pregnancy – the attempt in defiance of God to have the icing without the cake.

An Irish girl I spoke to has seven children; three of them were born by mistake – miscalculation of her fertile time. She wondered, 'Isn't the point that if you use the rhythm method you're not using devices – it's natural. That's why it's not a sin.' The encyclical agrees that making use of a natural disposition is justifiable; but it is very strange to say that if you can separate sex and procreation by a slick bit of timing this is not a sin, whereas if you have recourse to pills it is. Indeed it makes the whole position incoherent for it offends, if not God, at least the most fundamental law of reason, the law of non-contradiction. This states that no proposition can be both true and false at the same time. If 'This is a sin' is true of a proposition, 'This is not a sin' is false. The Church is saying 'Contraception is a sin.' Since the rhythm method is not a sin, but is undeniably a form of contraception, 'Contraception is not a sin' is also true. As a moral guide it is worse than useless; no one can act consistently with a principle that makes no sense. St Thomas Aquinas believed that God could do anything – except make a contradiction true. Popes are not likely to do better.

The only way to retrieve consistency is to say that some contraception is a sin. That is to say, it is not a sin to thwart God's will, only a sin to thwart it in certain ways. No one who believed in God could accept this. Better would be to allow that all contraception is a sin, but to show that the rhythm method is less of a sin than other methods. The Irish girl's response to that shows its weakness. 'Hell. If I'm going to be damned anyway then I might as well be damned for a method that works than for one that doesn't.' Unless the Roman Catholic Church could show there was some huge moral difference between different forms of birth control this second position would open up the flood-gates. Most people will think that all that is left is to allow all contraception, but to put the rhythm method top of the list as the one that will find greater favour in God's eyes – though only God will know why it should. Perhaps the best thing of all, then, would be for the Church to take the advice of the large Italian mamma whose comments on the present Pope and birth control enlivened His Holiness's visit to New York. At a televised news conference she roundly insisted: 'He no playa the game, he no setta the rules!'

A more studied refutation of the official Catholic position comes from a Jesuit, J.L. Thomas. He argues, 'In creating the human female with an ovulation cycle that renders her capable of conception during a relatively brief period in each menstrual cycle ... the Creator obviously intended sexual relations to serve a significant unifying function in marriage.' If we are constrained to act according to God's will, then it is vital that we know what the will of God is. Since the given arrangement of our reproductive system is open to a variety of interpretations, it is not obvious that we should embrace the one that is undeniably the cause of much human misery and is also, within itself, inconsistent. The idea that sexual intercourse is a God-given way for a couple to express the love they bear each other is profoundly appealing. It is also logically unassailable.

_ 6 _

ABORTION

Debates about abortion generate heat but very little light. At a recent seminar on abortion at a London college the floor was held on one side by the anti-abortionists, who were convinced that abortion was murder, and on the other by the pro-abortionists, who were equally convinced that abortion was a minor operation, the business of no one but the pregnant woman herself. Skittering uneasily between the trenches were those who believed that some, but not all, abortions may be justified. The only point of universal agreement was its definition: abortion is the destruction of life after conception and before birth.

What struck me most forcibly about this particular discussion was that each side was apparently impervious to the views of the other. Horror stories were produced, reasoned arguments laid out – and they all bounced off those whose position they might have undermined. People lost their tempers, or cried, but no one *heard* what others were saying. This is not altogether surprising: some people have an infinite capacity to stick to a position even when they have been given the best of reasons to abandon it. But in this particular case I thought the lack of flexibility had less to do with human weakness than with the subject itself.

If you genuinely believe that the foetus is a person, how can you possibly accept that it may be dispatched because its birth will bring inconvenience, or even suffering, to others? After all, you would not think it acceptable to kill other persons – for example a senile, demanding parent or a child handicapped through injury.

If, on the other hand, you believe that the foetus is just a pin-head of matter, not a person at all, then why should you grant it the same rights and considerations as adults and children – especially if this condemns those who certainly *are* persons to hardship and misery? Meanwhile, if you take the middle path you will almost certainly try to render unto everyone more than their due, and get into a dreadful muddle doing so.

I doubt whether any agreement will ever be reached between those who hold these incompatible attitudes. Indeed, discussing abortion in *The Sceptical Feminist* Janet Radcliffe Richards wondered, 'Are we left with no alternative but to try to force our will on the opposition?' She concluded that, in the last analysis, this would probably be the case. But the question is, 'whether we have actually got to the last analysis'.

There are, then, issues still to be settled. I am going to consider three of them. The first is really a non-issue, but it was so hotly debated in the seminar – arousing almost as much passion as abortion itself – that it seemed worthwhile to include it. This is whether men may take part in discussions on an issue that so crucially affects women. The second is the issue of exactly what the various stances on abortion commit their proponents to. The third is the issue of whether the middle-ground attitude which the majority of people seem to prefer can coherently be maintained.

Anna Raeburn once pole-axed Norman St John-Stevas by refusing to discuss abortion with him until such time, she said, as he grew a womb. Ms Raeburn was expounding a not uncommon view among women that discussion on abortion is something men should keep out of. As one girl in the college seminar insisted, 'Men have spent all of history telling women what's right and what's wrong – but what the hell do they know about us?'

It is a familiar truth that historically women have been ruled by men, usually to their disadvantage. It is hardly surprising, then, if women no longer wish to be told what to do by men. But abortion is not just about what women may do, and laws are not made only by the groups of people they will directly affect. As things are, if a woman wants an abortion she needs help from a doctor, and many doctors are men. It would be outrageous to deny these men, at least, the right to discuss abortion. Since the main aim of the medical profession is to save lives, any doctor who is to be asked to *take* life must of course be allowed to discuss the morality of it. To possess testes instead of a womb does not constitute a bar to this right.

Further, one of the biggest difficulties in deciding about abortion is that as yet we have no coherent account of the value of life that can be applied to the claims of all concerned. This is something that *all* of us – men and women – are responsible for establishing. It is a mistake to think that abortion is a self-contained issue. Whatever else is true, abortion is about taking life; as such it is, and must be, part of much wider discussions about taking life in other situations – for example, war, suicide, euthanasia, capital punishment. We need to establish some principle that will tell us when, if ever, it is defensible to take *any* life, and then apply this principle to all matters of life and death. Abortion is not a separate issue just because it is about destroying life inside, rather than outside, the womb.

Some women argue that man-made laws about abortion are yet another way of controlling women – of limiting their freedom. Even if this has been true in the past it could have been possible only because abortion *was* treated as a separate issue: principles that applied to abortion were conveniently forgotten when the issue was war, or execution. As Simone de Beauvoir points out in *The Second Sex*: 'Men with the most scrupulous respect for embryonic life are also those who are most eagerly officious when it comes to condemning adults to death in war.' Once the subject of abortion becomes part of a general discussion about taking life, there will be no way that one group can practise unacceptable discrimination against the other.

I discussed the issue later with a woman who sees abortion as the most important battlefield between men and women. She argued that there was some justification to the bar on men. 'I get disgusted listening to men sitting round discussing abortion. They never talk about feelings. Only reason and rational decisions – then they try to impose them on women. Abortion isn't about reason, it's about feelings.'

It is not obvious what it means to declare that abortion is about feelings. It hardly needs saying that the whole debate generates feelings – strong ones. Interestingly, a view that was given some support at the seminar was offered by a man: abortion should be made illegal, he said, to protect women from the feelings of guilt and loss it brings. This gave weight to feelings all right, but as an argument against abortion it was, of course, intolerably paternalistic.

Perhaps a better point would be that the way a woman feels about abortion should be her guide to action. But this will not do. One complaint made at the debate was that there are women who would be better off having abortions, but who do not because they are made to feel guilty and ashamed. These women, it was said, should be helped to put their feelings in perspective; there is nothing to feel guilty about, because abortion is morally acceptable. This is to say, in effect, that feelings are not always the best determiner of actions: sometimes you would be better off disregarding them.

Feelings do matter, of course. And despite the insistence that abortion is not about reason, reason can, in fact, be invaluable in considering them. A woman trying to decide whether or not to end an unwanted pregnancy will have many things to take into account – the effect on her future, the wishes of the father (they may not be paramount, but they do count), and her own feelings. She may be sure that abortion is acceptable but know that she will feel grief at the loss of the child. This knowledge may tip the balance in favour of her not having an abortion: a child will be inconvenient – perhaps very inconvenient – but she will be happier than if she had aborted it. On the other hand, while recognising that she will suffer if she has an abortion, she may decide that all in all it will be better if she does: she just cannot face the prospect of motherhood. Now, the only tool for assessing all the relevant factors is, in fact, reason. Reason does not cast doubt on feelings – their strength, their existence or their importance. To the contrary, it helps you give them their due in your calculations; the rational choice is the one that takes proper note of feelings. There can be no objection to bringing reason to bear on any issue – even one as emotionally charged as abortion.

One of the fruits of reason is that it can reveal the implications of some dearly held conviction. It can lay bare what you are, perhaps unwittingly, really committed to by a certain belief. For example, what is the anti-abortion lobby committed to? The high card of the anti-abortionist is the view that life is sacred. Albert Schweitzer's comment, 'I cannot but have reverence for all that is called life', sounds a chord in most people, a chord that echoes in the conviction that life is to be respected and preserved, that killing is *prima facie* wrong. A middle-aged Presbyterian with strong views on abortion aligned herself with the anti-abortionists at the seminar, declaring, 'I would hope that my daughter would never consider having an abortion. I hold to the principle that life is sacred – taking it is terribly wrong. Even if it hurts you have to stick to your principles.'

When people say that you must act from principle they are insisting you be guided by some rule which always triumphs in any conflict with your personal preference. Principles act as a rein on desires to limit what is morally permissible. This woman, then, is claiming that even if her preference would be to end an unwanted pregnancy, the principle that life may not be taken would override it. For whatever else a foetus may be, it is undeniably life.

The principle that life is sacred has implications far beyond abortion. As stated, it puts killing the human foetus morally on a par with killing anything – other animals, insects, perhaps even plants. The lamb that is sacrificed to the palate of the carnivore is as much a life as the human foetus, so anyone who holds that life is sacred is committed to the view that killing the lamb is as wrong as killing the foetus. Indeed, the gardener who systematically eradicates anything regarded as a pest and the holidaymaker who swats mosquitoes are both committing a crime which is morally indistinguishable from the crime of abortion.

The theologian Karl Barth was prepared to embrace this extreme position. He believed that if something was killed without specific authorisation from God then the killing was murder, even though it was an animal that had been killed. The 'life is sacred' lobby cannot wriggle out of this conclusion by insisting that it is acceptable to take some types of life but not others, for that implicitly abandons the sanctity principle: if you can kill animals and insects then it is not *life* that is sacred. Given that most of us are carnivores, and we do also kill inconvenient bugs, consistency demands that the 'sanctity of life' principle be dropped.*

We may begin, then, by adopting, as almost all anti-abortionists do, a narrower, more anthropocentric, principle: it is the life of a person that is sacred. Given that what is brought into being at conception is a person, its life is sacred and killing it is wrong. Those who hold this view will agree with St Jerome that abortion is 'the murder of the unborn child'. A nun working in a hospice for the terminally ill observed, 'People often say, "Wouldn't it be better to allow euthanasia for people in great pain who are going to die anyway?" But a person's life is sacred. It may not be taken – it would be murder – and that is as true of the person who has just been conceived as the person whose life is near its end.'

Anyone reflecting on the rights and wrongs of abortion may find this hard line persuasive; it is simple and powerful. You may be grieved, of course, by the harrowing stories of women exhaustedly trying to cope with handicapped children, or saddened by the misery and distress that may come with an unwanted child; but you will not have to agonise about what to do. If you believe that a foetus is a person, you will be quite sure that abortion is not an acceptable means of avoiding another person's suffering.

Many of those who in the abortion issue rigorously apply the principle that it is wrong to kill a person are reluctant fully to embrace its implications. For example, in the college seminar a woman insisted, 'With all the contraceptive devices available today it's just criminal if a woman gets pregnant when she doesn't want a child. If she can't be bothered to go on the pill why should society allow her to murder the result?' Someone pointed out that many contraceptive devices – the coil, the mini-pill – are in fact early-abortion techniques. They allow conception but then prevent the fertilised egg implanting itself into the lining of the womb. The response was, 'It's hardly the

---

* This does not necessarily mean abandoning other creatures to be treated in any way we choose. As Jonathan Glover explained in *Causing Death and Saving Lives*, 'When we have become clearer about the reasons for thinking it wrong to kill people we will be better placed to see whether the same reasons should make us respect animal or plant life as well.'

same as having a six-week-old foetus sucked out of a womb. Is it?' Mechanically it is not; but morally it is precisely the same. If a person comes into existence at conception, then a woman who has a coil, and knows how it works, is in the same position as a woman who has an abortion; there is no line to be drawn between them.

This view also commits its proponents to absolute pacifism. The next step from believing that no amount of human suffering justifies killing a foetus because it is a person is that it would be wrong to kill a tyrant – who is also a person – no matter what horrors and tortures he had inflicted, and then that it would be wrong to fight a war no matter how repressive and bloody the aggressor. It would even be wrong to kill to save your own life. In short, these proponents are committed to the view that there is no circumstance whatsoever that will justify killing a person.

Many people cling to the principle that human life is sacred for fear that if it is undermined our natural disgust at the taking of life will be eroded. An army officer who commanded tanks during the war explained, 'Of course I had to kill during the war. But if one comes right out and says that killing is justified this is surely the thin end of the wedge. People will soon stop feeling the horror of killing.'

The kind of attitude that it is feared will be engendered is explicit in the following excerpt from the diary of an Auschwitz doctor, Hans Herman Kremer.

> September 6, 1942   Today Sunday, excellent lunch: tomato soup, half a hen, with potatoes and red cabbage, sweets and marvellous ice . . . in the evening at 8.00 hours outside for a *Sonderaktion*.

A *Sonderaktion* is a 'special action'. An example of such an action in Auschwitz was one in which live prisoners were burned to death in a pit. It is incomprehensible that such an event could even be perpetrated, let alone reported as a footnote to details of lunch.

Such atrocities are a long way from abortion, yet a supporter of 'Life', the anti-abortion campaign, argued in a television interview that the mentality of the typical pro-abortionist was similar to that of the Nazis. Setting aside what on earth it would entail to be a 'typical pro-abortionist', and assuming that the comment was an expression of a genuine anxiety rather than a cynical piece of oratory, it raises this issue: is it true that questioning the sanctity of life principle contributes to such callousness as Dr Kremer's?

The crucial phrase in the army officer's comment is 'killing is justified'. It is easy to slip from the conclusion that an act is justified to one of its being good. But there is, in fact, a vast gulf between the two. It is perfectly coherent to argue, for example, that killing in self-defence is justified, while maintaining that any killing, including killing in self-defence, must constitute an evil. Sometimes, an evil may be justified, but an evil can never be good. Our abhorrence at killing is grounded in our perception of it as an evil; there is no reason why that perception should change, even if killing may be seen in some circumstance to be justified.

Without taking a step towards Dr Kremer's attitude, then, we may propound a weaker version of the sanctity of human life principle: killing is an evil, but it may be justified if it is the only means to avert a much greater evil. David Sheppard, Bishop of Liverpool, gave this principle support in a discussion we had about the problem for Christians of dealing with human weakness. He said, 'The toughest human decisions are when you cannot see anything facing you but a choice of evils – war is the greatest of them. But if there's a Hitler across the Channel it might be that not to go to war would be an evil. It is still worth calling what you do an evil though – and going through the pain of that.'

The war, then, against Nazi Germany, in which millions were killed, was certainly an evil, but it may have been a just war, aiming as it did to secure the quality of life of those who survived. I have no idea what David Sheppard's views on abortion are, but no one who agrees with him about the war could consistently hold that it is acceptable to kill innocent children in, say, bombing raids, to avoid appalling suffering for others, but not for the same end to kill a foetus in abortion.

One reply to this might be that it is acceptable to fight a defensive war against invading soldiers, but utterly unacceptable to fight an offensive war in which innocents are killed. The

aggressor somehow forfeits his right to consideration; innocence demands that life be respected. The innocence of the
foetus should, then, protect it from abortion. I imagine that in
war the practical difficulties of this position would be enormous, but at least the reasoning is consistent: killing may be
justified in self-defence but not at the cost of innocent life. It
would, of course, follow from this that abortion would not even
be justified if the mother would otherwise die, for even the
foetus that is unintentionally killing you is innocent; you may
not sacrifice innocent life for your own.

An absolute prohibition on killing people need not, however,
entail a prohibition on abortion. The pacifist insists that killing
a person is always wrong, but there are those who insist that the
tiny scrap of matter that is the fertilised egg is not a person. A
20-year-old student who wrote a thesis on abortion made this
observation: 'I thought I was pregnant once and decided if I was
I'd have an abortion. I never thought of the foetus as a person –
like a baby would be. It's just a blob after all.' Judith Jarvis
Thompson argued in her article 'A Defence of Abortion' that 'a
very early abortion is surely not the killing of a person'.
Professor Thompson's emphasis on 'very early' suggests the
view that the fertilised egg does not start out as a person; rather,
it becomes one some time after conception.

At what moment, then, does the foetus become someone to
be protected? A 35-year-old teacher with four children argued
in favour of early abortion on demand. She suggested, 'It's
when the foetus is viable. If its body can function independently of the mother's body then it's a fully fledged person.
Otherwise it's not.'

This has some bizarre consequences, for what is supposed to
be a morally significant moment varies alarmingly according to
the dictates of such diverse considerations as luck, medical
advances and geography. One foetus, for example, may by
chance survive a premature birth at three months. A recent
newspaper article describes how a nurse who was assisting at
an abortion found that the foetus was alive after the operation.
She then had to battle to save it. Another foetus, however, may
die of premature birth at seven months. It would be very odd to
be committed to the view that the least developed foetus was a

person while the most developed was not. Advances in medicine also mean that an early foetus which could not have survived independently of its mother five years ago can survive now. Today it is a person; then, at the same stage of development, it was not. Strangest of all, linking personhood to viability entails that in a country where there are few medical resources a foetus would become a person much later than it would in a country with well-developed resources. All of this clamours for an answer to the question: is being a person so crucially related to viability?

First, it would be dangerous to insist that to be a person you must be able to survive independently of *any* life-support system at all. This would commit you to regarding babies in incubators and people on lung or kidney machines as not being people. The idea, then, must be that you are not a person if your life-support system *is* a person. This is an arbitrary distinction with chilling consequences. In his book *Causing Deaths and Saving Lives* Jonathan Glover asks his readers to imagine that a woman with, for example, a severe kidney defect could be kept alive normally by being linked to a person with healthy kidneys for regular periods. The sick woman would not be able to function without the healthy woman: she would not be viable, and therefore on the 'viability equals person' theory she would not be a person. I cannot imagine anyone wanting to be committed to this view; but then, if being a person is not related to viability at one end of the scale, why on earth should anyone think it is at the other end?

Because of these difficulties, some people latch on to birth as the moment at which the foetus becomes a person. A 20-year-old student whose girlfriend had an abortion when she became pregnant by accident told me, 'You do just think of a foetus and a baby as very different. I didn't think it was wrong to get an abortion. But I wouldn't kill a baby. Once it's born it's a whole new ball game – I mean, you've got a little person on your hands then.' The idea is that there is some difference between a new-born baby and a foetus – at any stage of development – which allows the killing of one but not the other, for the foetus has none of the moral status of personhood that protects even a one-minute-old baby.

This seems to me to be a great moral weight to hang from the spatial fact of being outside rather than inside a womb. What might be the relevant differences between foetus and baby? There are two obvious ones: a new-born baby is independent and the foetus is not, and the baby is visible and present in a way that the foetus is not. The first should be rejected with the viability argument: being independent or not does not confer or debar personhood. The second smacks of an unsavoury morality; it is like being committed to the view that it is wrong to kill one person in hand-to-hand combat but acceptable to kill thousands by dropping a bomb from five miles up. Admittedly, human psychology is such that we do respond more caringly to what is before us than to what is unseen. A starving child on your doorstep will probably move you to sympathy and help; millions of starving children in another country may leave you cold. Similarly, if all that is seen of a foetus is the distortion of a woman's body, it must be easier to withhold the feelings of care, protection and respect that a tiny, helpless baby almost invariably arouses. But it would be disastrous to build a morality on this fact of human make-up: it would justify genocide as long as the perpetrator was far enough away not to be moved by the slaughter.

The philosopher Richard Wertheimer wondered recently during a discussion on abortion how differently people might feel about the moral status of a foetus if the mothers had transparent wombs and you could see the foetus growing and moving. A friend told me of her feelings when she saw her baby during a scan. 'There was this little thing about the size of a fingernail. Nothing like a baby to look at – but it was miraculous! I could see a tiny pulse which was its heart-beat. I could never think of it as a thing – or disposable. It was a baby – my baby.'

In the end, disputes about whether or not a foetus is a person are futile, for 'person' is a vague concept; it does not have a definite outline. This indeterminacy is exploited by those involved in the abortion debate. Antagonists of the idea that abortion is acceptable produce some sufficient condition for personhood – for example, the presence of the full genetic code – and then show that the foetus satisfies it. Friends of pro-abortion arguments produce a necessary condition for personhood – a concept of self perhaps – and then show that the foetus lacks it. But no amount of mental exertion provides 'person-hood' with the hard edges a concept needs if it is to be applied without uncertainty.

In this, it is like the concept 'bald'. A man without a hair to his head is bald. But what of the man with a few hairs scraped over his pate? Is he bald or not? And what of the fertilised egg, which is so different from what we normally think of as a person? Is it one or not? Some people are sure it is; others are equally certain it is not. Deciding the issue is not like deciding whether or not a certain tree is an oak: the tree's DNA structure will decide that. But there is no comparable fact to decide the issue of personhood. Uncertainties do not spring from ignor-ance of some decisive fact but from there being no decisive fact to be known. As Jane English puts it in *Abortion and the Concept of a Person*, 'Our concept of a person is not sharp or decisive enough to bear the weight of a solution to the abortion controversy.' She concludes, 'To use it to solve that problem is to clarify *obscurum per obscurum* [the obscure by the obscure].'

The vagueness surrounding the issue of personhood seems to allow room for someone's needs to dictate whether the foetus is seen as a person or not. A woman I spoke to had an abortion because she was told that she would not survive the pregnancy. She said, 'I didn't see it as a person. It felt more like a horrible kind of growth I had to get rid of.' Perceiving a foetus in this light would make you far more disposed to kill it than the woman for whom pregnancy was a minor inconvenience. In line with this a nurse told me, 'Women who have miscarriages – even very early ones – talk about losing the baby; but women who have abortions usually talk about getting rid of the foetus.'

This nurse expressed a regret that women abort healthy foetuses at all. 'I see so many women who are desperate to have children and they can't even adopt one. It seems tragic that babies are being lost that would be snapped up by loving parents.' A man I spoke to was adamant that this was more than tragic; it was unacceptable. He and his wife have been trying for nearly two years to adopt a child, but the waiting list seems endless. 'How can it be right to allow women to have abortions when so many people are desperate to adopt? It's a dreadful waste.' The distress that this man and others feel cannot be disregarded. But does it justify the interests of childless couples being given priority over the interests of unwillingly pregnant women? 'I can see,' he replied, 'that a woman may suffer if she is made to carry a child she doesn't want. But think of the happiness it would give. Doesn't that count for something?'

There may be grounds for saying that the morally decent thing for a woman who does not want her child is to bear it and then give it to someone who does want it. But what we can see as morally decent is not what we should necessarily make obligatory. Charities operate on the principle that it is morally decent that those who have should give to those who have not; but no one thinks it should be made obligatory for people to give to charity – especially if it will cause them distress and hardship.

If you think abortion is in principle acceptable you cannot deny it to a woman simply to satisfy another woman's need. Of course, if a pregnancy lasted only an hour you may think any woman who refused to see it to term callous and selfish – but even so, other people's interests would not provide grounds for forcing her to bear the child. As it is, pregnancy lasts nine months – months in which a woman may have to adjust to social and professional changes, not to mention physical and emotional ones. The end of pregnancy is not necessarily the end of trauma. Many women who give up their babies for adoption report a continuing feeling of sadness that their children are being brought up without their mothers. No group of people should be made miserable simply in order for another group to be made happy. If abortion is acceptable, then women must be allowed to choose it.

Anyone who argues that it is acceptable to force women to meet the needs of childless couples is also committed to believing that contraception should be outlawed. It may seem that it would be a gross infringement of liberty to prevent a woman taking a pill, but much less of an infringement to prevent the destruction of an already conceived foetus. But if the interests of pregnant women may be disregarded – because what matters most is making up a shortage in babies – then the interests of women who *could* become pregnant may be disregarded. If supplying the baby market takes precedence over a woman's freedom to choose, then all suitable women may be pressed into service. This would surely be unacceptable.

*

Opposing the anti-abortionists, whom they tend to see as repressive, as religious maniacs, or as anti-woman, are those who believe that abortion should be allowed on demand. Many agree with Jill Tweedie that it is 'a basic human right for a woman to decide whether she will have an abortion or not'.

What precisely is this right? A woman in her early 20s, who rather chillingly described an abortion she had had as, 'nothing more than the removal of an inconvenient growth', argued, 'Germaine Greer made it plain that it is crucial to feminism that a woman has the right of control over her own body. We mustn't go on being dictated to by men on issues like contraception and abortion – it's a kind of slavery. It's part of this right of control that a woman may have an abortion on demand.'

The Women's Abortion and Contraception Campaign echoed this view. 'Women must have control over their own lives. For this we must have control over our own bodies. The abortion issue is the cornerstone in the liberation of women.'

Even one who finds abortion acceptable in principle may be unconvinced by this women's rights argument. For there is a weakness in it, one that is often apparent when people start talking about rights – what must be allowed. Rights are so often produced out of a hat like magic rabbits to beg the very question they were supposed to deal with. And this is exactly what is happening here.

Even if it were true that denying a woman an abortion infringed a very important right, the question has still to be answered: is abortion acceptable? For it is not at all clear that a right can be exercised whatever the cost, or whatever the other moral considerations. The Royal Family have a right to privacy, but only the most rabid royalist would think it acceptable for them to machine-gun intrusive reporters. A woman has the right to control her own body, but may she exercise that right by taking life? Someone may perfectly well argue that this right – like the right to privacy – does not justify killing.

The argument that a woman owns her body – it is her property and, just like any other piece of her property, she has the right to deny anyone the use of it – is a common one. A young trainee solicitor thought this argument was unassailable. 'You can't deny that a woman owns her body – so surely she has the right to deny the foetus the use of it. It's surely obvious then that she has the right to an abortion.'

I will not deny that a woman owns her body – though it seems an odd way to describe the relationship we have with our bodies. But I do deny that on some scale of values a person's property rights obviously wipe out the obligation on us to refrain from taking human life. Such a grading would commit a woman to thinking it acceptable to throw a child out of a boat into shark-infested waters because it was her boat and she had the right to deny the child the use of it. This conclusion cannot be avoided by insisting that it is unacceptable to throw out the child because we have an obligation to refrain from doing what will kill it, but that this does not prevent abortion because we have no such obligation towards the foetus. This simply makes the argument redundant, whereas the point was to show when it was permissible to do what is generally thought wrong – that is, to take life.

Anyone who insists that the property rights argument is unacceptable is not necessarily anti-feminist. The feminist philosopher Mary Ann Warren has said, 'Mere ownership does not give me the right to kill innocent people whom I find on my property. It is equally unclear that I have any moral right to expel an innocent person from my property when I find that doing so will result in his death.' This is not solely a restraint on women. On this argument a man would be wrong to kill someone trespassing on his property: his undeniable property rights do not allow murder. A recent trial involved the captain of a Greek oil-tanker who threw twelve stowaways overboard into shark-infested waters. He argued that they had no right to be on his boat, that it was far too inconvenient to sail them back into port, and that he was therefore justified in forcing them over the side at gun-point – probably to get eaten. Along with his crew he was convicted of manslaughter. It was not murder, because the boat was only a mile from shore and the captain convinced the jury that he believed the victims could make it to safety. On this law, the most the 'property rights' argument will win for a woman is the right to expel the foetus – but in such a way as not to kill it. It is probable that science will in the end secure this argument for women. For if, as it surely will, it becomes possible safely to extract the foetus and rear it either artificially or in another woman's womb, we will be able to give due respect to the rights women claim on their bodies. As things are, though, this right will not in itself make abortion acceptable.

If the property argument wins too little for the pro-abortionists, the following contract argument wins too much. The argument in essence is that no one need take responsibility for another's life unless that responsibility has been assumed from the start. When a pregnancy is unwanted, especially when adequate precautions have been taken against it, the mother has no responsibility for the foetus, for she has no pre-established contract with it. A woman who fell pregnant despite being on the pill spelt it out. 'I didn't hesitate to go for an abortion. I felt no responsibility for the foetus whatsoever.'

It is arbitrary to establish that you contract only with a willingly conceived foetus. Why not stipulate that you have a contract with any foetus that is the product of sex in which you willingly engaged? But setting that aside – do we want to talk of contracts in terms of the responsibility human beings have for each other? It is a deeply-felt intuition that even strangers have moral claims on each other. America was outraged in the 1930s when singer Bessie Smith, the 'Empress of the Blues', died from loss of blood after a car crash because the nearest hospital did not treat black people. Similarly, an elderly woman living near me was mugged recently while a group of bystanders did nothing; the local newspapers were crammed with quotes from the police, community organisations and neighbours denounc-ing those who stood by. People were as shocked by the failure to help her as by the actual mugging.

The contract theory, however, commits us to saying we may ignore the plight – however desperate – of those we do not know and for whom we have no responsibility. But that is not all: since in abortion a woman instigates harm against a foetus, we would be committed to allowing that you do not need to refrain from hurting those with whom you have no contract.

This goes too far. It is perhaps grounded in a fudging of the notion of responsibility. A woman who tries to prevent concep-tion may not be responsible for the existence of the foetus; but it does not follow from this that she has no moral responsibility towards it.

During a discussion with a group of students, I was offered the thought that even if these arguments fail a woman has the right to defend herself from harm. 'When my mum was carrying me she was told she might die – there was some complication or other – and she had to think about whether to have an abortion. She didn't, of course. But I reckon if a pregnancy's going to kill you it's on to kill the foetus. I wouldn't hesitate.'

Every woman has the right to defend herself from harm, and it is generally accepted that this right may be exercised even if it costs the life of an attacker. The harm is, of course, presumed to be serious harm – it would not be acceptable, for example, for a woman to kill a man if she knew that all he intended was to pinch her bottom. But if you believe that your life is at risk you may kill to protect it. From this, some people take it as uncontroversial that, as part of her right of self-defence, a woman has the right to an abortion if the pregnancy is likely to be fatal to her. The foetus is not precisely an attacker of course, since it has no intention to harm its mother; thus to hold this self-defence view is to be committed to thinking it acceptable to save your own life by sacrificing an innocent life. Many people would baulk at that: few of us, after all, would give our own lives automatic priority over the life of a child – often the opposite, in fact. Nevertheless, innocent children are killed in wars and this is often justified on the grounds of self-defence. If infanticide is acceptable to save life, then the same principle will justify abortion.

If self-defence were the only justification for abortion, very few women would be morally entitled to have one. Although those who are pro-abortion produce harrowing stories of desperate women in need of abortion, the reality is that, in Western countries at least, women have abortions for less dramatic reasons. A baby would interfere with the mother's career; she is too young now, or too old; the father is the wrong man to spend a life with; there are too many children in the family already, and not enough money for another. It is this that creates a need for the women's rights arguments. These assume that if the foetus has rights – whatever they are – they are outweighed by the mother's rights. But justifying abortion by giving a trade-off value to the mother's property or contract rights is unpalatable; most of us would reject the idea that such rights have priority over life.

But why should the pro-abortionists have to argue from the priority of some kind of right or other? They do not have to reach the conclusion that abortion is completely and categorically acceptable. All that is needed is to put it beyond severe censure. This can be done by trading on the fact that any reasonable morality has to have space between great goodness and great wickedness, and that it is this space which most people inhabit. Very few of us, for example, do anything at all to help the world's starving children. But we do not condemn ourselves as moral hooligans, nor feel overwhelming guilt about our failure. We simply acknowledge that, morally at least, most of us are not heroes.

It could be admitted, then, that a woman who has an abortion is not a moral heroine. But this does not mean that she has done something appalling. For abortion is morally on a par with the way most of us behave towards starving children. In both cases there is a clearly specifiable and heroic course of action – to bear the child, and to give our earnings to charity. Doubtless women of the moral calibre of a Mother Teresa would choose such a course. But most of us cannot match up to such women: we fall short of heroism.

It might be said, then, that abortion deserves no more blame than doing nothing to ease the plight of children who are dying. That is to say, it deserves a rather theoretical kind of blame which is not very highly charged. While most of us complacently accept our moral shortcomings we are not in a position to demand moral heroism of a woman carrying an unwanted foetus.

The most common view concerning abortion has grown out of a modified version of the self-defence argument: abortion is an evil, but no woman should be forced to bear a child at the cost to herself of great suffering. This pays coin to the value of the foetus as human life, as well as to the promptings of humanity that suffering is to be avoided. So, for example, a man at my college seminar insisted, 'If a woman gets pregnant as the result of rape of course she can have an abortion. Of course she can.

But I don't believe that any woman who just doesn't want a baby should be free to kill it.' A schoolmistress teaching at a girls' secondary school agreed. 'I wouldn't hesitate to recommend a girl pregnant through rape to get an abortion. But if some silly girl gets pregnant because she can't be bothered to take adequate precautions I can't see any reason at all why she should be given an abortion.'

Why should a foetus conceived in rape be eligible to be killed, but not a foetus conceived of a voluntary act? Both foetuses may be healthy; neither is guilty of anything; and neither is a threat to the mother's own physical health.

There can be no difference in their moral status. Why, then, should it be readily assumed that it is acceptable to abort one and dubious to abort the other? The usual answer is that to force a rape victim to bear her attacker's child is tantamount to compounding her already appalling suffering and distress. Surely the mother's pain and horror cancel out any rights the foetus may have? As the schoolmistress insisted: 'This is the only humanitarian attitude it is possible to take.'

But anyone who believes this owes us an explanation of why the possible misery of the unwillingly pregnant woman does not have the same overriding weight. It is easy to imagine that *some* women pregnant by accident suffer as much as, if not more than, some women pregnant by rape. If suffering justifies abortion, then it is suffering that must be calculated. The method of conception is in itself irrelevant. For example, one woman I spoke to had become pregnant after being raped by her ex-husband. She was offered an abortion but chose to have the baby. 'I only had one son and I kept thinking, "This is his brother or sister." I couldn't have aborted it.' Clearly on some scale of suffering she would be likely to register less high than a frightened 16-year-old who 'went too far' at a party. Yet on the views being considered, the 16-year-old would be forced to bear her child while the rape victim would be sympathetically treated. This is just a muddle: either any woman suffering as the result of a pregnancy is entitled to an abortion on the principle that her suffering trumps the foetus's rights, or no woman is entitled to one, however much she may be suffering, on the grounds that nothing justifies killing the foetus. This latter view was actually offered – to much cat-calling – at the

seminar. A young woman who insisted that she had no religious base to her views argued, 'The child of a rape is at least
half the mother's child; it has done no harm; it is not its *fault*.
Why should it be made to pay with its life?'

This is a hard line to take. It seems uncaring and cold. But
although it offends our strong inclination to help those who are
the victim of misfortune, it also satisfies our disinclination to
help those who are the authors of their own predicament. It is
presumably this sort of feeling that made many people I spoke
to – men and women – argue that those who could have
avoided pregnancy should be made to carry the results of their
casualness to term. The issue of abortion, however, is not about
determining who deserves help; it is about whether a foetus
may ever justifiably be killed.

It may seem outrageous that even one who genuinely believes the foetus is a person should deny an abortion to a
woman who has been raped. But no one who thinks a foetus
has the same rights as an infant has any alternative. To allow
that a person – even an embryonic person – may be killed to
save someone else pain and suffering is a commitment to the
view that an old sick parent or a handicapped child may be
killed if it is the only way to relieve a miserable burden on
another. You cannot have your morality both ways: if you feel
morally obliged to treat a foetus as you would an infant, then if
in some situation it would be utterly unacceptable to kill the
infant it would be equally unacceptable to kill a foetus. Similarly, if it is ever acceptable to kill a foetus, then in that same
situation it would be acceptable to kill an infant.

One of the saddest imaginable cases of abortion to spare the
mother was told to me by a journalist. A woman asked for the
abortion of a 21-week-old foetus because her husband had been
killed in a car crash and she felt that she could not have his
child without him. The National Health Service duly performed the operation. That same day the Director of EXIT (the
voluntary euthanasia society) told me the story of a young man
who for several years had been almost completely paralysed
after an accident. For him, life was utter misery and he had
several times tried to commit suicide – unsuccessfully, because
of his physical limitations. Finally he managed somehow to get
hold of and take an overdose of sleeping pills. He was dis-

covered, and his stomach was pumped out. Thus he was forcibly dragged back to a life he found desperate. The NHS was prepared to override the carefully thought-out wish of a fully conscious, fully aware adult to terminate his life, while allowing a grief-stricken woman, hardly in a fit state to make a decision about anything, to terminate the life of a healthy foetus that must have had at least a chance of a happy life. This is madness: if it is acceptable to kill then it must be acceptable for someone to choose to die. If someone may not take their own life then no one may take another's life.

People who do want it both ways – an abortion in certain circumstances is acceptable, but not in others – are often responding to a feeling that people should take the consequences of their actions, especially when they are almost wilfully the agents of their own misfortunes. I spoke to a 23-year-old who had had four abortions because 'I just don't seem to be able to get it together with pills and things'. Many people would – with some justice – regard her as a 'silly girl' who deserved to be refused an abortion. 'She brought it on herself,' they might say. And most of us would feel some measure of sympathy with the sentiment. But nevertheless, it is being taken too far. You may feel in exasperation that you are entitled to withhold help from someone who persistently behaves irresponsibly, but what you cannot demand is that no one else should help her. If you believe that abortion is in principle acceptable then you may insist that the girl sort it out herself, without your help, but you cannot insist that she is prevented from sorting it out at all. Of course, there are circumstances in which we insist that a particular consequence should follow from a certain act – in particular. when we are punishing people for some offence. Perhaps a woman who has four abortions because of her own carelessness does seem to deserve some punishment. As people are fond of saying, 'It's the only way she'll learn.' But it would be a distasteful morality indeed to discipline a woman by forcing her to bear a child.

If strong objection to suffering justifies abortion, then of course the foetus cannot be allowed to suffer. Even someone strongly pro-abortionist is likely to draw the line at the point where the foetus would suffer. As one woman agreed, 'It's one thing to get rid of something that cannot feel pain; quite another to cause suffering to it.' In his article 'Abortion and the Golden Rule', R.M. Hare concluded that if 'foetuses really do suffer on the same scale as adults do, then that would be a good moral reason for not causing them to suffer'. The problem is knowing if and when foetuses do suffer. Professor Hare goes on: 'It will not do to show that they wriggle when pricked, for so do earthworms; and I do not think that the upholders of the rights of unborn children wish to extend these rights to earthworms.'

The medical profession generally allows that the foetus can feel at about twelve weeks; so if after that time the foetus would suffer this would provide a limit to abortion. But even if we are sure of the level of suffering, what about the abortionist who is sufficiently skilled to abort a much older foetus without caus- ing it pain, say by skilful use of anaesthetic? Most people have a gut reaction against aborting foetuses very late – perhaps because they are much more like babies – but if all that matters is not to cause pain then such restrictions would have to be regarded as purely sentimental.

If it is acceptable to abort a foetus because of the mother's suffering, why is it generally not thought to be good enough for an abortion that the future child is unwanted? Being unwanted is a cause of great unhappiness and disturbance. No one, after all, believes that it is wrong to commit suicide because you are miserable but acceptable if, however happy you are, your death will make others happy. Of course, we all yearn for people to be morally heroic, and we thrill to great altruism in a way that we do not thrill to self-interest. But even so, there is no justification for 'imposing' altruism – even on the unaware foetus.

A doctor I discussed this with thought I had missed the vital point. 'Look! It's relatively easy to calculate the suffering that a woman is enduring because of a pregnancy, but it's almost impossible to calculate the suffering an unborn child may have to go through in its life. It would be presumptuously god-like to do so . . . ' But is it not just this stance that doctors take all the time? It is almost a commonplace that the possibility of future suffering is often a deciding factor in the question of whether or not to abort a foetus. A couple I met had an abortion when a scan showed that the foetus had Down's Syndrome. 'What life is there for someone like that? We did what we thought was best for it.' It is assumed, then, that physical and mental handicaps so diminish the quality of life of the future child that it is better to have no life at all. But is that obviously true? Setting aside for a moment the strain on parents who must support and care for a handicapped child, is it obvious that the best thing for the *child* is to be killed before birth?

Candidates for therapeutic abortion include Down's Syndrome children. It is well known that these children have a capacity for joy and happiness that tends to exceed that of 'normal' children: if they are miserable it will be largely because they are badly cared for, not because they are handicapped. If the prospect for such a child is possible years of happiness, should it be denied those years? Interestingly, a woman I spoke to had an abortion at 18 'because I was just too young', but at 23 and married she found her baby had Down's Syndrome. 'I was ready for a baby, and so was my husband. We're comfortably off and had no other children so all we had to think about was the future of the child. We went to a home for children with the syndrome and it was an extraordinary experience. The kids just come rushing up and cuddle you and hold your hand – they're enchanting. Anyway we had Kelly – and she's happy – and we all love her.'

What of children who are handicapped in more horrible ways – for example, with spina bifida? Again, if the *only* consideration is the future happiness of the child, it is not obvious that abortion is the answer. I would have thought it better to allow the child to be born and then see what kind of life it could have. It will surely give anyone pause for thought that Beethoven – whose father, we are often reminded by anti-abortionists, had syphilis – would today have been a candidate for therapeutic abortion, as would the dreadfully handicapped Irish writer Christy Brown. In fact, the truly rational policy would be to allow the child to reach a certain age, whenever it might be expected to understand these things, and then ask it if it wanted to go on living. When I said this to a friend she described the whole idea as 'revolting and utterly disgusting'. But surely some chance of happiness is better than no chance, and voluntary euthanasia more acceptable than abortion?

The doctor I spoke to reflected that, even among the most

severely handicapped, those who wish to kill themselves tend
to be those who become disabled late in life, through injury or
illness. 'People born that way are nearly always better adjusted.
I suppose those of us who are normal find it hard to believe that
such people can have anything going for them at all – but that's
certainly wrong.' Philippa Foot commented on this in an
interview with Mary Kenny: 'I think that the term "quality of
life" is extremely dangerous. When we say "this person's
quality of life isn't high enough" – isn't high enough for what?
Nobody can judge who is going to be happy.' And, as Aristotle
once observed, those things that for one person make life worth
while may seem unlikely to another to have much to do with
happiness. In the *Eudemian Ethics* he reports that 'Anaxagoras
answered a man who was raising problems of this sort and
asking why one should choose to be born rather than not – "for
the sake of viewing the heavens and the whole order of the
universe".'

Most handicapped foetuses are, in fact, aborted because we do
not want them. Dress it up how you will, that is almost
certainly the reality behind the pious mouthings about what is
best for the child. And what, you may ask, is wrong with that?
Why should anyone want a handicapped child? Of course, no
one would *want* a handicapped child; the question is whether,
having conceived such a child, you may kill it. Perhaps this
seems to put the whole matter too simply; there are, after all,
the parents of the child to be considered – and what they may
suffer. One of the most harrowing documents I have ever read
was a letter to *The Times* from the mother of a severely
handicapped son. She described her day looking after him, and
it sounded utterly miserable, having no recognisable rewards.
How could we condemn her to this?

There are undoubtedly too many handicapped people living
wretched lives in institutions, and there is a heavy burden on
the parents of such children who look after them. Knowing this,
it is easy to argue that it is better for the abnormal foetus to be
aborted. But from the same premise you might argue that
anyone born handicapped should be given whatever is necessary to give them a chance of happiness. And people are not
necessarily condemned to misery by the refusal to allow

abortion. There is also the refusal to make available the resources to help parents and children – money for homes, equipment, medical staff. All of these would considerably reduce present suffering.

The argument that it is better, for its own sake, for the foetus to be aborted is doubtful. The lengths to which we will go to avoid having handicapped children born is brought home by the fact that people are prepared to risk aborting a healthy foetus if there is a chance that it may be deformed. Many people accept that a woman has a right to an abortion if she has contracted German measles in early pregnancy. The problem is that it is impossible to tell if the foetus has in fact been damaged, and to what extent. Women who carry haemophilia may also have an abortion, even though there is a 50 per cent chance that the child will be free of the disorder.

Anyone who finds this acceptable is in effect allowing that a foetus may be aborted, even though it is not definitely known what quality of life the child will enjoy. There are some doubts, the child may suffer, therefore it is acceptable to abort it. But these people are committed to accepting that *any* foetus about which there are doubts is a candidate for abortion. Being definitely unwanted casts a shadow over the life of the child, just as possibly being deformed does, so on their own admission this should be sufficient for abortion. One woman's response to this was, 'You can't just kill a foetus for frivolous reasons like being unwanted.' This misses the point; the foetus is to be aborted – or so the argument goes – to save it possible suffering. Since in many cases this is regarded as acceptable, there is no ground for dismissing it when the cause of the unhappiness seems not to be in some way as weighty as disease or deformity. The only ground for denying this would be that a healthy foetus with a chance of happiness must be protected from uncertain predictions – in which case *any* foetus which has a chance of being healthy or happy should be protected.

The proponents of this most common view about abortion – some are acceptable, others are not – are caught on the horns of a dilemma. It cannot be sufficient for abortion that there is a reasonable chance of future misery for the child, for then there will be many more abortions than middle-of-the-roaders wish to allow; it cannot be sufficient for abortion being denied that there is some chance of happiness, for then there will be many fewer abortions than they would allow. It is not possible to pick a way between these two points: abortion is all or nothing.

What is a woman to do if she finds herself pregnant and does not want a child? If she sincerely believes that taking human life is wrong and cannot imagine any situation – war, self-defence, euthanasia – which justifies such killing, then for her abortion is an unjustifiable evil. She may go ahead and have one because she cannot face the consequences of bearing the child – most people, after all, have been known to act inconsistently with their moral principles – but according to her own lights what she has done is wrong. She may believe, though, that taking human life can be justified – especially if it aims to relieve other people of misery and hardship. Then abortion for her is not necessarily wrong: if she thinks it is acceptable, for example, painfully to kill innocent people in wars for the sake of the survivors, then it cannot be unacceptable painlessly to kill a foetus for the same reason. Indeed, if the consequences of bearing the child would be misery for her and others, abortion will seem to her to be fully justified.

You cannot, however, infer from abortion being *justified* that it is a *good* thing to do. David Sheppard argued earlier that even though war may be justified in certain circumstances, it is always an evil. Being justified is not the equivalent of being good, and it is for this reason that we talk about having to choose between the lesser of two evils. Our choices are not always between good and evil. There the moral issue is clear. Often we are forced to choose between evils – and then the difficult, sometimes heartrending, issue is of how to identify the lesser evil. These sorts of dilemma are described by Thomas Nagel as 'moral tragedies': for some women the choice in such a tragedy may be abortion.

To a woman agonising over whether or not to have an abortion, this must seem like a recipe for confusion. On one side is the burden of unwanted pregnancy; on the other is the burden of choosing what is inherently an evil. She is caught in the middle, desperately trying to get out of the mess she is in. Those of us outside looking in want everything to be perfect; we want to maximise happiness and minimise misery;

we want all the rough parts smoothed out and everything tidied away. Equally, we want to cling to the idea that life is precious. But this should not blind us to the appalling dilemma an unwillingly pregnant woman faces. We can all agree that the taking of a human life should be considered very seriously. The price we must pay for this is that, inevitably, any decision about taking life will be very tough to make.

7

THE LANGUAGE OF SEX

Nothing is more talked about than sex. Children ask endless questions: 'Why does Mummy go in where Daddy comes out?' or, as my step-daughter asked her mother on a crowded bus, 'But how do the seeds get into your tummy?' Uninitiated adolescents speculate anxiously: 'You mean the girl puts her feet in the air?' And savants turgidly debate technique or the flagging libido.

This amateur chorus is swelled by ranks of professionals – doctors, psychiatrists, sex therapists, marriage-guidance coun- sellors – who talk for hours about the nature of impotence, the significance of fantasies, the way to achieve good sex, better sex, best sex. A shrill accompaniment to all this is the voice of the moraliser telling us how we may have sex, when we may have sex, with whom we may have sex . . . if, that is, we may have sex at all.

Then there are the gossips. 'You'll never guess who I saw last night.' And, of course, there are the jokes, the allusions and the innuendo. Sex is so readily insinuated into a non-sexual conversation that the most innocent remark, 'Did you get it?' 'Do you want it?' 'Hold it!' is likely to produce convulsions of winking, nudging, sniggering.

Nothing is more talked about than sex – in fact it is probably more talked about than done.

The words we use when we talk about sex are as intriguing as the fact that we talk about it so much. And one of the most compelling, vivid, sometimes shocking means of sexual expression is metaphor – our figurative descriptions of the sex act and our own anatomies. Samuel Taylor Coleridge thought that all metaphor was poetry. There is, however, little poetry in the most common metaphors of the language of sex.

'Cunt' is a slang term for the vagina; used metaphorically, as in 'You're a cunt', it is an ugly sound that is commonly regarded as a shocking insult. A male teacher in one of the roughest parts of Liverpool admitted to me: 'Although I'm used to being called filthy things, when some little snot-nose called me a cunt I wanted to take him apart.' It needs little acumen to understand that for this boy and man, 'cunt' is a powerful term of abuse. Similarly, 'fuck' is one of the most commonly used words for sexual intercourse. It is also a vicious expression of malevolence: 'Fuck you!' you scream in a moment of hatred.

This feature of the language of sex – that it provides the most powerful language of violence and insult – has led many people to feel deeply disturbed about our attitudes to sex. In an article in the New York Times, for example, Barbara Lawrence, who teaches Humanities at the State University, New York, observed of so-called obscene words that they all 'seem to serve a similar purpose: to reduce the human organism (especially the female organism) and human functions (especially sexual and procreative) to their least organic, most mechanical dimension'. She went on to argue that they 'substitute a trivialising or deforming resemblance for the complex human reality of what is being described'. And the American philosopher Robert Baker argued from our use of expletives that we conceive of sex as an activity in which the female is being harmed – 'screwed', 'fucked' – by the male.

An immediate response to this is that it is hard to see D.H. Lawrence's use of 'fuck', for example, as a deformation of identity and a denial of humanity. Talking of this novelist's use of language, Lawrence Durrell told me, 'It was the struggle Lawrence had to realise himself that made him what he was. It's obvious to me that he had to choose as targets those dreary attitudes that prevented him using four-letter words in a legitimate way.' Was Durrell suggesting, then, that D.H. Lawrence used so-called expletives to free us from the unhealthy attitudes about sex reflected in the traditional language of lily-livered 'prunes and prisms'? 'I think so. You want to adore from the guts and you want to say so. In sex it's terribly important to free that part of you. It has been a great liberation to allow four-letter words to breathe . . . it's astonishing. But to make the breakthrough you have to be extreme. That was Lawrence's game . . . and how right he was.'

At a student debate I attended, everyone present felt more in tune with Durrell's position than with that of people like Barbara Lawrence. It was generally ageed that the use of expletives was not a mark of unhealthy attitudes. Rather it was a sign of liberation, of freedom from hang-ups – linguistic or otherwise. The freedom to lard everyday discourse with what are seen as strong, earthy, rich words for the bodily functions – so-called 'Anglo-Saxon' words like 'shit', 'piss' and 'fuck' – was, as one student represented it, 'reality, honestly stated . . . not shirked'. Clinical latinisms that define these same functions – 'defecate', 'urinate', 'copulate' – were sneered at: ' "Copulate"! It's not attractive, is it. It reminds me of dogs doing it in the street.'

Those who eschewed four-letter words were regarded by the students as more or less the linguistic equivalent of those Victorians engaged in putting frilly pantaloons on piano legs. 'It's difficult,' one student remarked, 'to believe that someone who thinks "fuck" is dirty doesn't think sex is dirty. I mean – what's all the fuss about? It's only a small, four-letter word . . .'

'Fuck' is a small word, but that is no reason to dismiss a debate about the propriety of using it. 'Wog' is also a small word – even smaller. More important even than this is the need to reject any notion that a refusal to use certain words necessarily springs from disgust of the organs and activities those words label. As a professional musician I met at a women's group told me, 'I don't find sex dirty . . . to the contrary. Nor do I mind talking about it. When you're on tour with an almost all-male orchestra, that seems to be all that is talked about. Still, I don't like sexual obscenities – they're so ugly and harsh.'

This objection is not a moral one: it does not suggest that there is anything *wrong* with using words like 'fuck'. The objection is, rather, an aesthetic one; the words are ugly and unpleasing. Similarly, I use the word 'shit' without qualms but I very much dislike the word 'crap'. However, the aesthetic value of a word – the beauty or otherwise of its sound – is not always the best criterion of its appropriateness or otherwise. 'Doxy' is pretty enough, but I would resent its being applied to me: it has pejorative overtones I dislike. 'Ms', on the other hand, is not a particularly attractive sound, but I have no objection to being addressed in this way. The ugliness of the sound is more than compensated for by its being an appellation that does not identify me in terms of my relationship to a man.

Sometimes, however, an aesthetic objection is just a mask for prejudice. Many of those who claim to dislike 'Ms' because it is ugly quite happily use the clumsy 'Messrs' as a plural for 'Mr'. And I have heard people exaggerate the sibilance of 'Ms' to express contempt for the concept it labels. For example, a well-known actor proud of his reputation for Old Worlde gallantry towards 'the ladies', once said to me: 'My dear lady – I would never address you as "Msssssss". It's far too ugly for someone so attractive – it sounds like a demented bumble-bee. I reserve it for those ferocious women who eat men for breakfast and won't shave under their arms.'

You may find a word unpleasing because you are troubled or outraged by what it stands for, or you may feel certain that you simply dislike the word itself: 'fuck' is just ugly. The problem with this sensibility is that introspection may not be able to confirm that your dislike is directed solely at the word – that it is totally unconnected with the word's subject-matter. It is theoretically possible to separate the two: you may find a word in a foreign language ugly with no idea of its meaning. But when you do know a word's meaning you cannot rely on soul-searching to tell you that your emotional response is unconnected with it. You may be a closet prude. Still, no one is entitled to infer you are problem-ridden just because you eschew the word 'fuck', or any other obscenity.

Someone may refuse to use the word 'fuck' of some particular sex act on the grounds that it was inappropriate to what had taken place. A 42-year-old woman told me about an affair she had with a much younger man: 'I'd just broken up with my husband and I really needed some good sex. And that was what I got from him – he was lovely. Then one day I said I loved the way we fucked and he threw a fit. He was so angry – we were supposed to be "making lerrrrrv" or something.'

At a purely linguistic level the dispute between this woman and her lover was about the appropriate application of words that describe sex. He thought what they did was correctly described as 'love-making'; she thought 'fucking' was appropriate. There would be no dispute if the words were synonymous, but they are not. A quickie in a shop doorway may be correctly described as 'fucking', but only rather bizarrely as love-making. 'Of course, people use euphemisms quite often,' she added. 'They prefer them to an honest, straightforward description of the biological event – they like evasion. I suppose it might be out of embarrassment. Or perhaps it's just that suburban respectability will out!'

Do euphemisms invariably avoid the issue? Are they a deliberate evasion of reality? Suppose someone says to you, 'John has gone.' If you knew nothing at all about John you might think he had simply left town. If, however, you knew that John had been seriously ill you would recognise that your informant was using a euphemism for 'died'. So, in context, 'gone' does not avoid the issue; it points quite clearly to dying. On the other hand, a euphemism like 'powder room' does avoid the issue: 'ladies' were not supposed to have excretory habits, so when one disappeared for a 'pee' it had to be disguised as 'powdering her nose'. Of course, through use these terms often become transparent, leaving the reality exposed; they are then supplanted by a more suitably opaque term. 'Lavatory' – which literally means 'washroom' – dropped out of common usage once it was regarded as explicit.

There are, then, two kinds of euphemism. There are the 'soft options', which perfectly well identify the activity but are preferred by a speaker because they are less harsh or brutal than 'straight talking'. Then there are the 'innocents', which at a straight semantic level identify something else – a room to make up in, rather than a toilet. These are evasions.

'Make love' is the most common euphemism for sexual activity, and it veers between being a 'soft option' and an 'innocent'. If what a couple did was fuck, and you knew it yet called it 'making love', then you would be using the phrase as an 'innocent' – avoiding the issue. But if all you knew was that they had sex – you had no idea if it was romance, love or brute lust – and you called it 'making love', then you would be using the phrase as a 'soft option'.

We tend to treat sexual verbs as interchangeable, but it is a mistake to regard them as synonymous. 'Jack fucked Jill' has

THE LANGUAGE OF SEX   113

very different connotations to 'Jack made love to Jill'. The first
statement could be true while the second was not true at all. So,
as one man I spoke to pointed out, different words for sex can
be used to label very different acts. 'I'd say "have sex" if what
happened was maybe oral or manual sex. I wouldn't use "fuck"
unless there was – well, what word would you like – penetration? And then only if it was all pretty casual. I certainly
wouldn't use it about what I do with my girlfriend – we make
love.' My step-daughter Frances agreed: 'My friends would say
that if there's some emotional commitment then you make love.
If there's not – if maybe it's just a one-night stand – then you
fuck.' Even in this steamiest of activities, then, there are rules –
rules that govern the correct application of language. Someone
may resent your describing what they do as 'fucking' for the
very good reason that it is not, it is making love.

However, any moment of human coition that can be described as 'fucking' can rightly, though perhaps less richly, be
described as 'having sexual intercourse'. If 'Jack fucked Jill' is
true, then necessarily, 'Jack had sexual intercourse with Jill' is
true. Yet some people find that the second statement trips
easily off the tongue or pen while the first does not. They baulk
at it. Thus, a headline in a notorious Sunday newspaper read,
'VICAR HAD SEXUAL INTERCOURSE WITH SCHOOLGIRL'. It is impossible
to imagine it reading, 'VICAR FUCKED SCHOOLGIRL'. Similarly,
when I was a schoolgirl my headmistress gave the sixth-form
a 'don't just read the dirty bits' talk on *Lady Chatterley's Lover*.
She described passages in which the gamekeeper 'had sexual
intercourse' with Lady Chatterley. We would have fallen out
of our desks if she had said 'fucked Lady Chatterley'. This
was partly because we were well inculcated with beliefs about
what language it was acceptable for women to use. We were
taught to be restrained in our choice of words, for what would
count as blunt and forceful uttered by a man would be
unacceptably vulgar used by a woman. Restrictions on the
use of 'fuck' and 'cunt', however, have more or less applied to
both sexes.

In his etymological dictionary, *Origins*, Eric Partridge writes:

'Fuck' shares with 'cunt' two distinctions: they are the only
two standard English words excluded from all general and

etymological dictionaries since C18 and the only two standard English words that, outside of medical and other official or semi-official reports and learned papers, still could not be printed in full anywhere within the British Commonwealth of Nations until late 1961.

This Victorian squeamishness, or perhaps delicacy, is no longer a feature of literature, but it still permeates our most popular medium – television. Christopher Martin, a senior BBC producer, told me, 'No matter how tough, racy, or searingly honest a drama production may be, it would be inconceivable to write "fuck" into the script. It would be regarded as equivalent to throwing a hand-grenade into people's sitting rooms. There is a cut-off point at about ten o'clock, though. After that you can show feature films with expletives every two minutes. But even then, if I were making a programme – perhaps one whose integrity demanded that this kind of language was used – I'd have to make a case for it with the Controller. Otherwise there'd be a hell of a row.'

It may seem entirely mysterious that one group of words for human functions and human organs is acceptable while another is not, meriting the quaint censorship of a row of dots in books and a bleeping out in television programmes. Barbara Lawrence offered one explanation at the beginning of this chapter, arguing that words like 'fuck' and 'cunt' reflect a perception of sex which is unacceptable – obscene. Her point was not that sexual activity in itself is obscene, but that a certain way of looking at it makes it so. If, for example, a perception reduces a person to a mere gland – one piece of flesh – then that perception is obscene. This raises the following question: even though language is undeniably an index of what is going on in our minds, is it true that we can draw conclusions about our attitudes to sex from our use of certain words?

Since this is a question about the significance of the way we use words – how we talk about sex – it seemed to me that the best way to try and answer it was to ask people what they meant when they used the language of sex. So I gathered together a group of twenty people to discuss with them their use of – and their views on – so-called obscene language. The group was made up of several women from a counselling group on female sexuality, plus a number of men they had brought with them. My step-daughter provided a sprinkling of students and my husband persuaded a few of his friends to make up the numbers.

We began by agreeing that the following expressions were generally regarded as interchangeable with 'had sexual inter-course with':

* had sex with
* was intimate with
* slept with
* went to bed with
* made love to
* went all the way with
  fucked
  banged
  screwed
  poked
  did it to
  gave it to
  had

Everyone agreed that each of these verbs easily takes a man as its subject and a woman as its object (for example: 'Jack slept with Jill'). It was also agreed that the asterisked verbs will just as easily take a woman as subject and a man as object ('Jill had sex with Jack'). The group spent some time discussing who would actually use which of these terms. A plumber who says he's proud of three things in his life – his biceps, his bulldog and his missus – thought: 'This is the sort of language you'd read in The Times. You know [in a grossly exaggerated 'Oxford' accent] – "the Rt Hon. Member was intimate with his secretary during a Cabinet meeting".' And a student joked, 'I'd gag over "had sexual intercourse" – it sounds sort of furtive – reminds me of the Family Planning Clinic. I suppose if I didn't want to be shocking, or wanted someone to think I was a "naice girl", I might say "went to bed with" – though if you're living three to a room like me it's the one thing you never actually do.'

It was generally agreed that apart from 'make love' the asterisked verbs lacked all emotional force. Yet they do have a certain pleasing symmetry: if they are true of Jack, they are also true of Jill. If 'Jack slept with Jill' is true then, necessarily, 'Jill slept with Jack' is true. If 'Jack went all the way with Jill', there is no denying that 'Jill went all the way with Jack'.

But when I asked my group to compare 'Jack fucked Jill', we agreed that all that follows from this being true is that Jill was fucked by Jack; nothing at all is said about what *Jill* did. And the same is true of 'banged', 'screwed', 'poked', 'did it to', 'gave it to' and 'had'. An accountant who is as precise with words as he is with figures disagreed about 'had'. 'It appears to me that if Jack had Jill then Jill had Jack. Though I am aware that when a woman says she's "had" a man it sounds brash, even defiant.'

I told everyone of the time I heard a young model boasting to a group of women about her affair with an international super-stud. An older and wiser actress finally advised her: 'Darling, do stop going on about it. It's nothing special – we've all had him.' Now 'had' is a portmanteau word: it can mean almost anything and, depending on what it stands for, it can be asymmetrical or symmetrical. Thus, if Jack had the last cake, all that the last cake did was to get eaten; if, on the other hand, Jack had the last dance with Jill, then Jill had the last dance with Jack. So it seems that with 'had' there is more room for interpretation than with verbs like 'banged' or 'poked'. However, it is interesting that the actress chose the word 'had' to make her point – viz., that the model's pretensions were absurd since the man was readily available to any woman who cared to make the effort: he was, in fact, an easy lay. The sting in this denigrating implication is that it is typically said only of women precisely because the object of a sexual 'had' is more readily seen as the last cake than as a dancing partner. One pop star made it explicit when in an interview with a national newspaper he talked about the 'crumpet' he had 'had'.

Thinking about all this, the group concluded that, as they are commonly used, the so-called 'obscene' expressions for sex focus on *male* activity. The woman may be as joyful, active, ingenious a partner as could be wished, but all these verbs say about her is that she was there.

There were plenty of examples of these words being used this way. One of the group said that in a rape case it was reported that the victim lost her temper under pressure from the defending counsel and screamed, 'How can you defend him? He fucked me.' The verb carried no hint at all of any activity on her part – no suggestion of participation. Similarly, though less horribly, someone else recalled a friend bemoaning a row she had with her husband. 'I do admit,' the friend said, 'that since the new job I'm very tired – too tired for sex really. Anyway, one night I fell asleep half-way through. Bob didn't even notice – he just got on with it. When I told him he was an insensitive pig he wanted to know how he was supposed to tell whether I was awake or not. It was always like fucking a corpse anyway.' In other words, 'fucking' is quite uncommitted to the activity or otherwise of its object.

I find it interesting that verbs that are symmetrical – verbs that are equally comfortable with male or female subject and object – are unrevealing as to the activity of those involved. 'Had sex with' and 'was intimate with' say nothing about who did what to whom. One man suggested, 'Perhaps it's because they are not explicit that they can take a female subject without any sense of strain.' This is certainly consistent with the fact that verbs like 'fuck', 'bang', 'screw', which explicitly describe someone as *doing* something, carry with them the implication that this someone is male. A woman who had told the group she was a lesbian agreed with this and explained that it explains why she rarely uses the word 'fuck' or 'screw'. 'I might use them as swear words; but I'd never use them to describe what I do in bed. They're too male-orientated . . . which I'm not.'

All the women in my group of verb-watchers agreed that at some time or other men had said things to them like: 'I want to fuck you', or 'Please come to bed with me', or 'Let's make love', or 'I want to screw you'. But only one remembered ever having a man say, 'Please fuck me'. 'And that,' she said, 'was when he wanted to just lie there while I bounced up and down on him.' It may no longer be immoral for a woman to fuck a man, but it comes perilously close to being ungrammatical. 'Fuck' may seem like a liberated verb, but it is not liberated at all.

Some people in the group thought this was too extreme. A student said, 'I hear people saying things like, "She fucked him". And it doesn't sound odd or anything.' A French friend of mine thought this was related to nationality: 'I hear American women in Paris saying things like "I fucked him last night," but no French woman would say that. In France the equivalent to your English verb "fuck" never takes a female subject.' One member of the group was a slight, large-eyed actor who confessed to a deep dislike of aggressive women. He thought a woman who fucked was bound to be a man-eater. 'That's probably why I'd never ask a woman to fuck me. Nor would I ever say, "She fucked me." I might say of some other man, "She fucked him!" . . . but probably only if she'd made all the running.'

A woman in the group had a further point to make. 'I think it's pretty common to say things like "They fucked all night" or "They fucked in the back of the car" or something'. No one agreed that these were common exactly, but everyone did agree that 'fuck' can take both partners together as its subject. Nevertheless, it was also agreed that for the object of 'fuck' there are unfavourable overtones of being the passive recipient of another's sexuality. Also, although the verb is not restricted to a male subject this is its primary use. Burrowing through a dictionary of slang I found support for this conclusion. Of 'fuck' it said: 'As most taboo words this is primarily used by, but not restricted to use by, males.'

A 50-year-old housewife who could not bring herself to utter some of the words we had been discussing nevertheless proved to have a fine eye for detail: 'On that list of verbs men can do everything and some of the things can only be done by men – like these [pointing to 'bang' and 'poke']. But there's no verb that's just for women.'

Someone pointed out that the explicit obscene verbs for what women do sexually are typically confined to their hands and mouths. Oral sex can be described as 'She sucked him off', manual sex as 'She tossed him off'. Whether or not you find these pleasing, they do communicate that the woman is active. Of course, men – having hands and mouths – can do these things too, though to suggest they might have done so seems to be the worst kind of insult. I remember a banner displayed outside the White House at the time of the Watergate crisis which proclaimed 'Nixon sucks'. What is being missed from the list of verbs, however, is one that takes only a female subject, one that describes the unique activity of the vagina.

An advertising executive whose main client is a cosmetic house said, 'Look, the plain fact is that in sex the man *is* the active one; he moves, she doesn't. Language just mirrors the physical fact of the matter.' Who says men have to be the ones who move? Admittedly the penis is external in a way the vagina is not – little boys can do things with it like peeing to melt snow at a distance, and big boys can, with a pelvic thrust or two, put it into a vagina. But it does not follow that a man *has* to move. A woman can move on a penis every bit as easily as a man can move on a vagina. How is what she is doing to be described?

I asked the group for verbs to describe what a vagina does to a penis. Despite a certain ribaldry we arrived at these: 'Enclose', 'envelop', 'engulf'. (We left out 'swallow' in deference to male anxieties.) All these are action verbs that perfectly describe the unique action of the vagina in sex; they are the equivalent of 'thrust' for the penis. This encouraged a gentle, rather abstracted artist to say wistfully, 'It'd be great to shift our perspective a bit so we could say things like "She enclosed him". It sounds rather lovely – and it would take a lot of pressure off men if they didn't always have to be the doers.' The point was clearly made that a change in our vocabulary would allow a concomitant change in our conception of the relationship between penis and vagina. The nature of the change was highlighted by another man who said, 'If that was a familiar way to describe sex, it would be much harder to be macho about it. I mean, you're not going to sound like a Clint Eastwood hero if you go around saying "She engulfed me", are you.'

The advertising executive thought this was a silly game. 'It's all nonsense. "Thrust" is dynamic; "enclose" is static. The most expressive verbs for sex describe dynamic activity – so of course they are male-orientated.' What about this perfectly proper English sentence: 'The Germans enclosed the Belgium army in a wall of tanks'? This is about as dynamic as could be wished. The executive was expressing a bias – a bias that irritated many of the women. One of them, a divorcee who says she is having trouble getting to like men again, said, 'I bet you're one of those men who think the penis is muscle. My ex-husband used to call his "*The* Muscle". I ask you. When I told him it wasn't and that the only love muscle around was mine, he got so angry he went bright red and started gobbling like a turkey.'

It is true that the vagina has muscular tissue. I remember a friend of mine going through a phase of reading every sex manual she could find and then imposing its message on those around her. One of these persuaded her that the ultimate delight was a vagina with strong muscle. She used to say, 'You must keep your vaginal muscle toned up. Now. With me. Squeeze, hold, relax. Do that every day. You can do it anywhere – while you're cooking, in the bath, at the bus stop.'

The penis, however, is not a muscle, nor does it have any muscular tissue. It is interesting that a common use of 'muscle' is as a metaphor for strength. If you have 'muscle' you have power; if you 'muscle in' you violently intrude. It seems extraordinary that, even though the physiological facts are known, the language of sex should be biased towards character-ising the organ which literally lacks muscle as strong and powerful, and the organ which literally has it as a passive receptacle.

Looking at the way the language of sex is used, it is fair to conclude that sex is seen as primarily a male activity; it is something a man *does*, but something that *happens* to a woman. But what kind of activity is it? 'I think "fuck" is okay – redeemable,' a student observed. 'The way people use words changes after all – I reckon it could end up uni-sex! But I don't like "bang", "screw", "poke". They're sadistic – I mean, who in her right mind wants to be banged or screwed?'

Everyone agreed that used literally, these words denoted actions at least uncomfortable, and more probably painful. One man shuddered at the thought of it: 'You need a lot of force to get a screw into wood. The wood gets gouged out – mutilated.' The point was vividly made: 'screwing' is not a gentle process. This is underlined by other very common metaphors that use the verb. If you 'put the screws on' you oppress someone; if you 'screw money out of a person' you extract it with some force. 'Bang' is just as aggressive. It derives from the Old Norse *banga*, 'to hammer', and it has connotations of hard, relentless impact. This made one man thoughtful: 'I've talked jokingly about giving the wife a bang, but if I told my mates I'd hammered her they'd think I'd beaten her up.' He agreed that it was strangely selective to eschew hammering a woman while being prepared to bang her. 'Poke' is less violent. Still, it is not pleasant to be poked in the ribs and is not likely to be pleasant to be poked in any other part of one's anatomy. Deliberately to use 'screwing', 'banging' or 'poking' as metaphors for sex is to import connotations of brutality into the act; it is to identify sex as a mechanical and painful act performed by a man on a woman.

What about 'fuck'? In *Origins*, Eric Partridge traces the word 'fuck' through the German *ficken* and the Latin *battuere*, both meaning 'to strike', allied to *fustus*, 'a cudgel'. The commonest slang word for sexual intercourse derives from a series of wound verbs; and perhaps, given the above, it is not surprising that Partridge identifies this as a *male* activity. After pointing out that *ficken* is to strike, he adds, 'hence – of a man – to copulate'.

This made the young actor angry. 'It would be unfair – ridiculous – to impute this to those who use "fuck" now. It's a hell of a long way from source. I don't know where it came from . . . who does?' This is an important point. 'Bang', 'poke' and 'screw' are metaphors for sex which are also commonly used in a literal sense: 'I banged the door/ screwed in the nail/ poked the fire.' These actions are familiar to us all, so you may think there is little excuse for failing to recognise what is being graphically conveyed when the verbs are used as metaphorical identifications for sex. After all, if I say, 'He applied the screws to get that job', there is no doubt that I am implying he brought pressure to bear. 'Fuck', however, applies only to sex: it is not a metaphor for it. It does not literally apply to some other aggressive activity, so perhaps we are excused from picking up the connotations of its ancient origins.

But this is only half the story, for we do use 'fuck' metaphorically, and it seems to many to be a dismaying comment on the way we think of sex that these metaphors are usually expressions of hatred and malevolence. My youngest step-daughter, who had crept in to listen to the group discussion, was perturbed by certain anomalies in all this. 'Everyone says sex is beautiful, but then they tell people they don't like to get fucked. Why don't they tell them to "get un-fucked"?'

Wittingly or unwittingly, she touched on a mystery: the

prevailing attitude about men and sex is that sex enhances a man. One woman pointed out that it is only women who are seen as being degraded by sex. 'I had a boyfriend once who prided himself on being a famous fucker – you know, "If it moves I've had it": that sort of bloke. He once asked me how many men I'd had, and without thinking I said thirty-seven. It wasn't true – it was just my age. But, hell, what business was it of his? Anyway he went crazy. Called me a whore and a slag, said I was disgusting. And this from a man who was always trying to score.' If we think about the words that describe a man who is sexually very active, they tend to have overtones of praise: 'buck', 'stud', 'Don Juan', 'Casanova'. These terms have none of the pejorative overtones of 'slag' or 'whore'. Men gain status from sex; women lose it – they are 'loose' or 'fallen'. Men are enhanced by sexual conquest; women are diminished.

It makes perfect sense, then, if you think fucking degrades her, to tell a woman to fuck off. But where is the punch in telling a man to fuck off if you're one of those who think the activity enhances him? 'Get fucked' is clearer. It tells a man to adopt a degrading posture to the insulter, and many would agree with Plato that nothing humiliates a man more than playing the female role in sex.

'Fuck' is also a metaphor for trickery, deception and disaster. Everyone in the group, bar one, agreed that they say, 'I've really fucked it up' if they make some calamitous error, or the ambiguous 'I got fucked' if they were in some way harmed. As one man explained, 'I tend to use that if I think some bastard's conned me.' The most powerful metaphor for being harmed is a verb that literally applies to sex; our harshest expletive is our richest, strongest description of sex. It is instructive to note that although 'He was fucked' is likely to be taken as meaning the man was tricked or deceived in some way, 'She was fucked' is ambiguous. Is it a comment about sex, or about being harmed? It is difficult not to believe that at some level or other sex is regarded as an aggressive activity that hurts the recipient . . . who is usually female. This was thought to be consistent with the organ that is responsible for this activity being called in slang a 'prick'. From *Origins*, again, it was found that 'prick' derives from Old Norse words for 'beat', and for 'thorn', 'goad', 'sting'. Things that prick cause pain.

'Cock', the other slang term for the penis, is, of course, a male domestic fowl; its confidence and briskness gave Middle English the verb *coker*, to fight and strut. The sexual link is obvious – so much so that when a back-bench Member of Parliament was asked if a prominent member of his party was a homosexual, he replied, 'No, not at all – to the contrary, he's a capon.' In other words, a man who is uninterested in sex is a cock who has been castrated. And 'cock', too, has its metaphorical use for harm – it describes a painful disaster. 'What a cock-up', you groan. Or, 'I cocked that up', if it was all your fault. I told the group about a conversation I once had with Barry Humphries about the language of sex. He said: 'Many of the words for it are certainly aggressive. But I don't know whether they're untruthful . . . because, of course, human coitus is not always a pastel-hued adagio.' 'Too true it isn't,' was the wry response.

Just how intimately sex and violence may be linked in people's minds was brought home to me by a passage from Yvonne Roberts's book *Man Enough*. Ms Roberts had interviewed a selection of men about the problems of being male and 35. One of the men had this to say about his feelings for a certain princess. 'You don't know what I'd fucking do to her, do you? I'd make her fucking ache. I'd fuck her so hard all night it would hurt. To me she is an 'orrible woman. You can't go up and physically hit her but you could . . . get her to bed and do things that [her husband] and no one else has ever fucking done to her. I detest her.' Fucking is brutal, painful, punitive – an explicit expression of hatred. No wonder it is our favourite expletive. One of the students was by now hopping up and down: 'If I whisper to my girlfriend "I want to fuck you" I'm not talking about throwing her a fifteen-round fight. I'm talking about mutually pleasurable, mutually engaging sex.'

It would be simple-minded to suggest that *all* sex is aggressive. It obviously is not. But it would be very surprising if an activity as potentially intimate and revealing as sex did not also have the potential for causing harm. Rape is one proof of it. But even where there is mutual consent two people may enter a sexual situation with very different intentions, and one may do extremely unpleasant things to the other – things that could not have been done if both had kept their clothes on: something with the potential to be wonderful also has the potential to be dreadful. Perhaps our language focuses on the potential for aggression rather than the potential for tenderness. It certainly focuses on sex as a male activity rather than female – and men are more usually regarded as aggressive than tender.

The artist thought the time had come to put in a plea for men. 'Okay. So the language we use may imply that sex is some kind of violence. But it isn't just men who are into that. The first girl I went to bed with liked to be hurt; she wanted to be symbolically raped all the time. But I couldn't do it. Every time she started to "struggle" I'd go limp. One day we were walking past an army poster. You know – the one that says "The Army will make a man of you". She pointed to it and said "You should try it".'

The women were generally unsympathetic. As one said, 'So some women like being knocked about. So do some men. But it's still a man-made language in a man-made world.'

When the group finally disbanded after several discussions, I was left with a great deal of material about how we use the language of sex. But what is to be made of it all?

First, in spelling out how we use words like 'fuck', 'cunt' and 'prick', the group felt the tug of a sinister undercurrent: the metaphors we commonly use for sex seem to show that sexual activity is thought of as painful and violent. But is it right to infer this from the fact that sex is commonly described as 'fucking' or 'screwing'; or that a penis is a 'prick' and a vagina a 'cunt'?

Imagine someone first using 'screw' as a metaphor for sex. How exactly does it work? The essence of screwing is that one thing penetrates another slowly, rotating in one direction . . . and stops. To get out, it has to rotate in the other direction, a feat of acrobatics certainly beyond any man I have known. But perhaps this is simple-minded. For 'screw' to work as a genuine metaphor there only needs to be one way in which sex is seen, at some level or in some moments, to be like screwing. Perhaps this one way is not steady rotation but a harsh, gouging penetration in which the male is active and the female passive.

For whatever reason, the metaphor catches on. Some people see through it, and because they are in the grip of a certain attitude to sex – it is brutal and mechanical – they latch on to 'screw' as the ideal way to express that attitude. Others simply inherit the word; they hear 'screw' used for sex, and without detecting the metaphor they adopt the usage. They do not necessarily have a view of sex as being brutal. (Similarly, they might inherit and use the word 'nigger' without realising that it was profoundly disparaging, and without having racist attitudes.) Yet others use 'screw' as a public statement, not about sex but about attitudes to sex. They see that 'make love' shows a certain delicacy towards sex while 'screw' shows a certain coarseness. 'Screw' is used to deprecate delicacy – to thumb the nose at lily-livered 'prunes and prisms' – and to vaunt coarseness. They will not see this as displaying an unhealthy attitude to sex. Exactly the opposite; this displays a robust honesty, they will say.

Now there is no denying that a choice of words manifests a certain attitude. But the question is, which attitude? A friend confides to you, 'We screwed in the bath.' Does she see sex as brutal; is she just using a common label for the event; or does she loathe namby-pamby descriptions? Her use of the word will not in itself tell you, for what she means is crucially involved with what she intends to communicate. You understand what someone means by what they say only when you latch on to the thought concealed in the word. She may simply be telling you what sort of activity occurred: or she may be communicating that she did not see it in a particularly romantic light; or she may think that 'screw' is a word you are familiar and comfortable with – or she may want to shock you. There are many possible attitudes lurking behind a choice of words. It follows that we cannot accuse people of having reprehensible attitudes to sex just because they describe it as 'screwing', or, indeed, as 'fucking'. 'Right-thinking' people may very easily find these words on their lips.

One man I said this to was ambivalent about it. 'I feel that's how it is with me. I don't think sex is violent – but I do call it "fucking" or "screwing". And I can't honestly see me saying "copulate". I'd be making a right arse of myself. But on the other hand, what about insults? I mean – if we say "Screw you" or "Fuck off" aren't we showing that the words mean something violent to us?'

I once listened to a man describing a party he had been to: 'Fucking mountains of food, more fucking booze than you can imagine ... this fucking beautiful bird. I took her out to the fucking bushes and ... *married* her.' Any semantic theorist would have a case for saying that this man did not know what 'fuck' meant. Imagine someone using 'bloody' for everything except a blood-stained handkerchief, which he described as 'sanguineous'. You would be entitled to think he did not know what 'bloody' meant. It was just a swear-word.

Mark Sainsbury, a philosopher at London University, said this story made him wonder 'if "fuck" consists of two words, one a contentless insult, the other a word for sexual intercourse. Evidence for this would be that someone might master the insult use without realising there was another use – and certainly without realising that the insult value came from any link with sex. Then the best description of the phenomenon in this story might be that there are two words, of which the man knew one.'

The idea, then, is that 'fuck' is like 'row': there is one word as in 'row of bottles' and another word as in 'row the boat'. There is one word 'fuck' that has no content but is used to insult or swear, and another word 'fuck' that means sexual intercourse. Someone who speaks no English could easily learn to use 'fuck' as an insult by being told, 'If someone English upsets you, say "fuck off".' He might never know that it also applies to sex. Or someone could be taught by an English lover that 'fuck' meant sex and then – associating it with loving activity – be as surprised to hear 'fuck off' as you or I would be to hear 'hug off'. If this is right, though, why should it be the words for sex that have this insult 'twin'?

Our whole vocabulary of insults is odd. Why are some words used to insult but other very similar ones not? For example, 'piss off' but not 'shit off'; 'you shit' but not 'you piss'; 'fuck off' but not 'screw off'; 'a stupid prick' but not 'a stupid cock'. And why may you call a man a 'cunt' but not call a woman a 'prick'? Perhaps the answer to the last question is that it is commonly supposed, with Freud, that women suffer from penis envy; therefore to call a woman a 'prick' would not be an insult but the ultimate benediction! A young neighbour thought that men were indeed too proud of their appendage for it to be unequivocally an insult. She recalled this conversation with her younger brother. 'He's got this teacher he really hates and he said he was a cunt. I told him I'd rather he used "prick" to insult people. He said "It's too good for this bastard." ' This ambivalence (is it an insult or a compliment metaphorically to identify someone as a penis?) is displayed by the common uses of the word 'balls'. It is a slang word for testes and is used as a not too vicious expletive. But it is also used to indicate courage and endurance. To say of a man, 'He's got no balls' is not usually to point out an anatomical deficiency but a character deficiency: the man is a coward or a weakling. 'He's got balls', however, is a compliment. A friend who is a cricket buff related this incident. 'David Gower – you know, the England batsman – was hit on the head by a vicious delivery from a West Indian bowler. But he played on even though he was bleeding and he must have been shaken. Next day – you know Test matches go on for five days? – well, the next day someone in the crowd displayed this banner: "It takes balls to play cricket". So there you are.'*

All this suggests that insults may grow up by fairly *ad hoc* conventions – conventions that would be self-sustaining. You ask, 'What have I found insulting?' or 'What have others effectively used as insults?' – and then you adopt it.

Why should it be that slang terms for certain sexual organs are used as insults? Is it significant that they are the most effective way of denigrating someone? It is often said that words like 'cunt' serve so well as a contemptuous epithet because of their phonetic properties – not because of the organ or activity they name. A friend who used to live in Brazil told me: 'Words like "fuck" and "cunt" have got such satisfying sounds – hard and vicious. Even if you don't understand English you know from the sound that they are insulting. In Portuguese, though, the word for "cunt" is *babacca* – a lovely

---

* This reminded me of the time when Evonne Cawley injured an ankle at Wimbledon and tried to play on for what was an obviously agonising few moments. No one to my knowledge commented, 'It takes pussy to play tennis', even though traditionally tennis players have needed cat gut for their rackets as much as cricketers have needed balls. (If you think this slogan is ridiculous, that in itself is a measure of how strongly we identify power with male sexuality and how little we identify it with female sexuality.)

sound. It is used as a term of endearment: "beautiful cunt". The word just doesn't have the phonetic quality to be an insult so it is never used as a term of abuse.' French seems in this more like English than Portuguese: the French word for 'cunt' is con, a good, vicious sound, and one you hear about 500 times a day in the streets of Paris.

The power of a word like 'cunt', then, is not just what it means; it is also the violence and disgust that the sound itself transmits. Saying the word carelessly, lovingly or wearily may defuse much of its power. I remember a friend of mine whose lawn-mower failed, telling me that the odd-job man was overheard lamenting with ingenious economy: 'Fuck, the fucking fucker's fucked.' It was said resignedly – without rancour and without viciousness.

You may feel sceptical about this. There is nothing ugly sounding about 'punt' or 'rick'; so why 'cunt' or 'prick'? A test that would prove that certain words make good insults because of their sound would be to get people who did not know what the words meant to rate them on an 'ugly' scale. If 'cunt' was consistently rated as very harsh and ugly, then we perhaps could conclude that it was an insult because of its auditory properties. Ethel Strainchamps, an American feminist, offers some evidence in support of this. She has spent years studying words, and she has noted all the dirtiest words in English begin and end with one of the blowing sounds – k, f, p, s or sh. She insists, 'they can be no more cleaned up by open and high-minded usage than can the Bronx cheer or the symbolic gesture of spitting'.

This fails, however, to explain why 'kiss', which satisfies all Ms Strainchamps's requirements, is not a dirty word. The answer is, surely, that the content of a word – what it stands for – must be, at least originally, part of the insult value of the word. I think the most that can be said about the auditory thesis is that insults survive better if they have the right kind of sound.

For 'prick' and 'cunt' to serve as really powerful insults, then, someone, somewhere, must have considered the organs they labelled distasteful. Clearly Lord Rochester felt some disgust for his sexuality when he wrote:

Worst part of me and henceforth hated most
Through all the town the common rubbing post.
On whom each wretch relieves her tingling cunt,
As hogs on gates do rub themselves and grunt.

Why should anyone think of sex as disgusting? Perhaps Yeats had the answer: 'But Love has pitched his mansion in/The place of excrement.' We have sex somewhere between peeing and shitting – in spatial proximity to activities that we see as shameful and disgusting. It is a common thought that sexual shame derives from this physical fact. The disgust we feel for human excrement encourages a view that we have parts that are 'dirty' – parts that we are encouraged to cover and keep hidden. Freud supposed that there survives in us the notion of a dirty secret – dirt that relates to hidden pleasures. It is said to be some such thought that colours our attitudes to sex.

I do not know whether this is so; but even if it is we cannot infer from 'cunt' or 'prick' being an insult that these attitudes of disgust are held by the user. The inference is simply not good enough. This may outrage those who, recognising that the vilest thing you can call a person is 'cunt', deduce from this that women are thought of as degraded creatures. Even so, the inference from language to attitude is a poor one and should be rejected. This does not mean that the conclusion about attitudes to women is false. In fact, we can reach that conclusion by another, better, route. The language we have been considering is just not a strong enough plank to fight on.

Consider, though, the words 'humankind', 'mankind' and 'womankind'. In any sentence with 'mankind' you could substitute 'humankind' without any change of meaning. For example the Museum of Mankind becomes, with no violence to meaning, the Museum of Humankind. The History of Mankind becomes the History of Humankind. The Art of Mankind becomes the Art of Humankind. Now substitute 'Womankind'. In the Museum of Mankind you would not be surprised to find embroideries and needlework by women. But in the Museum of Womankind would you expect to find work by men? In an exhibition called 'The Art of Mankind' you might find paintings by Bridget Riley. If the exhibition were called 'The Art of Womankind', would you expect to find a Leonardo? Of course not. For 'womankind' is not synonymous with 'mankind' or 'humankind'. It has its own meaning. I remember a philosophy lecturer once declaring 'It is a truism to say man is a rational animal.' To laughter, he added, 'Of course, "Woman is a rational animal" is a substantive thesis.' That is to say, it is not implicit; it is debatable. Language does reflect discrimination: man is unequivocally human; woman is debatably so. And that secures the conclusion that women are regarded as some kind of inferior species.

The fact that words like 'prick', 'cunt' and 'fuck' are used as insults hints at certain attitudes to sex: that it can be violent and degrading. Nevertheless, this conclusion cannot be inferred from our individual use of these words, for they may be employed by people who are innocent of these attitudes – in which case we do not need to see the suspect usages banished to be sure that we have straightened out our attitudes to sex and each other. We will know this when 'mankind' is an ellipsis for 'humankind' equivalent in meaning to 'womankind'. The least graphic parts of our language turn out to be the most revealing.

_ 8 _

SEX OBJECTS

'How do you feel about being a sex object?' I asked a volup-
tuous, fortyish friend. 'Very grateful,' she replied.

Many people would be surprised by such a frank acceptance
of the role of sex object; it is generally regarded as profoundly
demeaning. And women today are likely to be particularly
outraged, for to delight in being sexually pleasing and desirable
to men is often seen as a betrayal of the women's movement. It
lets the side down. In *The Sceptical Feminist* Janet Radcliffe
Richards notes, 'There is unquestionably a strong element of
resistance to being an object of pleasure for the male.' In
support of this observation she lists quotes from feminists: 'It is
degrading to make yourself attractive to men.' 'To make yourself attractive is to make yourself a male plaything – a sexual
object.' 'Any woman who tries to make herself attractive to men
is as good as a prostitute.' It is this sense of outrage that
underlies a basic tenet of feminism: men must stop seeing
women as sex objects.

It is clear from such comments as these that being a sex object
is often equated with deliberately being attractive to men. This
equation generates a tension for those women who wish to look
good but do not wish to be thought of as a degraded species.
And this tension makes feminism unattractive to many. It even
encourages women whose general views could certainly qualify them to be counted as feminists to distance themselves from
the movement: 'I am a feminist, but . . .' is an all too familiar
disclaimer.

The aim of this chapter, then, is to establish what it is to be a
sex object. Although the phrase is so well used as to be almost a
cliché, its meaning is hardly ever explained. Once it is clear

what a sex object is, it will be possible to ask if a necessary result of rejecting the role is the refusal ever to be sensually pleasing to men.

In his article ' "Pricks" and "Chicks": a Plea for Persons', Robert Baker proposes that since a known object is an object that is known, and a desired object is an object that is desired, a sex object is an object to have sex with. 'Hence to think of a woman as a sex object is to think of her as someone to have sexual relations with.' If this were all that the term meant, then, as Baker points out, it would be quite mysterious to consider the role of sex object an unacceptable one – unless, of course, someone happened to think sex itself was degrading. There are, of course, men for whom sex is dirty, and it is certainly demeaning to be regarded by *them* as a sex object. No one, man or woman, would wish to be inveigled into an act which is perceived by the partner as obscene. It would follow that there is nothing wrong in being a sex object *per se*, only in being one for a certain kind of man. Even so, many women feel strongly that even if a man has a healthy and wholesome attitude to sex, it is still wrong to be seen by him as a sex 'object'.

The feeling seems partly to be that however healthy or otherwise their attitudes, men should not want women for sex and sex alone. In *Pornography and Respect for Women*, Ann Garry writes: ' . . . even if I believe intellectually and emotionally that sex is healthy, I might object to being treated *only* as a sex object. In the same spirit, I would object to being treated only as a maker of chocolate chip cookies or only as a tennis partner, because only one of my talents is being valued.' It is, however, generally thought quite acceptable to want someone for only some aspects of themselves. If a man goes along to the tennis club in search of a partner for mixed doubles, he may be interested in nothing else in a woman but her tennis abilities. It is difficult to see what could be wrong with this. Similarly, if a man hears a woman give a lecture on feminism, he may find her views sufficiently intriguing to want to discuss them further. With this intention he pursues her. He is quite uninterested in any other aspect of her – her tastes in music, what makes her laugh, what she is frightened of, what she delights in. All he cares about is the prospect of having a

mutually pleasurable discussion about the women's movement. Would the feminist be degraded by his being interested
only in this? Would he be in some way discreditable for
wanting only this of her? As things are, he would probably be
congratulated for being liberated enough to be interested only
in a woman's intellect.

If it is acceptable to base a relationship in common intellectual interests, why should it be unacceptable to base it in a
common interest in sex? Where is the moral difference? So long
as the woman has not been annexed by a man who is interested
in only his own pleasure, there is surely nothing wrong in a
purely sexual relationship.

There is, nevertheless, a huge moral difference between being
a sex object, in the sense of being an equal partner in a mutually
pleasurable activity, and being an object to be used merely to
satisfy a man's own desires. When the focus of enquiry is
shifted from the term 'sex' to the term 'object' it becomes clearer
why there is such strong resistance to being considered a sex
object.

The crucial feature of an object is that it is subject to the will
of others; it is buffeted about according to other people's
desires. An object has no will of its own, so the only limitations
on how it is to be treated relate to other people's interests. You
do not refrain from kicking a car because the *car* would not like
it, but because the *owner* would not. (In much the same spirit,
men have been encouraged to respect other men's wives.)

An object is inferior to a person, for a person has needs and
desires that must be considered. Because people have bodies
they are vulnerable to being treated as objects, but they are
essentially subjects – they each have a domain in which they
determine what happens. To borrow a term from Sartre, treating someone as an object is to ignore his or her 'subjectiveness'.
Rape is the ultimate form of objectifying – of ignoring subjectiveness. In rape, the woman's domain is abrogated by the male:
her 'space' is invaded in total disregard for her existence as a
person. She is treated as an object.

For Sartre, the way in which people interact reflected a
perpetual conflict between subject and object. He speaks, for
example, of 'le regard' – the gaze of others in which a person is
judged in ways that can never fully be grasped because no one

can penetrate the mind of another. Thus a sense of self and self-identity is constantly being threatened by the assessment of others, over whom the 'victim' has no control. Most women will know what it is like to feel defiled by the kind of look from a man that reduces her to feeling that she is nothing more than an object – a thing whose subjectivity, as Sartre would say, has been stolen.

In sex, a woman is so clearly a means to a man's satisfaction that she is always on the verge of becoming *merely* a means. To return to Sartre: 'intercourse counterfeits masturbation'. Sartre also noted how men tend to focus on parts of the body – the breasts and thighs, for example; in obviously having no will of their own, they resemble objects. A sex object, then, is a mere piece of flesh, an instrument to be used by men for the satisfaction of their sexual desires. Such a role is clearly demeaning and degrading. Someone who is trying to be a sex object in this sense is, for a start, one who has no self-respect.

If Sartre is right, there will always be the danger that a man will see his sexual partner as an object for his own gratification. Sex is essentially an activity which focuses on possessing the body, so there is inevitably a sense in which each partner wants to reduce the other to an object. Yet since the normal man has little interest in a woman who is unconscious or dead – a woman who in sex would be unequivocally nothing more than a depersonalised, will-less, manipulated object – Sartre concluded that in normal sex there is a need to retain the other's subjectiveness. This may be achieved by protecting autonomy: each partner remains a subject and each wishes the other to be a subject. Instrumentality vanishes because sex is mutual and mutually desired, and, crucially, because preserved within the act is respect for the person who is also the partner.

It might be argued that we have good reason to doubt that respect can redeem the sex object. Men have always respected women, it might be said; they have stood as women entered a room, doffed their hats, given up their seats on buses, restrained themselves from swearing or telling dirty jokes in the presence of women. Yet these men have also been prepared to treat women as sexual objects. Ann Garry resolved this apparent anomaly: 'The "respect" that men have traditionally

believed they have for women – hence respect they can lose – is
not a general respect for persons as autonomous beings; nor is it
respect that is earned because of one's personal merits or
achievements.' She adds that it is a respect which grew out of
the 'double standard'; it was given to women who displayed
the qualities that men deemed appropriate. This respect was
always withheld from 'bad' women, and bad women were
invariably sexual. Almost by definition, the sex object could
not be given the 'respect' that was given the good woman.

Women demand that all men grant all women the respect
that is due to them as fully fledged persons – not a spurious
respect that is earned only by women prepared to perch on
man-made pedestals. But one man I spoke to thought this must
be too comprehensive: 'When I married my first wife I was
absolutely crazy about her. But she was hardly out of her
wedding dress before she was in bed with someone else. She
said there was nothing wrong with us – she just liked having
lovers. She'd had so many that in the end people were calling
her "The Knicker Dropper Glory" ... Okay, I suppose it's
funny now – but then it nearly killed me. She's doing it to her
third husband now. Why should I respect her? She's a lying
immoral bitch.'

This man does not believe that everyone is entitled to
respect, and there is surely something in what he says. Why
should anyone respect an incompetent teacher, or a crooked
politician, or a congenital liar? It makes perfectly good sense to
say that someone does not deserve respect or has forfeited it.
We could not say this, however, if everyone was entitled to
respect, whatever their behaviour. Given this, the question of
whether a sex object deserves respect is open to discussion.
Perhaps being a sex object is morally on a par with being a liar
or a thief: it is reprehensible. In which case, of course, men
would be justified in treating sex objects with scant respect,
and women who complained would be wrong-headed.

Since it is perfectly acceptable to feel sexual desire, why
might a woman who sets out to arouse it lose respect? One
reason might be that she is simply inept. After all, if a secretary
forgets to pass on important messages, types erratically, cannot
get the hang of the photocopying machine, and books her boss
on a flight to Paris when he was supposed to be in Geneva, then

she is a poor secretary. She does her job badly and there is no
reason at all to respect her for it. A woman who wants to be
desirable to men may be equally inept in her way of going about
it. She may wear the wrong clothes for her shape, smear her
make-up on to make a garish mess, wear her hair in an
unbecoming style. However hard she tries, she ends up looking
a fright – less enchanting sylph than nightmare. It would be
difficult to respect such ineptitude, but that is not the same as
despising her for trying to be a sex object, per se, any more than
despising a tennis player's patsy serve or weak vollying is to
despise him for being a tennis player.

There are also times when it is simply ill-advised to be
deliberately sexy. As one woman told me, 'It would be stupid to
flash your boobs during a board meeting – or in an army
barracks full of men who hadn't been near a woman in months.'
My guess would be that in the barracks few women would
have to go so far to be arousing. Indeed, J.R. Lucas argues in
Because You Are a Woman that 'Miss Amazon' should be
prevented from pursuing a military career because, whatever
her intention, 'she would be a disturbing influence in the mess
room'. It is a dubious morality that allows discrimination
against women on the grounds of men's lack of self-control; it
would, after all, be unforgivable to refuse to employ blacks
because it might disturb prejudiced whites. Still, it makes the
point that there are occasions on which it is neither appropriate
nor sensible fully to display sexual charms. Such folly is not, of
course, the prerogative of women. It would be equally ill-
advised for a wealthy man to flash his money in a back-street
slum.

There may be reason to withhold respect from what is foolish
or immoral, but that does not justify failure to recognise that the
one who is behaving in this way is none the less a person. It is
easy to fall victim here to a confusion between respecting a
person as such, and respecting what a person is and does. Being
a person is not the same as being a human being. Being human
is a biological fact of the matter, like being an oak tree or a
worm. A 'person', however, is a social concept – a person is a
bearer of rights. To be recognised as a person, then, is to be
recognised as having certain rights. In his article 'Respect of
Persons', R.S. Peters – locating himself firmly in the Kantian

tradition – insists, 'Respect for persons implies having due regard for a person's dignity as a self-determining agent; it therefore implies as well, the refusal to interfere with another's capacity to be self-directing.' In other words, persons have the right to decide what will happen to them, what they will do, how they will shape their world. They may not be exploited or manipulated; no one may arbitrarily disregard their needs and wishes.

It is this that gives the punch to the phrase 'sex object', for any woman who has a sense of herself as a person will find it intolerable if others block her attempts to be self-determining. This will be particularly irksome if those who frustrate her do so because they think she is no more than an instrument to satisfy their needs, and so are indifferent to or contemptuous of her vision of how she wants her world to be. This is why so many women see something pernicious in being a sex object. Displaying charms may act as a jamming device on her being seen as a person: she is seen instead as an instrument, an instrument which one woman described to me as 'a masturbatory machine for him to ejaculate into'. There would be something profoundly demeaning in any woman setting out to be nothing more than a service machine for men. Feminists are right that this is something women should not consider, and that men should not expect. But does it follow from this that women should not be prepared to be sensually pleasing to men? If they reject the role of sex object, must they also reject the role of object of pleasure?

One argument against women using tricks of make-up, hair-styling and clothes to make themselves pleasing to men is that they have better things to do. A woman who is thoroughly disparaging of such artifice told me she thought it ' . . . trivial to spend time dolling yourself up when there are so many important and valuable things to do. Spending time on lipstick and powder encourages a certain flightiness.'

No feminist would wish to see the situation described by Betty Friedan in *The Feminine Mystique*, in which women completely abandoned their studies to concentrate on the trivialising business of being feminine. But it does not follow from this that whatever alternatives you may have, making-up is bound to be the least valuable. If your option is to sit mindlessly in front of the television, then arguably you would be better off playing with powder and paint: at least making-up is active and creative. Mary Quant suggested to me that cosmetics have a wide range of value. 'They make a woman feel good – she can play a part, have fun, be more than she thinks she is.' Of course, it might be thought that it would be 'better' for a girl to read a Jane Austen novel, say, rather than ply Mary Quant's products. But this is simply a statement of personal priorities with which you may or may not agree. Or even if you do agree, you may just disregard it on some occasion. Fun, after all, is important, and any attempt to dismiss its pursuit as flighty should be resisted. It would be a dour world if everything we did had to be 'meaningful'. As Yeats observed, 'constant sacrifice makes for a stony heart'.

It is worth taking note of a point made by Jeremy Bentham in *The Theory of Fictions*. He identified the form of argument in which an action is decried because there is some other action – which is not being performed – that is preferable. But for any activity you care to name there is bound to be one more valuable: reading good novels is arguably not as worthwhile as working to raise money for Oxfam. If any activity which was less valuable than something else had to be given up, then we would lose most of what makes life worth living. This is not to say that we should never make judgments about what, at the moment, it is most important to do. If Gainsborough had seen a child drowning in the river and blithely continued to paint Mrs Sissons, we would have condemned his sense of priorities. Yet no sensible person would think Gainsborough's painting trivial, nor that he should have given it up to do charity work, because that was 'better'.

A friend to whom I made this observation thought I was making odious comparisons. 'You can't compare a work of art and a painted face – there are huge differences.' Of course there are. *Guernica*, Picasso's passionate protest against war, is considerably more significant than even the most pleasing arrangment of 'Vibrant Peach' foundation and 'Bronze Goddess' eye-shadow. But many works of art are simply created as beautiful objects, and valued as such. Our sense of beauty, after all, is as much a part of what it is to be human as our sense of morality, and someone who has no aesthetic sense is surely worse off than one whose aesthetic sense is finely tuned. Because we value beauty, we put time and effort into beautifying our homes, our gardens and our cities. In the present anxiety about our polluted world, aesthetic values are, rightly, high on the list of what must be taken into account in sorting the mess out. Why should anyone draw a line between beautifying ourselves and beautifying our environment? If beauty is valuable it is valuable wherever it is found. Why should anyone think it trivial to make a face beautiful and yet somehow morally elevating to clamour for beauty elsewhere?

An interior decorator I spoke to told me that – for all her well developed aesthetic sense – she was not prepared to make any kind of effort to make herself look attractive. 'Doing up homes is my career – and I wouldn't have time for it if I had to spend hours doing myself up. Who's got the time to make herself look like Raquel Welch?'

I read somewhere that Ms Welch spends three hours a day making-up, not to mention the time she spends exercising to keep in trim and choosing clothes to display all the resulting pulchritude. It does seem excessive; yet she and other perfectly beautiful creatures are the standard that the rest of us are urged to emulate. Never mind if your nose is too big or your eyes are too small; forget the spider's web of wrinkles on your face or your irretrievably sagging stomach – do your darnedest to look beautiful. This is the message that is shouted at women from advertising hoardings and magazines. The outrageously high standard set by fashion plates is the Procrustean bed on which the rest of us are supposed to lie to be suitably hacked and stretched until we fit. Most of us will never come anywhere near it – at least, not without the vast expense of plastic surgery. The rational thing is to give up the attempt.

Nevertheless, most of us can make some improvement on the raw material. I look better for a touch of powder and a lick of mascara. It takes five minutes to put on and interferes with nothing. Refusing, quite sensibly, to spend hours vainly trying to look like a film star does not entail refusing to spend five minutes in order not to look like the wreck of the Hesperus. Most of us are not going to be Einsteins, either, but that is no reason to give up on trying to improve the mind.

In *Femininity* Susan Brownmiller argues that the 'nature of feminine dressing is superficial in essence'. For Brownmiller, wearing trousers is a feminist statement, and she gives a long list of reasons – most of them unconvincing – why she will never again wear skirts. For example, 'I remember how cold I used to feel in the winter wearing a short skirt and sheer stockings.' This is an argument not for giving up skirts, but for wearing them with woollen tights and boots. It also sanctions skirts for the summer because they are, of course, cooler than trousers. She goes on, 'I don't wish to start shaving my legs again.' She does not have to – even in skirts. 'I recall the anguish of an unravelled hem.' Trousers have hems too. 'I remember resenting the enormous amount of thinking time I used to pour into superficial upkeep concerns.' Trousers, too, need to be bought, repaired and cared for. Unless Brownmiller goes into the nearest shop and buys the first pair of trousers that fit her, she is spending time buying and selecting clothes. There is no reason to suppose that less 'thinking time' is involved than for a woman who chooses only to buy skirts.

The only reasons that carry any conviction are, 'I don't like this artificial gender distinction', and 'I'm at peace with the freedom and comfort of trousers'. There is nothing to be said against this. One advantage of women's successful opposition to the rigid demands of feminine dressing is that it has left us free to establish our own priorities – to please ourselves. But Brownmiller does not see women who wear skirts as simply pleasing themselves; she sees them as 'backsliders' – those who have reneged in the battle with men. Of course, if what men wanted were women in short, tight skirts that hobbled their movements, and stiletto heels that sent them teetering into the arms of the first male they saw, there might be good reason to scorn women who went along with it. But fashion now, and at the time Brownmiller wrote her book, accommodates women's demands for freedom of movement and comfort. Fashionable shoes are often flat; flared skirts allow the wearer to stride.

What seems to happen in arguments like Brownmiller's is that some activity is seen, quite rightly, as having been given too high a priority in the past. Women have been required, for example, to spend valuable time in dressing to please men. This activity is then condemned as pernicious. In fact, what was wrong was the *time* wasted, not the activity itself. Dressing up is, at least, harmless; it may even be good. Brownmiller herself admits that 'dressing feminine' can be creative. And what could be wrong with that?

One woman I spoke to thought that even a small preoccupation with looks could be unacceptable: 'Isn't it just degrading to spend time pleasing men? Sort of – well – boot-licking.'

It cannot be degrading in itself to set out to please someone – even if that someone is male. Of course, you may get a thrill from reflecting that since you do not care what a man, or all men, think of you you can be deliberately unpleasing; you can get a wonderful sense of freedom from being thoroughly unlikable. But this will not do as a way of life – at least, not for most of us. Most of us want to be liked and loved, and the only way to achieve that is to be pleasing; as Radcliffe Richards writes, 'there is no other possible basis for love than what is in some way pleasing to the lover'.

Of course, if you are forced to please a man because you are dependent on him, and so feel you have no choice, then you are bound to feel demeaned by it. It is rather like having to be nice to your jailor. A woman I know watches video nasties with her husband because if she refuses he does not speak to her for days. She feels humiliated by it, and helpless. In the past, most women were dependent on men and therefore had to please them. Men were not dependent on women to anything like the same extent, and so they were free to be gloriously indifferent to what women wanted while rigorously exercising their 'right' to be pleased by them. As Germaine Greer observed, 'men, in their arrogance demand to be loved as they are'.

The remedy is not to refuse ever to please a man, but to become independent so that you do not *have* to please. Where equality of dependence and independence exists, there can be nothing demeaning or degrading in deliberately being pleasing.

Many people I spoke to thought that if by some happy chance you were in all ways pleasing to someone, this was well and good. But if you had to make an effort to be different in order to please – if you had to change your style of dressing, for example – then there was something wrong. As one woman said, 'If you love a man you do want to please him. But you can't just expect people to change, can you?'

Why not? There is nothing wrong with change. Indeed, life demands it. There is also nothing wrong in asking people to change; after all, this is what women have been demanding of men for the last twenty-odd years. A woman who feels she may justly ask men to change cannot consistently refuse to consider changing herself for her man. To do so would be sexist, and no woman should want to be that. I am not suggesting that anyone should slavishly make herself over to suit her man, whatever her own inclinations: 'I'd do anything for you, dear . . .' Anything is a warming sentiment for a song, but in real life it needs to be tempered by a consideration of everyone's needs and personality. But with this proviso, where is the virtue in stubbornly clinging to what you are? You may be horrible – a stuffy, sanctimonious prude or a habit-ridden, unimaginative bore. A bit of change could do wonders for you, and those around you.

It might be thought that austerity pays big dividends and should not be given up. Perhaps it separates those men who want women for the right sort of reason from those who want 'only one thing'. As one woman complained to me, 'Women who worry about clothes and make-up are just letting men like that think that all is well with their world – nothing's changed, there's still plenty of crumpet and they can go on being chauvinist pigs.'

There is no reason to suppose that a woman who worries about the way she looks is trying to be the ultimate turn-on for every man in sight: she may simply want them to think she is attractive – or she may want only to be liked. We all respond much better to people who are well turned out than to those who are dirty and unkempt. A woman, then, may try to look 'nice' for a variety of reasons. However, will men automatically assume that she is there just for sex?

Many men say they no longer know what to think about women. As one told me 'I can't deny that men haven't always treated women properly – especially in sex. We were selfish and we did use women. But now we do think about what a woman wants. We want them to enjoy sex, and I was delighted when women said they wanted to be sexual equals – you know all that stuff about not being passive. But then they say they don't want to be sex objects!' He paused and added bemusedly, 'I got lost when they burned their bras to prove it. When I see a pair of boobs bouncing under a tee-shirt what am I supposed to think about? England?'

There can be nothing wrong in a man thinking about sex and wanting a woman for that reason. Nor can there be anything reprehensible in a woman making herself pleasing so that a man does think of her as a sexual partner. But it would not be satisfactory if that was *all* a woman was seen as *all* the time. If it is true that sex objects encourage men to see women only in sexual terms, then that is something to worry about. Women want to be other things – friends, business equals, intellects, lovers. Certainly these one-track-minded men should be discouraged, but is the way to do that for us all to embrace austerity?

It is tritely true that only the attractive attracts. If a woman sets out to be deliberately unattractive to all men because she does not want to be of sexual interest to those men whose attitudes she despises, she will probably achieve the doubtful satisfaction of seeing every one of them disappear over the hill in pursuit of other women. If the worst of men are attracted only by beauty and glamour and she possesses neither of these attributes, they will probably not spare her a glance – but what about the best of men? Are they to be expected to excavate beneath the unappealing surface layer simply in the hope that there is something valuable there? It seems rather like making a job sound dreary and dull in an advertisement because you do not want the wrong applicant, and then sitting back and expecting the right person to divine somehow that it is a truly wonderful opportunity.

Bertrand Russell pointed out that what arouses a man's interest is largely a matter of social conventions. 'To an early Victorian man a woman's ankles were sufficient stimulus, whereas a modern man remains unmoved by anything up to the thigh.' It is also a matter of convention that a certain type of looks is considered beautiful. It is often hard to see – at least from portraits – why a woman of a different era should have been an acknowledged beauty. But women of all times have used make-up and careful dressing to compensate for what the current standard of beauty regarded as defects.

If women were required to give up such artifice, some would suffer a great deal in terms of their looks. But it would not put an end to certain of them being seen as sex objects: for there are bound to be some women with better complexions, shinier hair, a neater figure, bigger eyes – or who are just younger. The way people look and are is a matter of cosmic unfairness that cannot be compensated for by banning make-up and stylish clothes. These women, though unadorned, will still be seen by men as sex objects: there will just be fewer of them. Meanwhile the rest of us who want a relationship with a man or just admiration and attention, and who with skill and artifice manage to compete with the high fliers, would be condemned to dreary 'naturalness'.

Of course, looks are not everything. As one woman said to me, 'A nice man won't want you for your looks. You wouldn't want a man who did.' She was partly right. I would not want a man who cared *only* for my looks – who would? After all, looks fade, and if they were all a man saw as valuable in you, you would be likely, at the sign of the first wrinkle, to be unceremoniously abandoned. I would hope and expect that a man would care more for lasting things – like personality. But why should he care *only* for this?

If a man is presented with two women who are identical in all respects but looks – one is beautiful, one is not – it would be absurd to expect him to opt for the less beautiful woman. But this does not mean that he will go *just* for looks. The majority of men have their priorities in good order. They look for a partner who is kind, or interesting, or shares their interests – whatever personal qualities it may be that matter to them. If she looks good too then that is a bonus. Of course, good looks will not be enough if she turns out to have nothing else going for her, but the good-looking woman is going to make a stronger initial impact than the unattractive one. It may be a virtue to give up looks for other things, but there is no virtue at all in just giving them up. It would be absurd puritanism to refuse to have anything to do with someone attractive because it made you somehow 'nicer' to go for someone plain: a perfectly nice man may start out hoping for looks as well as personality – even if in the end he finds a less-than-beautiful woman whom he would not swap for anyone. As Radcliffe Richards points out, this man

' . . . might still know that she would please him even more if she looked like the centrefold from the latest *Playboy*'.

Attractive women are often subjected to unpleasant behaviour from men – the leer, the obscene remark. And it is too often assumed that since she has made herself look pleasing she has 'asked for it'. A beautiful girl I knew was attacked by a man in the street one night. Fortunately, she managed to fight him off. But her distress was compounded by the police officer's explanation of the attack on her: she was 'rapable' because she was attractive.

This sort of attitude is a powerful incentive to give up being attractive. But that would be capitulation. Translate the argument for a moment into the intellectual sphere. It is well known and acknowledged that many men dislike clever women, and most such women have had experience of the hostility that their intellects arouse. A friend of mine who is a don at Oxbridge never unleashes the full power of her mind in any argument with her husband because he cannot bear to be worsted by a woman, and ridicules her for being a 'blue stocking'. In other words, she capitulates. But the whole point of the women's movement was to release women from such absurdities and pressures. A woman, like a man, should be free to display what peacock feathers she may have without having mud slung at her. It is worth taking a tip from Israel's only woman prime minister, Golda Meir. When there was a horrifying spate of rapes in Tel-Aviv, her all-male cabinet suggested that a curfew should be imposed on women to keep them off the streets at night. Meir insisted, however, that since the rapist was a man, there was no reason why *women's* freedom should be curtailed. If there was to be a curfew, it should be imposed on men. It must be better to lay responsibility in the right place, and then attack that battlement.

For men to subject women to violence – physical or psychic – is, quite simply, wrong. Any woman, however beautiful or sexy she may be, should be free to walk the streets without having to go through a barrage of insolence, insults, attempted pick-ups or rapes. A step towards that freedom is to insist that men see women not just as suitable objects for their demands and fantasies, but as fully integrated persons. No woman should refuse to try this on the grounds that if men have not yet seen women as persons they never will. Women, after all, did not always see *themselves* as persons, which is why consciousness-raising groups sprang up – to encourage women to be aware of themselves as more than just wives, mothers and sex objects.

Jean-Paul Sartre identified as 'bad faith' the tendency of *many* people, men and women, to see themselves only as 'beings for others' – that is to say, as nothing more than what others want them to be. And it is not only men who have been guilty of failing to see the opposite sex as persons: many women seeing a man garlanded with the trappings of success – the big car, the expense account – may lose sight of him as a person and see him only as a bank balance.

We may all be guilty of 'bad faith'. When my step-daughter Frances took a part-time job as a waitress, she complained constantly that customers (of both sex) saw her as nothing more than a 'food-shovelling machine'. There is no reason to believe that the best way to get insensitive customers to rethink their perceptions of waiters is by encouraging waiters to give up their jobs. Similarly, there is no reason to believe that the best way to get men to rethink their perceptions of sex objects is for us all to sink into scruffy unfemininity.

A man I spoke to agreed: 'I once took an absolutely stunning barrister out to dinner. She was beautiful, so I put on a real show – expensive restaurant, champagne, the whole lot. Half-way through the first course she suddenly stood up and told me that my attitudes to women were smug, patronising and insulting. And she left – leaving me with two plates of smoked salmon and Châteaubriand to come. Christ, it was embarrassing – and a shock; but it made me think hard about what I'd said, and the way I was with her. I decided she was right. When I got it sorted out I saw her again, and it was better. Now we're friends. If she'd been plain or mousy I don't think her behaviour would have had anywhere near the same impact.'

This barrister surely had it right; she was prepared to be sensually pleasing and desirable, and so she had a wide range of men to choose from. She was also prepared to jettison speedily any man who did not treat her as she thought she deserved. If men's attitudes to sexy women are to be changed, sexy women must take the lead. Radcliffe Richards points out, 'You cannot touch the cause of the leer and the wolf-whistle by making yourself unwhistleable at.'

Deliberately to be attractive to men is not to invite all-comers. Helena Rubinstein once said that whenever a woman titivated before a mirror she was 'aiming to get laid'. Anna Raeburn warned: 'Certain kinds of clothes and make-up are, of course, a message. At the extreme it's the short skirt, the fishnet stockings, the very high heels, lashings of mascara and lipstick, the cleavage slit to the waist. It's a public offer of a certain kind of private behaviour.' But even when the message is screamed out so raucously, what is being offered is a possibility, not a guarantee: any woman must be free to say 'no'. Too many men are inclined to confuse a woman's being attractive with her being available – and to regard themselves as having been led on if they are rejected. Such men are the victims of confusion. And if women agree with men that men are being led on by this, then they are guilty of the same confusion. If these women then opt for sensible flatties and shapeless smocks, men will probably conclude that women who do not wish to be objects are incapable of being sexy, which is not acceptable, and that sexy women are indeed man-fodder, which is worse. A woman's desirability can get in the way of a man seeing her as a person; but this unfortunate fact is no argument for insisting that women refuse to be desirable at all. Do this if it suits you, but it is not all – nor the best – you can do.

_ 9 _

PORNOGRAPHY

An active sexual relationship can be both difficult and risky: one partner may make demands that the other does not wish to meet, or impose behaviour that seems distasteful, or refuse to do what is desired. The likelihood of someone getting precisely what they want in sex is circumscribed by the sometimes inconvenient presence of the other.

To escape from this reality, it is possible to create a private world in which all that conflicts with our wishes is excluded. This is the realm of fantasy – where everything and everyone is pliable to the will, where there is no clash of desires, where no one else's needs intrude, where the fantasist is sovereign. For all the freedom of such a private world, some fantasies are ordinary, even banal: the fantasist dreams about sex with a beautiful and famous film-star rather than with an unprepossessing spouse. Or perhaps the dream is of sex with two, three or even four, as a change from one. By contrast, some fantasies are bizarre. Do you get a buzz from imagining yourself trussed up like a rubber ball to be bounced about by a naked Amazon? This is what one man described to a psychiatrist as his cherished dream. And fantasies of flagellation, bondage, rape, buggery, fetishism and murder go beyond the bizarre into the 'obscene'. The possible combinations for actual coitus are necessarily limited by the organs and orifices available, but the possible embellishments seem endless.

People who admit to having fantasies at all usually insist that they figure in their sex lives no more than monosodium glutamate figures in their diet: as a touch of flavour – spice to a jaded or flagging relationship. In her collection of women's fantasies, *My Secret Garden*, Nancy Friday was asked, 'Who needs fantasies? What's the matter with good old-fashioned sex?' She replied, 'Nothing's the matter with good old-fashioned sex. Nothing's the matter with asparagus either. But why not have the hollandaise, too?'

Friday reported that in compiling her book she had difficulty 'getting through to women, getting through the fear of admitting their fantasies', not to her, but to themselves. She attributed this to a fear of rejection – a fear perhaps of seeming disgusting to others. Some such fear may affect us all: very few people are prepared to disclose their intimate imaginings.

Nevertheless, fantasies are taken out of the secluded corners of our minds and put before us in words and images. This is pornography: in books, pictures and films a public form is given to inner, often secret, worlds. Public opinion divides between those who believe that pornography is harmless, or even beneficial in its effects, and those who see it as degrading, corrupting and an inducement to violence. Lord Longford described it as 'a manifest evil'; Kenneth Tynan argued that it 'deserves a few words of exculpation and thanksgiving'. On the one hand, forceful efforts are made to ban pornography; on the other hand, there is a profound anxiety about censorship. Somewhat bizarrely, a 'Luscious Lorraine' spread on the cen-trefold of Playboy has become a battlefield on which the vanguard fight for free speech, liberalism and the rights of the individual.

As you peruse some of the available pornography, you may be tempted to leap aboard the bandwagon of the anti-permissives on the grounds that so much pornography is crude and badly crafted – because the one clear problem with this particular art form is that it is very bad art. If aesthetics were the only issue, the bulk of pornography could, without regret, be consigned to the bottom of the sea. But aesthetic arguments of taste and style are not all there is to it: there is also the question of morality.

People want and enjoy pornography. Since we no longer live in an age when sexual pleasure is suspect, this can be said to be an argument in favour of making pornographic material avail-able. Of course, the pleasure derived from an activity is not in itself sufficient to justify it: some people get intense delight from causing pain to others. Trading on this, those who wish to see pornography banned argue that, despite the obvious pleasures, its effects are significantly harmful and provide a very good reason for them to do so. This is a weighty claim which, if proved, would surely carry the day. But can it be proved?

These, then, are the issues involved in any discussion of the rights and wrongs of pornography. But before they can be considered, it is necessary to decide just what pornography is.

A woman who described herself to me as a 'trendy mum' was nevertheless revolted to find what she called 'girlie magazines' buried under her son's bed. 'I suppose it's only to be expected at seventeen – boys will be boys. But I can't help it, the whole thing's indecent. I suppose that's what pornography is – sex shown in such a way that it offends someone's sense of decency.'

The Longford Report, surprisingly, made no attempt to define pornography – but it did extend the legal definition of obscenity to cover anything whose effect, 'taken as a whole, is to outrage contemporary standards of decency or humanity accepted by the public at large'. This criterion has precisely the same fault as that offered by the 'trendy mum': it is dangerously subjective. People have an infinite capacity to be outraged, and if this response were the deciding factor in classifying what is pornographic, it would condemn just about the whole corpus of our art, from Shakespeare to *Coronation Street*. The ladies of Melbourne, for example, were deeply offended by the naked genitals of Michelangelo's *David*, and insisted on sticking a plastic figleaf on a replica of the statue. And it was once – seriously – suggested that the relationship between Enid Blyton's Noddy and Big Ears smacked of homosexuality and was therefore potentially corrupting to children!

Anything at all, however innocent and well-intentioned, may be perceived by someone as indecent. Fortunately, many such judgments are dismissed as misguided. Most of us would think it ridiculous to condemn the *David* as indecent, and therefore pornographic, because of the stupidity of a coterie of Melbourne ladies. If we accept Bertrand Russell's advice to consider the mass of historical evidence, we will see that a great deal of censorship has been grounded in nothing more admirable than prejudice. Russell described how in the 1920s a pamphlet arguing that women might get pleasure from sex was condemned as indecent.

A book or a film cannot, then, be described as pornography just because some, or even many, people think it is. Havelock Ellis's *Studies in the Psychology of Sex*, for example, is a learned and serious work. The fact that it was banned in England under the terms of Lord Campbell's Act of 1857 does not make it indecent. It is precisely because pornography is not defined by its effect on people that a distinction can be made between 'soft porn' and 'hard porn'. Most people will find hard porn offensive and indecent, and soft porn pretty tame and less likely to offend. But soft porn is still pornography.

If pornography cannot intelligibly be defined by its effect, can it be defined by its content? A common view of pornographic material is that it consists of explicit depictions of sex. An advertising agent defending his profession against charges from a women's group that advertisements exploiting sex were pornographic said in an interview, 'Of course advertisers are going to use sex – why shouldn't they associate something that powerful with their product? But the sex isn't made explicit. It is much more subtle than that. Whereas pornography is nothing but explicit sex.'

Even though this is certainly true, the explicitly sexual content of pornography is not its defining characteristic. Other things deal in explicit sex too – sex manuals, respectable medical books, much 'high' art and any serious, sober account of sexual activity. It cannot be argued that *any* picture of a couple making love is pornographic – far from it. The fact that something is explicit does not make it pornographic.

Consider these two passages:

Naegele took a bull-whip from a hook on the wall. Jacques was naked. 'On your knees,' said the Gestapo agent . . . Naegele raised the whip and dealt Jacques a terrible blow on the soles of his feet. Jacques fell forwards. Naegele forced him upright again. Jacques twisted and turned to avoid the whip . . . He screamed . . . The Gestapo were more excited by those who resisted than by those who wept, screamed and groaned. And Jacques screamed his head off. The whip lashed his calves and thighs.

And:

> The lash of the bull-whip caught him across his naked
> shoulders. In spite of himself he screamed as he fell to his
> knees. The Gestapo officer forced him to his feet and raised
> the whip again. Pete twisted away and screamed again as the
> whip lashed like fire across his thighs.

In content – and out of context – the two passages are virtually
indistinguishable, but in intention they are miles apart. The
first is from a book called *Dora*, a serious account of the
humiliation and suffering endured at the hands of the Gestapo,
intentionally explicit since the author wants us to know exactly
what it was like. The second is a leech, exploiting these horrors
for what is called the 'fladge' market. Pete's agonies are set out
in a nasty, amateur little volume called *The Scourge of the Nazi
Bull-whip*. The intention is to appeal to those who get their
erotic kicks from sado-masochism, and it is this that makes it,
and other volumes like it, pornographic: if some visual or
verbal representation is intended to stimulate sexual desire,
then whatever effect it actually has, even if it makes you yawn,
it is pornography.

The converse of this is that works with a serious, non-sexual
intent which happen to titillate certain people are protected
from being categorised as pornographic. Lord Russell of Liverpool's book *The Scourge of the Swastika* was a best-seller. It is
not far-fetched to suppose that of the many people who read it
some were stimulated by some of the accounts of sado-
masochistic activity in concentration camps. Such activity has,
after all, become a stock subject for sadistic pornography. It
would be unacceptable, however, to condemn Lord Russell's
book because of the unsavoury pleasure people may have
derived from it.

Pornography, then, is defined by the author's intention. The
only problem with this is that there may be instances when the
author's intention is not known; thus *we* will not know if the
work is pornographic or not. If, for instance, you knew nothing
about Goya and you stumbled on his series of prints *The
Disasters of War*, could you state unequivocally that none of
the gruesome scenes of flagellation and castration were pornographic? Could you even be sure of Rubens, or Renoir and his

sugar-pink nudes? Of course, if Renoir were painting now you might feel more certain: it tends to take stronger fare than Renoir to stir the fires of twentieth-century libidos. But you might imagine a youth who had never seen a naked woman, who desired women and longed to take their clothes off but had never had the opportunity. Renoir might be very exciting to him – just as exciting as *Playboy* is for many adolescents. How would we decide which was 'high' art and which was not?

In *Sexual Desire*, Roger Scruton makes this distinction between genuinely erotic art and pornography: the genuinely erotic invites the reader to re-create in the imagination 'the first-person point of view of someone party to an erotic encounter'. Pornography, by contrast, offers you the position of the voyeur; it 'retains as a rule the third-party perspective of the voyeuristic observer'.

This distinction is not shared by Geoffrey Gorer, who in a collection of articles called *Does Pornography Matter?* considers the work of artists such as Fuseli and Rowlandson, and writers like John Cleland, all of whose 'main talent or output has been pornographic'. He argues that if aesthetic considerations are set aside there is no value in maintaining the distinction between the erotic and the pornographic. In the same collection, Sir Herbert Read acknowledges that where there is great artistic skill it is tempting to use it to justify pornographic material. He adds, though, that an apologia for such material in great artists like Chaucer and Shakespeare is that it forms part of their 'realistic integrity'. 'Realistic integrity', as Read points out, is a cant phrase that may be used to justify just about anything. Nevertheless, it is certain that a serious artist is likely to have a breadth of vision and interest the pornographer conspicuously lacks. In pornography the world is reduced to the manufactured fantasy of sexual excitement. Scruton compares Cleland's *Fanny Hill* and Laclos' *Les Liaisons dangereuses*. In the former, Cleland's 'keyhole' technique enlarges the bodies of those having sex so that they are nothing more than their sex organs. In Laclos' book the sexual organs are simply instruments in a vicious game of psychological possession.

Obviously the artist cannot determine the stance of the viewer. Freud believed that if a work of art stirred someone at all, voyeurism would have played a part. 'The essence of the voyeur's position is his removal from action. He watches and participates in fantasy ... The simplest and most obvious subject of the male voyeur's enthusiasm is the naked female.' It may, then, be more difficult to secure the first-person perspective in pictures than in books, and so harder to pin down the erotic from the pornographic. On the other hand, Kingsley Amis is probably right when he observes that even if it is not always easy to pontificate about what is pornography and what is high art, 'in practice the reader can usually make out where he is'. The same goes for the film-goer and the art-lover.

Why should anyone believe that pornography is in some way immoral – that it is wrong to use pictures or words as a direct stimulus to erotic desires and impulses? Pornography works by evoking some of the physiological concomitants of sex: it gives a man an erection, for instance. The only qualities necessary in such material are those needed to produce those effects. Equally, an advertisement for food works by evoking some of the physiological concomitants of eating – it makes your mouth water. We have all seen pictures of Robert Carrier confections that would have a gourmand drooling every bit as lustfully as the reader of *Playboy* drools over a naked playmate. Since it is perfectly acceptable to want to eat, it is generally regarded as acceptable to arouse people's desire to do so. Thus, it is not thought reprehensible to produce deliciously evocative pictures of food. If it is also acceptable to want sex, how could it be wrong to arouse a desire for it?

One response to this might be to deny that it is always acceptable to arouse a desire for food. People on a special diet may be put at risk if they are enticed to eat what is bad for them. So, even if in principle it is acceptable to arouse a desire to eat, it may not be acceptable to impose pictures of food on us so that we want to eat even when we are sated or when it is bad for us. It is not pretty to contemplate people rushing off like modern Romans to shove their fingers down their throats to make room for more. Similarly, people going about their daily business should not be subjected to a barrage of pornographic images so that they are constantly in a state of jangling sexual excitement. In *The Puritan Jungle* Sara Harris described the outrage of people who receive unsolicited pornography through the post from pornographers gambling on 'hooking' at least a percentage of those who read it. We can sympathise with the lawyer who fumed, 'Using the mail to send pornography to nuns makes me mad.'

Stimulation should not be imposed on people, either inadvertently or against their will. But there does not immediately seem to be anything immoral in selling a product guaranteed to make a person feel sexy. If someone wants to arouse the need in themselves because satisfying it is so blissful . . . well, why not? It is certainly a more understandable, or at least rational, urge than the desire to feel fear that presumably prompts people to read horror stories and see films like *Psycho*.

There is also some evidence that pornography may be beneficial. Many psychologists and psychiatrists believe it can help people to overcome the blocks and inhibitions that damage their sex lives. I found it interesting that many people I spoke to accepted that *fantasy* could be a useful and good ingredient in their sex lives while believing that *pornography* was in some way unacceptable. Why should the unimaginative not be allowed to have manufactured fantasy available to them? It seems unfair that because someone lacks the mental agility to conjure up fantasies they should be deprived of such a benefit.

One woman told me that although she thought 'sex in real life is fine', there was 'something altogether shoddy about men in dirty raincoats getting their kicks from what someone's doing on a screen'. But if you go to a film like *Deep Throat* or *Emmanuelle* you will not find lonely men in dirty raincoats – only well-scrubbed, middle-class married couples. The only macs around will be Burberrys. The image of the pervert slavering over a blue movie or a book in a brown cover is simply a prejudice, and a long way from reality. Some of the most respectable people enjoy pornography. Samuel Pepys, for example, described struggling with the wish to buy 'the most bawdy, lewd book that I ever saw'. Eventually he bought it 'in plain binding, because I resolve, as soon as I have read it, to burn it'. Having read it, he masturbated, then concluded, 'A mighty lewd book, but yet not amiss for a sober man to read over to inform himself in the villainy of the world.'

Is there anything wrong with people getting vicarious pleasure from others having sex? Some people believe that all spectator sports are bad because they encourage passivity; we should be doing it ourselves. This is too extreme. In sex, human physiology sets its own limits on physical activity, but this capacity does not necessarily delimit sexual interest. And why, when as well as getting a great deal of pleasure you may learn something from, for example, watching tennis played by experts, should you not enjoy the same benefits from watching sex? A pornographic movie may increase your interest and enthusiasm and introduce you to novel techniques. During Wimbledon fortnight local tennis courts blossom with the creaky bodies of the under-exercised trying to emulate the skill and style of Becker and Navratilova. Perhaps blue movies inspire acrobatics as well.

A surprisingly common view among people I spoke to was that those who enjoy pornography may find sufficient satisfaction in fantasy not to want sex in reality. If they get all they need from masturbating over a video nasty or a Page Three lovely, they may be encouraged to eschew active sex.

It says a great deal about people's views of sex that they genuinely fear a solitary wank could replace the joys of sex with a loving partner. There is no historical evidence at all to suggest their fears are well-grounded: pornography is as old as literate man, yet the human race still, by and large, prefers sex with a chosen partner to the lonely pleasures of masturbation. By this token, it would be far-fetched to suppose that one who would otherwise have had a normal, satisfying, sex life could be robbed of it by Hugh Hefner's periodicals.

This is not, of course, to deny that pornography may never act as a substitute for sex. Someone who lacks a sexual partner, or whose fantasies cannot be acted out, may find great relief in pornography: it may help to discharge repressed desires and compensate for sexual deprivation. But this is an argument for pornography, not against it. If some people have been deprived of sexual pleasure by illness, travel or bereavement, and explicit sexual material can alleviate some of their distress, who could object? In his article, 'Is Pornography Beneficial?' G.L. Simons is emphatic that, 'pornography provides sex by proxy and in such usage it can have a clear justification'. He goes on, 'It is difficult to see how anyone could object to the use of pornography in such circumstances, other than on the grounds of morbid anti-sexuality.' In similar spirit, Kenneth Tynan observed that for men who are away from their women, 'pornography can act as a portable memory, a welcome shortcut to remembered bliss, relieving tension without involving disloyalty'. Women, too, may claim the same benefit.

Simons and Tynan are discussing the rights and wrongs of material that depicts socially accepted forms of sexual behaviour. A great deal of pornography, however, focuses on acts that are not acceptable, such as rape and murder. One woman I spoke to took the opposite line from that which saw pornography as replacing active sex: she argued that it 'recommends the behaviour it shows. All that pleasure people get from sadism – doesn't that imply it's acceptable to do those things to each other?'

It is not obvious that depictions of behaviour can be said to recommend that behaviour. Murder stories set out all the gory details of a murder, often with every sign of enjoyment on the part of the killer, but we do not think of this as a recommendation to kill someone if we are inconvenienced by their existence. Nevertheless, there may be something to this view if stories are distinguished from photographs and films. A photograph shows that something has happened – as they say, 'the camera never lies'. If you see a picture of a man tearing a girl's knickers off, that event actually happened. And this recognition may perhaps be a barrier overcome: if some people do this sort of thing, why should I not do the same? Pictures of sexual behaviour may be a thin end of the wedge with regard to other people's behaviour. A few years ago I saw a film called *Not a Love Story*; it was made by a group of women in protest at what was done to women in pornography. In one clip, a woman was dressed in a full-length black leather suit, hung with chains and suspended, in the most tortuous pose, by her hands from a meat hook in the centre of the ceiling. My neighbour turned to me in horror. 'How could anyone do that to a woman?' So far as she was concerned, this was for real. And, of course, in some films it has been. In the infamous 'snuff' movies in California girls were actually strangled – 'snuffed' – at the moment of orgasm. If, then, you see a film in which something dreadful is done, the thought that this actually happened – you saw it with your own eyes – may liberate a wish to do it yourself.

It is very different with a written story. If some sexual activity is presented in words, it is just a story, pure fiction. A story may have less impact on behaviour than a film because there is less room for the belief that these events actually took place. This undermining does not happen with, for instance, films of Agatha Christie mysteries. As the victim is throttled, we may feel all the thrill of fear, or sadistic pleasure; at the same time we are perfectly sure that this is acting – it is not for real.

Why can we not accept this suspension of reality with pornographic films? It may simply be a matter of detail. You can simulate a strangulation, but if you see a close-up of a penis going into a vagina it has to be real – it is impossible to fake. Once it is clear that the main action is actually taking place, it may be easier to believe that everything else is real. I do not know; but it may be so. In support of this, by the way, a supplier of pornographic movies told me that the most successful 'hard porn' films tend to be those where there are no professional gimmicks. The viewer does not feel that this is illusion, that the wool is being pulled over his or her eyes: this is life.

An editor for a small British film company told me that he thought producing pornography was simply irresponsible. 'People making porn movies, for example, can't control the way that customers satisfy the desires they've got going. You may come out feeling so horny you jump on the first woman you see!'

Violent films always create a furore; people are frightened that those who go into the cinema perfectly normal will come out violent psychopaths. There is simply no evidence to support this. It may be so; it may not. But it is a genuine fear, and out of it comes a sense that film-makers who persistently produce violent films are indeed being irresponsible. There is, however, a difference between violent films and sexual films that contain violence. If what is aroused is desire to harm someone, satisfaction is bound to be evil in every way. If you want to cause pain the only way to do it is to hurt someone. But if it is a desire to have sex that is aroused, this may be satisfied without any harm being done at all, even if what turned you on in the first place was violence. You may still leave the cinema to have a perfectly peaceful encounter with your lover. The difference between the man who makes violent films and the man who makes pornography is the difference between the man who sells a sawn-off shot-gun and the man who sells a hammer. It is absolutely clear what the shot-gun is to be used for, so the seller does have a responsibility. But no one has a reason to believe that a hammer is going to be used to beat someone's head in, so there is none of the same responsibility.

It is not at all obvious precisely what desires pornography does arouse. A woman who enjoys rape fantasies told me, 'I suppose I do identify to some extent with the victim in rape films – that's what excites me, I guess. But I don't end up longing to be raped. In real life the pain and fear would be so terrible – I can't bear to think about it. But I can enjoy a fantasy.' Similarly, a man who owned up to enjoying flagellation pornography said, 'I get quite a buzz from Amazons in stiletto heels forcing a man to have sex – but Christ – I wouldn't want it for real. I'd be bloody terrified! All I want is nice straight sex with the wife – and the odd bit of fantasy.' So pornography does not inevitably arouse a desire to act out the fantasy. Indeed, for some the thrill is there only if reality is, as it were, put in brackets. All the fantasist may want is a spectacularly good orgasm.

If a desire is acceptable there is not likely to be anything wrong in arousing it; but if the desire is reprehensible, encouraging it must be wrong. There is, then, a distinction to be made between pornography that arouses a desire to hurt someone and pornography that simply arouses a desire for sex. The first is unacceptable; the second is not.

The film editor I interviewed, however, thought this was inadequate. 'It's obvious that not everyone who watches or reads porn is going to turn into a raving nutcase. I've watched porn myself and it hasn't made me want to rape schoolgirls or bugger little boys. But there is a genuine fear that some people may be tipped over the edge into carrying out what they see. There was a horrible rape case recently – the boy said he'd been influenced by video nasties.'

Bertrand Russell – discussing the dangers or otherwise of indecent photographs – once observed, 'Conventional men are of the opinion that such things are extraordinarily injurious to others, although hardly one of them will admit that they have been injurious to himself.' Given the supposed virulence of pornographic material, it is remarkably to their credit that censors – who are required to peruse the most extreme versions of it – are not utterly depraved. Perhaps they are moral giants; or perhaps, and more likely, very few people, are going to be encouraged to emulate what they find repugnant just because it has been seen or read in a work of pornography.

No good case can be made for banning pornography simply by showing that some harm is caused by it. Some harm is caused by many things – those hammers, for example. It is not even enough to show that people who revel in pornography commit more sexual offences than clean-living souls who eschew it. There may be some underlying cause of both the addiction to pornography and the need to commit crime. As a psychiatrist told me, 'Someone with strong internal prohibitions against sex – who thinks it's wrong – may be impelled both to read pornography and sexually to abuse women.' The crime, then, is the result of the prohibitions, not the pornography. Just because two things turn up together you cannot deduce that one is the cause of the other.

Of course, the whole picture is muddied by exactly the sort of claim that a rape – or some other sexual crime – was committed under the influence of pornography. This might very well catch on as an excuse, for it is obviously an advantageous position for a sex offender to be in. He gets off; the video industry carries the can. Geoffrey Gorer, in his contribution to *Does Pornography Matter?*, has also observed that, 'Magistrates or reformers with bees in their bonnets can frequently get juvenile delinquents to admit exposure to whatever form of mass communication they themselves hold in abhorrence.' He reminded readers that juvenile delinquency was once blamed on the BBC serial *Dick Barton*! Once such a defence was allowed, it would be impossible to distinguish the truth from the expedient lies.

A women's organisation set up to help rape victims is certain that it is dangerous to identify pornography as the cause of rape: it removes attention from the real issue. Judit Kertesz, from 'Women Against Rape', said, 'We get very angry indeed when people say that pornography is the major cause of violence against women. Why don't they look at the facts? In many countries where there is little or no visible pornography there is no evidence of less violence towards women as a result. In the light of this it's absurd to suggest that pornography is the major cause of rape. It's also dangerous. If you focus on the morality of images you just push the real issue out of the limelight. Women are forced into financial dependence on men and men are put into power over us. *This* is what encourages men to take out their violence and frustration on us as some compensation for unemployment and low wages.'

Clearly, the connection between any sort of fantasy and the behaviour of people exposed to it is obscure. There is no real evidence to show that Dr Jekyll becomes ravening Mr Hyde as a result of blue movies featuring curvaceous blondes. Indeed, in the Longford report on pornography Dr Maurice Yaffe observed that his detailed research tended to show that pornography has remarkably little effect on its users' behaviour. Regrettably, Lord Longford's committed stance precluded any objective consideration of the doctor's findings, which were insultingly dismissed.

At present, the anti-pornography crusaders can admit only that the evidence is inconclusive. We are in the dark. But as Simons points out, once this is admitted the case for repressive legislation falls apart: 'in a free society, or one supposedly aiming after freedom, social phenomena are, like individuals, innocent until proven guilty'. He adds the further point that, in such a society, 'an activity will be permitted unless there is clear evidence of its harmful consequences'.

People want pornography – the fact that they are even prepared to pay for it is an unerring guide to the pleasure it gives them – and you would need compelling reasons to take what people want away from them.

That there are side-effects from pornography is undeniable. A psychiatrist told me, 'I wouldn't want to suggest that the sum of human happiness has been *greatly* increased by pornography. But some couples have certainly benefited from it.' And the same goes for single people. A student confided, 'I know you're not going to believe this – but I swear it's true. Until I saw a hard porn movie I didn't know it was all right to make noises!' Pornography can be liberating.

Some psychiatrists go further, and suggest that pornography can cut down on delinquency by purging the embryonic rapist of his aggression. This is the theory of catharsis, developed by Aristotle, according to whom certain art, for example what he called 'orgiastic music', can stir the emotions to a frenzy and, by doing so, purge them and restore the person to quiet. Catharsis is a healing process; it does not encourage strong emotions to erupt into violent action – just the opposite. It is possible, then, that rather than depraving or corrupting the consumer – inciting the weak-minded to act out activities described in fantasy – pornography purges the prospective villain of his villainous urges. The man driven to a frenzy by a fantasy of bondage and rape is not necessarily driven to translate his fantasy into real life. Instead he may be purged of violence by the cathartic action of pornography. As a pornography aficionado earnestly assured me, 'One *Playboy* sold is a maiden saved.'

This has its attractions, but unfortunately it is pure speculation. We simply do not know. Nor are we helped by simplistic dictums like: 'Pornography reduces violent crime' (the view of some who are pro-pornography), or 'Pornography encourages violent crime' (the view of many who are anti-pornography). We can perfectly well imagine the situation as being one in which some people are satisfied with violent sex by proxy and are kept off the streets by it, while on others pornography has the reverse effect. So both propositions could be true. Any rational policy on pornography would depend on knowing what the facts are, but the facts are just what we cannot establish. It is absurd meanwhile to prate on about the hypothetical consequences of pornography; we need to establish some causal connection between the availability of pornography and the crime rate.

Most people accept that if the crime rate soars as a result of pornography, it is the hard porn that is likely to be responsible: violent films and books that peddle some of the nastiest fantasies imaginable. Soft porn, by contrast, seems harmless. Even if, as *Mayfair* promised, 'You will be zonked by Zoe's 38 ins', it is unlikely that those magic inches will pitch you slavering on to the first woman you see. Nevertheless, this kind of pornography is also said by some to have unacceptable consequences: it reinforces traditional and unacceptable attitudes to women. As one woman complained to me, 'All those naked bums and boobs on the cover of soft porn magazines blatantly appeal to those dreary men who think that all women are just here to service the male member.'

There is a difference between art that propounds unacceptable attitudes and art that is enjoyed by those who happen to have unacceptable attitudes. Some Nazis revered Beethoven to the extent of playing his music as Jews were herded into gas chambers. Even such a horror as this does not make Beethoven immoral. Similarly, if a man has a certain image of women – as sex objects – this may be a factor in his enjoyment of pornography. But you cannot simply condemn something because people with deplorable beliefs enjoy it. Rubens's women may be particularly suited to being enjoyed by men who have a sexist attitude to women in general; but this does not, of itself, make Rubens immoral. The point, then, must be that pornography does not merely accord with what sexist men want to enjoy. More, it propounds particularly sexist attitudes.

This is Ann Garry's argument in her article 'Pornography and Respect for Women'. Pornography, she says, 'treats women as mere sex objects to be exploited and manipulated and degrades the role and status of women'. Bearing this in mind, it is illuminating to compare 'soft porn' for men and 'soft porn' for women.

When women are spread on the glossy pages of magazines like *Playboy* they are turned into goods – morsels for the observer to devour. All the posing, the nakedness, the pouting and smouldering, is for 'you wonderful guys out there'. It is an explicit affirmation that these women have what it takes ... and that what it takes is whatever men want. Any touch of individuality is carefully limited so that men can project their fantasy on to the sex object. Camilla, a *Playboy* playmate, claims to have a degree in economics – 'But', she gushes, 'it's so much more fun getting all this attention.' Any intelligence she may have is carefully confined to a place between her thighs. But not, of course, to be active. The whole message – the whole boring, repetitive, ancient message – is that women are just longing to be the grateful and passive recipient of male sexuality. It is phallus worship, the libation being all those juicy females. The stories in these magazines confirm the prominence of the active penis. One man calls his penis 'Mike Hammer': 'Its size struck fear into the hearts of several damsels in the course of my love life.' (Can you believe it?) Another insisted, 'I can really do a lady up. I've got ten inches.' And so on . . . and on . . . and on.

Now flip to *Playgirl*. The first thing that strikes the reader is that the display of hunky maleness is in danger of being ludicrously undermined by there being not an erection in sight: it is illegal to show them. Women's arousal can – of course – be taken for granted – narrowed eyes and a pout and we can assume she is panting for it. But a stud without an erection? To compensate for their shrunken and well-scrubbed organs, the lads are equipped with a wide range of more or less dangerous phallic objects: rifles, knives, swords, motorbikes, stallions. These attest to their virility; we can all be sure that if they are not up it is not because they cannot get there. These models are free to gaze challengingly out of the page with a look that is straightforward and aggressive; it is the viewers – women – who are the objects, not the models. It is a stunning macho coup. Female models promise men, 'I've got what you want.' Male models challenge women, 'Have you got what I want?' Men must be active, even men offering their bodies to women's fantasies. Women, by contrast, are always passive, dehumanised instruments of male sexuality. This is the attitude reflected in so called 'soft porn'.

As Roger Scruton points out, the world of fantasy does not exist comfortably with reality. The 'reality principle' by which the sex act is regulated is a principle of respect for others. But fantasy obeys no such rules. Instead, it is governed by 'monstrous myths and illusions which are at war with the human world'. The myths are familiar to us all – the myth, for example, that women want to be raped.

Are these myths and illusions imposed on women in real life? In his book *The Fantasy Factor*, Dr Peter Dally observed of a patient: 'Since Aubrey was nine he has masturbated while looking at photographs and drawings in soft porn magazines, imagining himself copulating with the women shown there.' Dr Dally explains, however, that Aubrey 'has never considered them to be real people, nor has he ever related them to anyone he knows.' It is perfectly possible for men to respond to pornography without leaping to the conclusion that this is what women are like in real life.

It is worth reflecting on the way men are portrayed in fantasy – for example, in James Bond novels. They are shown as having little interest in anything but surviving and satisfying bodily appetites; in other words, they are either killing or fucking. This is as much a degrading of men as pornography is of women. Now is it true that we extrapolate from a particular type of story to the assumption that this is what everyone is like? Perhaps some people do, and some do not. It is hard, though, to hold on to the view that on the one hand men see creatures in pornography and assume all women are like this, and on the other that pornography is fantasy. If it is fantasy, then by definition it is not seen as corresponding to reality. Men launch themselves into soft porn as into a world of make-believe, not as into a representation of reality. A self-styled king of porn told me, 'I don't want to be disrespectful. Okay? But what men really want is women on their knees sucking their cocks. Now you women's libbers won't stand for it (sorry, no joke intended), so that's what I give the poor bastards: the macho dream!'

Suppose it is true that the characterisation of women in pornography does not affect the way men see them in real life. Suppose we also knew – as we do not – that pornography does not tip those who use it into violent sexual acts. Would this be good reason to be morally neutral towards it?

It seems to me that Roger Scruton is right that none of us with what he calls a 'normal conscience' could adopt such a stance. I cannot help feeling that even though there is nothing wrong with sexual excitement in itself, there is something at least distasteful about arousing it in the way that hard core pornography sometimes does. It is not pretty to think of people getting a sexual buzz from seeing someone whipped and tortured, just as it is not pretty to think of people getting a thrill from seeing someone's head bashed in, even if it is only on film.

Most pornography – in the words of D.H. Lawrence – 'is an attempt to insult sex, to do the dirt on it'. Let me offer an analogy of what happens in pornography to sex and sexual relationships. Imagine an endless supply of exquisite Chinese vases. Some people enjoy plastering these vases with mud; others get great pleasure from watching. No one is actually harmed: the mud washes off, people who might have defaced other works are purged of the desire to do it, the whole thing gives pleasure and in addition stimulates the economy. But even if it is not obvious that there could be anything *wrong* in all this, it is profoundly distasteful. A beautiful object is made into an ugly one. And this is horrible whether the object is a vase, a human being or a human relationship.

This is an objection to pornography – but it is not an argument for making it a crime. Very few people feel neutral about adultery: equally few would wish to see it made illegal. The general liberal principle about interfering in other people's lives is that you should not do it without a just case. The just case for censorship follows from a reasonable, well-founded likelihood of danger. But however much you may disapprove of pornography, it cannot be because of its dangerous consequences: we do not know what they are. Also, it is not an intrinsic part of pornography that it should be sexist and brutal. If this kind of pornography proved to be dangerous to our moral well-being it would simply be an argument for good – non-sexist and non-violent – pornography, not for banning it altogether. This is, in fact, the proposal put forward by Ann Garry: ' . . . it seems preferable to try to change pornography instead of closing one's eyes in the hope that it will go away. For I suspect that pornography is here to stay.'

The probable effects on adults of pornography are so uncertain that there is currently no ground for interfering with its production. But what about children? Are we to let 9-year-olds have *Playboy* instead of the *Beano*?

When people express anxiety about pornography they nearly always do so in terms of the unfortunate effect it may have on others – never on themselves. It is the young or the weak-minded (two categories, not one, as people tend to assume) that are likely to be damaged. Lord Soper, in an article on pornography, writes: 'The girl who is encouraged to see nothing wrong in pleasing herself with somebody else's body will be unlikely to see any moral objection in pleasing herself with somebody else's money. Pornography is so often, particularly among adolescents, the first breakthrough into an atmosphere of delinquency.' It is hard to believe that anyone would find such nonsense compelling – or that someone of Lord Soper's stature could believe it. A girl who is sexually free may still think it wrong to steal, and may never do it. The notion that sexual freedom is in some way equivalent to immorality across the board is absurd and refuted by the facts. Not even the rapist is necessarily a thief.

What about the claim that sexual immorality is all the fault of pornography? First, pornography is not alone in the ideas it markets – romances, televison soap operas, even women's magazines display attitudes to women and sex that are unpalatable. Great art may also do so. Sir Herbert Read speculated that the very excellence of such art may encourage people to adopt the attitudes expressed. In which case, *pace* Lord Soper, Titian's *Rape of Europa* is more dangerous than the hack work of a porn magazine. Whether this is true or not, scientists have established that for any phenomenon – even human ones – there is likely to be a multiplicity of causes.

It is simple-minded to attribute, or try to attribute, all the ills of delinquency to a single cause. We really should have grown out of making this kind of mistake by now – especially when the evidence simply does not support the conclusion. Just as the effects on adults of pornography are incalculable, so are the effects on children.

Should we protect the young? Our grandparents were far too paternalistic, shoving prudery and propriety unthinkingly down children's throats; it certainly corrupted healthy growth as much as pornography is said to do. But we do not want to veer too much in the opposite direction in our determination to throw off repression. Pornography *is* debasing, often coarse and brutal, and I do not believe that children should be exposed to the risk of stumbling across it: I would not want my child to learn about sex from pornography. I am quite certain that even if we do not censor its production we need laws about where pornography is supplied and to whom. I simply would not go so far as denying it to any adolescent who was sufficiently curious to seek it out.

Bertrand Russell would most strenuously have disagreed. He

was certain that 'even frank pornography would do less harm if it were open and unashamed than it does when it is rendered interesting by secrecy and stealth.' Given this view, it is not surprising that he concluded, 'I am firmly persuaded that there ought to be no law whatsoever on the subject of obscene publications.' Of course, had it been proved that there was some causal connection between violent crime and pornography, Russell would certainly have wished it banned. But this returns us to the central problem of the whole issue: our ignorance.

Time and again with the issue of pornography we are bedevilled by our lack of knowledge, by the fact that we are in the dark. And when the question is one of whether children should be exposed to such material, how are we to find out? It seems too risky to subject them to a diet of pornography so that we may learn. We can only play a hunch, and the hunch is that it is better to protect them from unsolicited exposure. But even if we agree that much current pornography is cheapening and debasing, we should not deny it to adults who want it. Until we know it is dangerous beyond all compensating good, there is no ground for wielding the pen of censorship.

_ 10 _

PERVERSIONS

'We all have our funny little ways.' This was my grandmother's invariable judgment on anyone whose sexual behaviour was seen to deviate from the so-called 'norm'. Her cousin's tortured homosexuality, her neighbour's uxoriousness, the sweetshop man's penchant for little girls – all were neatly wrapped up in this one observation. My grandmother's comfortable acceptance of human variety made many of those around her profoundly uneasy. For it offended a well-entrenched, wide-spread view that only certain sexual behaviour is acceptable.

It is, of course, commonly thought that all sorts of human behaviour – not only sex – have a proper form of expression. Part of the whole process of being socialised is that we are brought up to act in certain approved ways. We are taught, for example, that there is a correct way to eat food, and we are encouraged to adopt that way so that we do not offend others. But clearly the idea that there is a proper way to have sex has considerably more import than the idea that there is a proper way to eat soup. The man who slurps his soup off a plate is likely to be censured as bad-mannered or uncouth; people may not invite him to dinner, or wish to sit next to him at table. But they are unlikely to censure him as a moral delinquent who should be barred from teaching their children, or jailed, or committed to a lunatic asylum – or even executed. It is a testament to the seriousness with which we regard people's sexual orientation that all these punishments have been meted out to those whose activity has been perceived as deviant.

This is not altogether a thing of the past. We may believe that we have progressed from the dark ages into the enlightenment, and it is true that there is not the same universal hysteria about sexual idiosyncrasies as there was even a century ago. But sex is still divided into the normal and the perverted, and perversions are still regarded with loathing and disgust. More, they are all, in a variety of ways, punished. In her autobiography *Being Myself*, for example, Martina Navratilova explains, 'Once I started travelling to the States, I realised I felt more comfortable around women than men . . . I just never thought there was anything strange about being gay.' But avowed homosexuality is not acceptable in Czechoslovakia: 'there they would put you in a sanatorium for crazy people . . . literally.'

None of us is in a position to be patronising about Iron Curtain moralities. What in Czechoslovakia is regarded as lunatic is treated elsewhere as criminal: anal sex, for example, is quite simply illegal in some states of America . . . and here for that matter. Indeed, it is an astonishing fact that, as an American lawyer told me, 'There seems to be no sexual activity except "normal" relations between husband and wife which is not forbidden by the law of some state or other.'

Even where attitudes to perversions are not institutionalised, they are unequivocally displayed in the denigrating epithets that are used of those who do not conform to the norm. Barry Humphries described to me the rich field of invention afforded him by the risible attitudes of his countrymen to homosexuality. 'In the 60s', he said, 'I wrote a comic strip with Nicholas Garland for *Private Eye*, centred on an invented character, Barry McKenzie. Richard Ingrams finally withdrew it; he thought there was too much "gratuitous smut"! Anyway, it was Australian attitudes to homosexuals that I satirized first through McKenzie and then through Sir Les. Australians call homosexuals "poofters", "shirt-lifters", "pillow-biters".'

The strength of some people's horror when confronted by a so-called perversion may dominate even the deepest and best emotions. A lesbian I spoke to told me that her father had cruelly wished her dead rather than having sex with a woman. Whatever paternal love and devotion he may have felt had been quite swallowed up in bitterness and disgust.

But why should anyone think that perversions are morally unacceptable? Why should it be seen as crucial to our concept of a moral life that certain forms of sexual activity should be condemned? If someone has a preference for oral sex, or anal

sex, or sado-masochistic reciprocity – if one feels breathlessly
tender towards a stiletto-heeled shoe or the neighbour's Great
Dane – why should it matter?

The question is not frivolous; to the contrary, it is vital that
we discover an answer, for the division of sex into straight and
perverted, good and bad, has caused a great deal of human
misery and justified many restrictions on and intrusions into
individual freedom. Such an edifice of condemnation and
control had better have an unshakable foundation.

Some philosophers have argued, however, that there is no
such foundation, for there is nothing to which the word
'perversion' can coherently be attached. As Michael Slote,
professor of philosophy at the State University, New York,
argues: 'the ordinary concept of perverted behaviour (or acts) is
inapplicable in principle . . . when we call certain behaviour
"perverted" . . . we express and counteract our own impulses
and fears'. It is just a sophisticated way of saying 'Ugh!' .

However, the corollary to the notion of perversion is the
notion of normality. If we can spell out what is normal then,
pace Professor Slote, we will know what behaviour may
coherently be described as perverted. Freud, for example,
describes a perversion as any sexual impulse that does not aim
at what is biologically normal in sex. The French psychiatrist
Dr Jean Fanchette, who has written widely on the subject,
explained:

> The classical definition of perversion goes like this: Devia-
> tion in regard to 'normal' sexual intercourse defined as
> reaching orgasm through genital penetration with a partner
> belonging to the opposite sex. So by definition there is
> perversion: when orgasm is reached with other sexual ob-
> jects as in homosexuality or bestiality, or through other body
> zones – anal or oral coitus, or when orgasm is only possible
> at all in certain external conditions, for example: fetishism,
> transvestitism, voyeurism, exhibitionism, and sado-
> masochism.

We have, then, a definition of perversion as being any sexual
activity which does not aim at the insertion of the penis into
the vagina of the human female. But this definition is not in

itself adequate to support the whole weight of moral disapproval that is hurled at deviant practices. A definition is simply a way of marking one thing off from another: it does not necessarily carry any moral import. It would be perfectly possible to accept that there are perversions as Freud has described them without accepting that they are abhorrent. As a colleague said, 'Without being morally censorious, I do believe that homosexuality is a perversion.'

'Perversion', then, need not be pejorative. There is no concept of perversion, according to Professor Slote, which identifies perverted acts as repellent and yet rests on a foundation as objective as Freud's account of biological normalcy. In short, he is saying we cannot have it both ways. A coherent account of perversions will not show them to be morally unacceptable. An account which identifies them as morally unacceptable will not be coherent.

Most people believe that there are perversions, that they can be identified and that there is something very wrong with them. What do they come up with when asked to justify this conviction?

A backbench Member of Parliament I spoke to suggested, 'The point about perversions is that they are sexual activities that instigate harm against others – think of incest and paedophilia. That's why so many perversions are also crimes. And, of course, anything that hurts other people is wrong.'

There are, of course, some sexual activities that instigate harm and therefore count as criminal. Voyeurism, for example, is a particularly unpleasant invasion of people's privacy, something that no one could reasonably be expected to allow. A Peeping Tom I interviewed was, however, both distraught and mystified at his preferred avenue to sexual pleasure being blocked. 'I wasn't hurting anyone. I just like looking at girls . . . I don't want them to know I'm there. Where's the harm?' The harm comes from the outraging of our strong inclination to hide our bodies – especially our sexual organs – from the unsolicited attentions of others. We feel very strongly that we must have the choice of allowing or disallowing an intimate view of ourselves. And we want this right enshrined in law.

Similarly, although the 'flasher' does no physical harm to his victims, he does intend to frighten them – that is the point. As a man who was undergoing treatment for compulsive exhibitionism told me, 'That was when I felt powerful . . . really dominant.' Unlike the voyeur, the flasher wants the woman, or child, to be aware of him as the agent of their discomfort, to experience what Germaine Greer once described as 'petit rape'. Clearly this is harmful, and clearly the flasher's victims should be protected by law.

What of paedophilia? Those for whom this is a desirable practice argue that it should not be illegal. They point to the fact that a child has sexual urges and can be sexually excited, and they infer from this that the child can want and enjoy sex. In reality, however, the paedophile does not want a fully responsive, fully responsible human being. He or she wants a child precisely because it is none of these. As Roger Scruton points out in *Sexual Desire*, the whole point of desiring a child is that one desires a lover 'whose personal nature is as yet unformed, who cannot bear the full weight of interpersonal responses and in particular who is regarded as only partly responsible for what he does.' The paedophile's desire is stunted, aroused only by those who are incomplete. This lack of completion, however, demands that the child be protected, for it cannot understand, and therefore cannot give consent towards, an adult's desires.

Strictly speaking, incest is not a perversion. A father may, for example, desire his daughter when she is adult. Apart from the family bond, their relationship may have precisely the same character as that of other normal heterosexual acts. A man who was convicted of incest with his 20-year-old daughter argued in a newspaper interview that love is a personal matter, and that individuals should have the choice of expressing their love as they wish. He also added that his relationship with his daughter was normal and that no harm had been done; indeed, they had both benefited.

It is not absolutely certain that an incestuous relationship is harmful. A psychiatrist told me about a patient of hers who had been classified in need of psychiatric help because it was discovered she had lost her virginity to her brother. 'The girl had clearly been in some terror at the thought of the act and had recoiled from any so-called normal contact. She was nineteen when she had sex with her brother and she claimed that he taught her not to be frightened of it. I couldn't definitely say that it had done her harm.'

Why, then, does the common morality regard incest as abhorrent? Part of the answer is that the commonest form of incest is not usually a relationship between adults but between adult and child. Objections, then, to paedophilia would be enough ground to condemn it. But there are other issues unique to incest.

A woman I spoke to who as a child had had an incestuous relationship with her father told me, 'My mother knew about it but pretended at the time that she didn't. And I just felt very confused. I loved my father but I wasn't sure that I wanted this.' The common view that incest is abhorrent and should be illegal is perhaps a response to the recognition that it substitutes a sexual relationship for the immensely valuable, non-sexual relationship of parent and child. As a result of the relationship between father and daughter or mother and son as lovers, mother and daughter or father and son become sexual rivals. The tensions are enormous and must have a destructive influence on family life. Further, the bonds of feeling between parent and child make it difficult, if not impossible, for a child to know precisely what its desires are for a parent who wants it sexually. The fear of losing parental love and affection, the desire to please, the child's own love – this must be a breeding ground for emotional turmoil. As the woman I interviewed said, 'I just felt very confused.' The parent who imposes this on a child is surely betraying their obligations as a parent for the sake of pleasure as a lover, and this cannot be defended by arguing that the child wanted it too. How can you tell?

Some perversions instigate harm, and there are grounds for thinking they should be illegal. The most dedicated *laissez faire* legislator could not reasonably argue otherwise. Liberalism does not entail letting people do whatever they choose. As John Stuart Mill explained, ' . . . power can rightfully be exercised over any member of a civilised community against his will . . . to prevent harm to others.'

However, this clearly will not do as a comprehensive account of perversions, for many do not cause harm at all. The fetishist mooning over a fur coat or a shoe is not hurting anyone, nor is the homosexual. If the possibility of causing harm is the reason for thinking perversions unacceptable, then many acts commonly thought of as perversions will no longer count as such. It would, of course, be a huge confusion to suppose that because some perversions are rightly classified as criminal, there should be an across the board legislation against all perversions. Heterosexuality, after all, may lead to crime – to assault or rape, for example. No one could reasonably think this a valid reason to outlaw heterosexuality. It is a purely contingent matter that some sexual activity may be a public nuisance or a danger.

The account of perversions as instigating harm offends a common intuition – that perversions are wrong for their own sake, not for the effect they have on others. Certain sexual acts are supposed to be in themselves heinous. A receptionist for an international firm of clothes manufacturers offered her view as to what this amounted to. 'We get a lot of homosexuals in the clothes world, of course, and some real oddities . . . people who are obsessed with fabrics like silk or satin. There's one man who carries a piece of fur around with him wherever he goes. He even puts it beside his plate at lunch time! That must get in the way of his having a normal sex life, mustn't it?'

Kant thought the paradigm of the perverted act was one in which desire is aroused 'not by its real object but by his imagination of this object and so in a way contrary to the purpose of desire since he himself creates the object'. The person who can desire only objects of their imagination – objects that are malleable, with no desires or interests of their own – can clearly not have a relationship with a person. But do acts classified as perversions inevitably have this consequence?

Fetishes can be the comic relief in what is often a tale of tragedy. It is hard, for example, not to be amused by this letter to a woman's magazine. 'My husband has a fetish for "ticklers" – condoms with knobs on. But when he gets an erection and puts one of them on he looks to me like a randy sea-anemone! I try not to laugh but I can't stop myself – then he goes down. What am I to do?' This makes it clear at least that a fetish need not be a substitute for an active sex life. True, if the fetish is itself the object of desire, the person may not be able to move to having a relationship with another person. The fetish may be needed as a stimulus to consummating desire with another person. In other words, a fetish may be complementary to, rather than exclusive of, active sex.

This is true of other perversions. The woman who masturbates to ease the longing she feels for her absent lover is not blocking off the possibility of normal sex. On the contrary, she is creating in her imagination the normal act she yearns for. Of course, some people may masturbate as their only sexual activity – the usual channel for satisfaction is blocked for them. They do seem, as Kant suggested, locked in their own fantasy world. But this is a fact about masturbation, not about perversions generally. Similarly, the homosexual clearly has a relationship with a person; he or she may even be bi-sexual and able to enjoy heterosexual sex. A perversion, then, cannot be defined as that which blocks off the possibility of 'normal' sexual activity.

A common blanket condemnation of perversion is that it is 'unnatural'. An elderly woman I spoke to said, 'It makes me feel funny thinking what some people get up to in sex. I can see why homosexuals are called queer. I call them unnatural.'

There is, among many people, a strong supposition that certain sexual acts are 'natural' and others are not. Further, unnatural acts are perversions. These two words, 'natural' and 'unnatural', tend to wear the trousers in any argument, for they have a moral edge based on a generally unchallenged assumption that the naturalness of something is a gilt-edged guarantee of its goodness. As John Stuart Mill pointed out: 'That any mode of thinking, feeling or acting is according to nature is usually accepted as a strong argument for its goodness.' By contrast, the unnatural is inevitably bad. Following this siren call, people assume that things like breastfeeding are good because they are natural; things like disliking one's child are bad because they are unnatural. Any challenge to these categories usually takes the form of denying that some activity is indeed unnatural. And many homosexuals I spoke to defended their sexual practice by saying things like, 'It's absolutely natural for me to want sex with a man.'

Obviously, people disagree about what things are or are not 'natural' and if this is to help us distinguish perverted from non-perverted acts, we need to know exactly what 'natural' means. A Roman Catholic priest offered me an answer. At a sexual guidance group run by the local church he insisted that homosexuality was unnatural 'because it is abhorrent to God and a pollution'. But many things apparently abhorrent to God are not regarded as unnatural. Abortion, divorce and pre-marital sex are all said by some to be unacceptable in God's sight: none of them, to the ordinary way of thinking, is unnatural. Ask adulterers about their activities, and they are likely to insist that after twenty years of marital sex it is perfectly natural to stray to fresher pastures.

Purveyors of religion have, of course, found it expedient to threaten divine displeasure for certain acts. It encourages people to eschew what is regarded as unacceptable. Prudence surely dictates that if there is a God and He dislikes some act it is better all round to stop doing it. As the priest observed, 'Eternal damnation is a heavy price to pay for a transitory pleasure.' Indeed. But all this presupposes that we know there is a God, and that we know what He dislikes; both of these are open to debate. Even if they are conceded, it is still not obvious that perversions may never be indulged. For example, anyone may find homosexuality, masturbation, even bestiality, accept-able alternatives to screaming frustration. We live in a twilight, troubled world in which it is not always possible to do only what is good. Killing, lying and stealing are all evils, but they are often accepted, if not condoned, as the only alternative. Talking about sexual suppression, the British philosopher H.L.A. Hart says, 'It may create misery of a quite special degree. The suppression of sexual impulses generally is something which affects the development or balance of the individual's emotional life, happiness and personality.' If, in the name of liberty or justice, moral generosity may be extended to activi-ties which are in themselves evil and hurtful, the moral majority owe us an argument as to why the same generosity may not be extended to activities that hurt no one and that may be of great value in achieving happiness. If, that is, the horrors of war may be countenanced as the lesser of two evils, it is hard to see why certain sexual activities, as the alternative to the misery of sexual suppression, may not.

What of the other arm of the priest's claim – that perversions are unnatural because they are pollutions? The view that certain sexual activities are polluting has a long and religiously impeccable history. St Augustine of Hippo condemned as pollutions the night-time emissions which, despite his celibacy, bothered him. And as late as 1925 Ferrer's *Compendium theologiae moralis* was keeping the clock firmly at the hour of Augustinian anxiety, trumpeting about 'the intrinsic malice of pollution'. Such balderdash has been much diluted by common-sense. A modern man's own and splashy exploit is not likely to generate the hysteria it once did – and as for women: as a friend remarked, 'Thank God there is something we can do in sex that does not demand we look our best!'

Still, to describe something as a pollution is to imply that we would all be better off without it. 'Pollution' is this age's dirty word; pollutants are the industrial spilt milk that people are now beginning to cry over. However, many substances classified as pollutants are of enormous benefit in the right place: radiation does good in a cancer ward; it is only in the atmosphere or the sea that it becomes a pollutant. A pollutant, then, is a substance in the wrong place; the process that puts it there is polluting. On the subject of unnatural sex, the idea may be that there is a right and proper place for the male seed to be spilled: the womb of a woman. Anywhere else, as in masturbating into a handkerchief, anal sex or whatever, places the seed in the wrong place. Then it is a pollutant, and the process that put it there is polluting.

As far as it goes, this idea seems unassailable, but it does not go very far. First, it will not do as an explanation of what is wrong with all unnatural sex. Transvestitism is counted unnatural and a perversion, but it does not necessarily involve spillage of male seed; conversely, sadism and masochism are counted as unnatural, though seed may be ejaculated perfectly properly into the womb. And, of course, female masturbation involves no spillage of this morally significant seminal fluid at all, but is nevertheless unnatural sex. On the principle called Occam's Razor, that it is better not to multiply entities beyond necessity, one does not want a batch of different explanations for the term 'unnatural'. It is much simpler just to accept the inadequacy of the idea that unnatural sex is a perversion because it is a pollution.

A more sophisticated attempt at explaining why homosexuality and other perversions are unnatural came from a 35-year-old biologist who uses the word 'nature' as a personal trump card of his own views. 'I wouldn't go so far as to say homosexuals are sick or criminal, but I think they're confused. The natural development of their sexuality has gone astray – become deformed.'

This man seems to be saying that there is a natural path for our instincts. In the case of sex it leads straight to heterosexuality; but it can be forced unnaturally in other directions. Interestingly, homosexuals often concede this point. A lesbian told me, for example, 'I reckon I'd have been all right if it hadn't been for my mother. She wanted a doll to play with really – so she used to dress me up in ribbons and frills and curl my hair. Christ . . . she even made me curtsey to visitors. I hated it. I got to be a real butch little tomboy – and that's how I've stayed. She says it's nearly killed her.'

Certain sexual developments, then, are the result of 'alien' forces – they are unnatural. Something is unnatural if we can point to influences which are alleged to be the cause of brainwashing or distortion.

This cannot be true, for everybody's sexuality is influenced by something: the husband, prying apart scarce-willing thighs in the arid bed of the good woman, might wish indeed that she had not been influenced by Victorian morality – he may regard her lack of desire and pleasure as thoroughly unnatural. No one does or could live in a vacuum removed from all outside influences. Everyone is bombarded with them, all the time, from family, friends, school, books, television, films. One's sexual tastes are every bit as much the product of the environment as tastes in music, clothes or food. There is no way of wriggling off this particular hook by saying that the natural is the product of certain influences only, for the only way of identifying these desirable influences would be through the fact that they led to heterosexuality. But that presupposes what it was supposed to prove: that heterosexuality is the natural aim of human sexuality.

I have heard it suggested that the definition of unnatural is 'rare', or 'atypical', sex. One man I talked to remarked, 'When we're talking about perversions we're talking about a very few people indeed.' This view can only be the product of ignorance.

Masturbation, after all, is counted a perversion, but it is neither rare nor atypical. As a psychiatrist confirmed, 'Most people masturbate at some time in their lives – certainly all children derive erotic pleasure from playing with their genitals.' A teacher at a boys' public school agreed. 'Of course the boys masturbate . . . they have contests!' By contrast, feats of sexual prowess may be rare, but they are not counted as perversions. Don Juan's seduction of an apparently unlimited number of women is a quite uncommon act of sexual enterprise, but it would not be regarded as deviant.

The other side of this dud coin is the notion that natural sex can be defined as what is customary. One woman suggested, 'What's natural is what most people do . . . most of us are normal, aren't we?' This is a staggering pre-supposition, with unpalatable consequences, for what is customary changes from place to place and age to age. In Ancient Greece, for example, the prevailing ethos was homosexual – so much so that in vase-paintings of sex between a man and a woman she looked for all the world like a boy, though without a male's dangling appendage. Whatever the artist's conscious intention, the act looks perilously close to being anal rather than genital.

By the eighteenth century in France, however, homosexuality was considered such an appalling vice (homosexuals were being burned at the stake there until 1760) that Voltaire could not accept that the civilised Greeks could have been guilty of it. In an ingenious reconciliation of two different moralities, he concluded that 'this abuse' was a circuitous way of paying homage to the 'fair sex': men buggered beautiful boys because they looked like beautiful girls. This must be nonsense. Whatever there may be of rum sodomy in the Navy, in Ancient Greece men loved other men quite simply because they were considered the embodiment of all that was spiritually and physically ideal. As an anonymous Arab pithily concurred, 'A woman for duty, an ass for pleasure, a boy for love.' The sexual preferences that twentieth-century Europe regards as impeccable would seem a tiresome business to such men.

England in the nineteenth century waged a pious public war against private morality by locking up Oscar Wilde. But as W.T. Stead wryly commented, 'Should everyone found guilty of Oscar Wilde's crime be imprisoned, there would be a surprising emigration from Eton, Harrow, Rugby and Winchester to the jails of Pentonville and Holloway.'

All this shows just how naive it is to consider unadorned heterosexual genital sex as customary. It has not always been . . . and perhaps never was. Many couples enjoy fellatio or cunnilingus, after all, and these are counted as perversions. An early Kinsey report revealed that 95 per cent of American men had indulged in so-called perverse activities. The American philosopher Robert Solomon is explicit that we cannot declare morality by numbers: 'the fact that thousands of middle-aged, middle-class New Yorkers paid five dollars to watch the swallowing of giant genitalia in *Deep Throat* does not constitute a defence of fellatio or voyeurism'. If what the majority do is counted 'natural' and what the minority do is counted 'unnatural', then, as David Hume wrote, in the moderate tones of the eighteenth century, 'perhaps virtue will be found in the unnatural'.

There is, of course, a very common meaning given to the word 'nature'. What is natural is the world around us – trees, grass, birds, animals, anything that is non-human and non-supernatural. This natural world is supposed to be the repository of all that is wholesome, good and clean. It is pure, untouched by the corrupting influence of man. The power of this message is attested by all the advertisements that exploit nature. 'Nature' as a guarantee of goodness is attached to anything from shampoo to laxatives to padded bras. So how is nature to act as a criterion of straightness in human sex?

Richard Mabey has been described as the 'most influential nature writer of the 1980s'. He told me that if we took as our guide the behaviour of other animals, we would be released to indulge in just about any sexual activity we chose. 'All mammals masturbate, for example. It's a notorious spectacle at zoos – the wanking monkeys. Many lower mammals commit incest, usually between brother and sister, and homosexuality is common as a solution to over-population. Then there are mallard ducks. They are so sexually ruthless, quite beyond the bounds of biological necessity, that it's hard not to describe what they do to females as rape. We've even found that foxes who live near a golf course get obsessed with golf balls! It's always difficult, of course, to know what language to use in describing such behaviour. Perhaps you wouldn't want to categorise it as sexual at all. But if a human were doing it we'd probably – almost certainly, in fact – describe it as a fetish.'

These observations make two things clear. First, what is natural is governed by the demands of the species. Second, this naturalness may be unacceptable to rational beings – to those with the possibility of choice. It may be natural to a mallard duck to be sexually ruthless, but we would not think it acceptable if a man treated a woman in the same way. We would describe it as rape. Nor would we accept as a defence that such behaviour is natural because other creatures do it. Similarly, the female mantis devours her mate during intercourse (as a biologist noted, he provides her with both bed and board); we would not count this as justification for a human female to devour her mate.

Mabey resists applying the concept of perversion to animal behaviour, for if an animal, for example, puts its penis into an anus rather than a vagina, we can explain its action by pointing to the similarity of the two orifices. As far as the perceptions of the animal go they do not differ at all – both are warm and accommodating. There is no need to explain the activity in terms of a perverted instinct. It follows that anal sex could not be regarded as unnatural in the animal world, and therefore by the above argument could not be compared to a human perversion.

We are left to conclude with John Stuart Mill: 'In sober truth, nearly all the things which men are imprisoned or hanged for doing to one another are nature's everyday occurrences.' Nature in this sense is not going to serve as the champion of heterosexuality – though I am told by a biologist that you never find a fetishist beetle!

Linked to the view that sex should be 'natural' is the view that there is in all of us a shining nugget of purity, the 'natural' person, which has been tarnished out of all recognition by social needs and pressures. If we were all able to act according to instinct – as other animals do – we would not perform the thoroughly undesirable acts that humans now do. Distasteful habits are the result of socialising. This view is very appealing – but it will not carry the weight required of it. No doubt social pressures do produce undesirable traits in people, sexual as well as non-sexual – but 'civilising' people can also bring out the best in them. It is just not true that the only good actions are those that spring from the guts. The Nazis surely proved it with their demonic cry to 'think with the blood'.

We get a more interesting perspective by turning this view around: the natural is right and the right is whatever is according to reason. This view was invented by the Stoics; morality is a matter of encouraging reason to suppress unacceptable, anarchic desires. The seventeenth-century philosopher Thomas Hobbes made reason into a law-giver. 'We ought to judge those actions only wrong which are repugnant to right reason. But that which is done wrong, we say it is done against some law. Therefore true reason is a certain law: which . . . is termed natural.' So, if we all think straight we will all be straight.

In any moral climate it may be rational to act in certain ways. Until 1862 the homosexual in England could be sentenced to death: it would be rational in those circumstances to be circumspect. As Epicurus insisted, 'Fear is the rational man's response to the external world.' Even today, in a more liberal climate, overt displays of homosexuality may be unwise. A homosexual friend of mine was attacked on the Thames Embankment and tossed into the river by a group of self-styled 'queer bashers'. He had been strolling along holding his lover's hand.

It may also be rational to accept that one way of life is preferable to another. While in conversation with me, Jilly Cooper admitted she would not like it if one of her children turned out to be homosexual. 'I think your chances of happiness are less if you're gay than if you're not. One of the great sadnesses is if you can't have children.' If one agrees with her that certain things are necessary for the good life, then it is perfectly rational to regret being someone who cannot enjoy those things. So it may, in some hostile climate, or if you wish to have children, be rational to wish to be heterosexual. But this is within an already established moral code; if one starts cold, as it were, with no moral presumptions, how is reason supposed to take us to the conclusion that a perversion like homosexuality is wrong?

One briar-strewn path to this conclusion might be that society needs its members to reproduce, and that it is therefore reasonable to require that everyone engage only in those activities that may produce children. There have, of course, been societies with a need for population increase. Kate Millett observed of warrior societies that population growth is closely linked 'with the ambitions of a military state; more children must be born to die for the country'. Minority groups — especially those that are at risk from others — will also wish to increase their population so that they are not swamped by their enemies. And some people have recently expressed concern at the diminishing birth-rate in the Western world on the grounds that a population of old people is neither appealing nor stable. If, then, it is rational for people to engage only in reproductive acts, homosexuality is contrary to reason and the conclusion drops easily into the lap: homosexuality is wrong and unnatural. Other conclusions are more startling. Sex with one known to be infertile would be as wrong as masturbation or bestiality. But sado-masochism would not be counted a perversion so long as it was part of an act intended to reproduce.

Similarly, the Roman Catholic Church would have to embrace the conclusion that celibacy is contrary to reason and unnatural in precisely the same way as homosexuality. For although priests can reproduce, and some do (a Spanish friend told me, 'We call the priest "Father" except when he is; then we call him "Uncle"'), celibacy by definition excludes procreation. Further, the Ancient Greeks proved that their need for children could be easily met within the homosexual ethos, which would mean that the acceptance by homosexuals of a bisexual life would be morally preferable to the abstention practised by the Church. Reason can take one to some unexpected conclusions.

Considering the world's great problem of over-population, the rational preference might be for homosexuality, with its built-in guarantee of low productivity; heterosexuality might come to look like a self-indulgent irrationality — like getting very drunk when one knows the hangover will be a bone-crusher. And if it were irrational, it would count as perverted. It is unlikely, however, that anyone would wish to approve this conclusion — for it is unacceptable that we should draw conclusions about sexual activity without having as a premise the fundamental importance of sex to the individual, not just to society: it matters very much that people should be able to express their sexuality freely. The rational response to the population explosion is contraception – not preventing hetero-sexuality, but limiting its output. In the best of all worlds, people would be free to give expression to the passions they have, not forced to try and make them into something else. And this must be true for the so-called 'pervert' as much as for the 'straight'. Reason will condemn perversions only if the dice are loaded – if the individual's emotional needs are excluded from the equation.

I suspect, however, that rational sex is really supposed to be minimal sex – the less the better. Augustine of Hippo, who gave up sex in his 30s to become a saint, plotted this mean little path. He found sex of any kind shameful; what shamed him was that lust is independent of the will. However virtuous a man may wish to be, given the right stimulus Old Adam defiantly stirs. A penis is not subject to man's will, as are his other members, but virtue demands that the body is controlled by reason's factotum, the will. Hence sex is irrational and incompatible with the perfectly holy life.

Those of us who enjoy our sex lives will wince at all this. But it will also be unpalatable to anyone trying to drive a wedge between straight sex and perverted sex with the sledge-hammer of reason. If the only acts that are acceptable are those that are rational, and sex is irrational, then *all* sex is unacceptable. This has the charm of comprehensiveness . . . but not much else.

And so to nature's big gun, the human reproductive system. Male and female sex organs seem unlikely pegs on which to hang a whole morality, but it has been tried. Let us see if they can bear the weight.

Elizabeth Anscombe, in her article 'Contraception and Chastity', has argued that sex is an essentially generative act. Normal sex is an expression of the intention to perform such an act, and it is this intention that makes the act moral. Where it is absent – where sex is, by its nature, divorced from reproduction – the act is deviant and therefore immoral. This makes homosexuality perverted, since no one could knowingly intend a generative act with someone of the same sex. Similarly, masturbation, bestiality, oral sex and sex with one who is sexually immature would all be perversions. However, it would also follow that contracepted sex, or sex with one known to be infertile, or with one too old to bear children, would also be perverted. They would be as easily condemned as, say, necrophilia. This runs counter to most people's intuitions. Hardly anyone will accept that loving heterosexual sex with, for example, a woman who has had a hysterectomy is perverted.

Norman St John-Stevas argues from the premise that human sex has a God-given purpose: 'The Catholic natural law tradition accepts as self-evident that the primary purpose of sexual intercourse is procreation.' He acknowledges what he could hardly deny – that a great deal of sex is not as a matter of fact aimed at reproduction. People use sex to get to sleep, get even, get ahead, get pleasure – but he thinks this is wrong. And it is wrong because, 'Man is free only to act within the pattern imposed by nature.' So any activity which does not have procreation as its aim is a thwarting of God's purpose; it is unnatural and a perversion.

St John-Stevas is cosily tucked up in the warmth of an old Western tradition: St Thomas Aquinas exploited St Augustine's view that God had designed sex for procreation and proved what every full-blooded heterosexual male had always known: homosexuality is unnatural, a deviation from the natural law laid down by God. But is it self-evident – impossible to deny – that God designed the intricate mechanism of human sexuality for one and only one purpose? Well . . . no. The apertures and protuberances of the human body seem as well suited to anal, oral or manual sex as to genital sex. It does not immediately follow that because one can do one thing, it is the only thing to do. The design of the human body suggests all sorts of possibilities, depending on how ingenious one is. But let us race by the Church's rules and accept that there is a God, that He designed all that is, that some things have a quite specific purpose imposed by God and that we know what these purposes are. Let us now see how far the argument will run. I will begin with a tale.

I have a brass lamp in my room; it was designed by a craftsman to cast light. When I bought it I wanted something attractive that would light a particular corner of my room, and that is what I originally used the lamp for. Thus the craftsman's purpose and mine happily coincided. One hot summer's day, however, with all the windows open, a through draught kept slamming my door shut. So I propped it open with the lamp . . . which still does duty as a door-stop. My purpose in using the lamp is now quite different from the craftsman's; but I had a need for it to satisfy and without a qualm I set it to do so.

Apply this to sexuality: God designed my sexual organs for the purpose of bearing children. Let us say that for some years I dutifully did just that – God's and my purpose coincided. But then I grew tired of disturbed nights, dirty nappies and school runs: I went on the pill. Now any sexual activity I indulge in is for the sheer fun of it, for pleasure. My purpose and God's no longer coincide. Similarly with homosexuals. God, we may say, designed their sexual organs to impregnate or to be impregnated; but they have a greater need to satisfy – they make love to members of their own sex. Their purpose in sex is not God's; they aim simply to feel pleasure. To go back to my lamp, it is rather as though the homosexual had seen its possibilities and, indifferent to the craftsman's purpose, bought it as a door-stop. The point is that human purposes may diverge from divine purposes, and that the God-given physical arrangements accommodate them.

What is wrong with this? Nothing – unless one assumes that it is immoral to make use of the coincidental side-benefits of God-given designs. But why believe that? God, perhaps, designed our digestive systems for the purpose of providing the body with nutrients. Nevertheless, we eat chocolate or drink fine tea, which have no nutritional value but are immensely pleasurable. As I make my way through a box of Black Magic chocolates, I do not imagine I am thwarting God's purpose and am guilty of unnatural and perverse behaviour. Why should sex be different?

Almost as delicious as these chocolates, by the way, is the reflection that anyone who takes this line is perilously close to damning the Catholic clergy as perverts. For if one buys a lamp and never switches it on one thwarts the craftsman's purpose every bit as much as if one uses it as a door-stop. To freeze one's sexuality in the pious mould of celibacy surely diverges from

God's purpose just as much as, say, homosexuality. On its own argument, celibacy is as unnatural as anal sex. St John-Stevas's theory, like Anscombe's, places contracepted sex and sex with those known to be infertile on a moral par with any so-called perversion – from incest to bestiality, coprophilia, necrophilia. Surely any theory that carries this consequence is a theory to be rejected?

But even if, despite this, one were dedicated to keeping in line with the Almighty's purposes, how is one supposed to know what they are? The clergy are notoriously unreliable. Even the Pope is fallible: in 1832 Pope Gregory XVI condemned 'freedom of conscience' as a 'delirium and pestilential error' – a degree of humbug one would not expect from the holder of the Keys. And in 1984 the present Pope insisted that a man who lusts after his own wife commits adultery in his heart – apparently failing to appreciate that by definition one cannot commit adultery with one's spouse, in one's heart or anywhere else. So who do we turn to? St John-Stevas admits that perceiving God's purpose is a 'practical difficulty' for his regime. Surely it is more than this; it casts serious doubt on the whole enterprise. For why follow signposts to virtue that may or may not be pointing the right way? Apart from the *fiat* of the Church, there seems no reason to discount other coherent views about the purpose of sex. Perhaps God is benevolent and gave us sex as a blessing so that we might feel great pleasure, enhance a union with another human being . . . or produce a child. Why assume that God is a bigot?

Where does all this leave us in the quest to identify the immorality of certain sexual acts? Nowhere much, so far as I can see. The idea was to find out why those activities classified as perversions by Freud should be regarded as unacceptable – why those who practised them should be condemned as morally delinquent. Nothing has so far succeeded. Each account of the baseness of perverted activity fails to capture all and only perversions in its net. Either acts that are commonly thought of as perverted are missed out, or acts that no one could wish to classify as deviant are included. What seems to emerge is that the reasons people offer for thinking perversions at least distasteful are either inadequate to cover all the acts they deplore or can provide good reasons for deploring acts they think of as morally impeccable.

There is a further confusion to consider – the confusion between our aesthetic views and our moral values. It is very easy to assume that these are identical, but they are not. Being revolted by something does not guarantee that it is immoral. For example, coprophilia – sexual obsession with excrement – is a nasty perversion likely to revolt anyone, but however much one's aesthetic, let alone hygienic, sense is outraged, the question of whether the act is morally unacceptable is still open. What is ugly is not necessarily the same as what is bad.

There is, of course, ample evidence that certain sexual activities arouse a deep feeling of disgust. These can be so great that those who are tolerant of such activities may reap an unpleasant harvest of hatred. Rabbi Julia Neuberger told me that after she had publicly displayed her rather liberal attitude to homosexuality she was almost drowned in a torrent of the vilest abuse. Anna Raeburn had a similar experience when in a radio phone-in programme she counselled a seriously disturbed adolescent that his masturbating was not grounds for painful guilt. For ages thereafter the lines buzzed with the shrill, hysterical voice of the Dark Ages revisited.

Many of the people I spoke to about perversions expressed similar feelings. They were 'repelled', 'turned off', 'revolted' by certain acts, the acts being 'sordid', 'nasty', 'shameful', 'dirty'. Clearly the whole subject arouses deep emotions. The problem seems to be finding good reasons for the resulting moral qualms. In their absence there is nothing left us but to agree with Michael Slote that the word 'perversion', as it is commonly used, is just a way of saying 'Ugh'.

_ 11 _

ROMANTIC LOVE

The longing for love, more than any other emotion, drives us all. It is love we ache to induce in others and love we yearn to feel. Even a man as dedicated to the intellect as Bertrand Russell placed love alongside his search for knowledge as one of the overwhelming passions that governed his life. Few of us unremittingly aspire to truth as he did, but all of us aspire to love.

In searching for love we are searching for a great source of happiness. We see around us the joy that love can bring, and we also see that anyone who misses love – who is neither loved nor loving – suffers a grave misfortune, one that may make their life grey with despair. For those who do find love, the emotion comes in different forms. There is the love of parents, love of children, love of friends, love of God or love of humanity at large. But the love that is central to our culture is romantic love. It is the main theme of myth, drama, literature, music, exemplified by Romeo and Juliet, who fell in love at first sight and were swept away by passions they were unable to control. Other pairs of lovers have been tossed in the same torrent: Tristan and Isolde, Antony and Cleopatra, Heathcliffe and Cathy, Mr Rochester and Jane Eyre, besides countless heroes and heroines of the slop literature that provides today's debased form of romance.

In however debased a form romance is commonly peddled – it sells. And it sells because this particular kind of tragi-comedy is irrefutable proof that not just the rich and beautiful may have an irresistible impact on others. In real life, unremarkable men and women find that through Cupid's good offices they become the purveyors of magic. For a brief span they induce madness, transforming sense and sanity into lunacy and obsession. Hardly anyone has not at some time or other been the cause of the little mischievous god loosing his arrow to bewitch, bother and bewilder another.

The thrill, the stimulation and the sense of power are one side of this story. Romantic love is a mixed passion of pleasure and pain. Most of us will have looked back on some experience of being in love and felt, 'I must have been crazy . . . out of my mind . . . mad.' But then, love is not supposed to be sane and sensible. You certainly do not walk clear-eyed into love. Your control is dissolved, and with minimum assistance from gravity you fall . . . in love, as into a pit.

This compulsion is generally regarded as the only unequivocally acceptable motive for marriage – so much so that the nation was faintly outraged when Prince Charles, whose choice of wife could not be determined solely by love, agreed on his engagement that he was in love, 'Whatever that's supposed to mean.' He was perilously close to breaking the rule that even royal couples must be 'head over heels'.

While it is anathema to suppose that a marriage may not be grounded in irresistible passion, it can hardly be denied that even such a good start is no guarantee of success. The divorce rate and the air of disillusion that hangs around so many marriages testify to failure. It may be as well to begin by seeing the loved one through a glamorous mist, but something more is needed to sustain a lifetime together. The effects of a *coup de foudre* are by definition short-lived, and they are produced quite independently of any knowledge of the person or any real esteem. Marriage demands an altogether more realistic love, unmixed with illusion.

Such observations lend credence to Mrs Malaprop's principle that since both love and aversion wear off in marriage it is better to start with aversion. Fortunately, such contortions of sentiment are unnecessary; all that is needed is to pull one's emotions into line with one's reason.

There is a widespread conviction that reason and emotion are two separate, self-contained elements that cannot occupy the same space. Where there is emotion there is no foothold for reason; where there is reason emotion is expunged, leaving

only cool calculation. To say that a love is rational is nearly to
say it is not love at all.

It seems to be only love that generates this disinclination to
bring reason to bear. Other emotions are often subjected to
rational scrutiny. People say things like, 'It's irrational to hope',
'It makes no sense to be jealous', or 'It's silly to be frightened'.
They are saying that, given the situation as they see it, it is
sensible to hold certain beliefs, and that if you hold those
beliefs it is not rational to feel certain emotions. A woman was
reported recently still to be keeping vigil for her son, believed
lost in an air battle in 1940. The wreckage of his plane was
washed up on the coast but his body was never found. However
much she may need to hope – however much we may warm to
her for loving so much – it is in the circumstances sadly
irrational to do so.

Not all emotions are irrational, of course. It is perfectly
rational to feel fear if you have good grounds for believing the
object of your fear is dangerous – if, for example, a spider
known to be poisonous is heading in your direction with
nothing to stop it. So long as the spider has some objective
quality – something independent of your apprehension of it
that makes it dangerous – then your fear is rational.

Another way of saying that an emotion is rational is to say
that it is well-grounded. Fear is well-grounded when it springs
from the correct perception of something as dangerous, grati-
tude when it is elicited by the recognition of a kindness being
done. It is obviously preferable that emotions should always
have such firm foundations. No one would want to be frightened of what is harmless, or grateful for an injury. But can we
talk of love as being well-grounded?

For fear to be well-grounded the object of fear must be
dangerous. Since 'dangerous' simply means 'whatever justifiably elicits the response of being afraid', it seems that for love to
be well-grounded the object of love will need to be lovable.
That is, he or she will need to be someone who justifiably
elicits the response of loving.

It is precisely this notion that is the core of the idyllic
situations celebrated in romantic myths and stories: she loves
him madly and thinks he is eminently lovable. This unshakeable belief about his lovability essentially involves the belief

that he is the repository of all sorts of valuable qualities – qualities that are pointed to when the love is challenged. 'I love him,' she may say, 'because he is kind and thoughtful.' The qualities identified will probably vary from person to person. Someone else may value a sense of humour or sexual prowess. Still, if love has even the smallest pretensions to being well-grounded, whatever is identified as lovable will have to be a characteristic that shows there is good reason to love the beloved. Inevitably, not every possible aspect of the human personality will qualify. We could make no sense of Romeo insisting, 'I love her because she's *such* a bore.' Or Charles Dickens's Nancy explaining that Sykes was lovable 'because he's a callous brute'. Tediousness and brutishness do not justifiably elicit love.

The problem with this is that it seems incompatible with a familiar experience, for it is part of love's divine madness that you may love someone who at the same time you can see to be silly or loathsome. Emotions may drive you to love a person whom, had you been free to choose, you would have avoided like the plague. So to find yourself in the situation where you can say, 'I love him/her but I don't think he's/she's at all lovable' seems to be perfectly possible. The analogy with fear is not fruitless, though, because it is also familiar to hear, 'I'm terrified of spiders – but I don't think they're dangerous.' As my husband scoops a hairy little arachnid out of the bath while I stand petrified with fear, I do not think the creature is danger-ous, exactly. What seems to happen in such situations is that there is some kind of breakdown in rational connections; somewhere a wire or two has got crossed. How might this happen in love?

Before there is love there is, of course, the turn-on. You are crazy about him or her, but this involves no beliefs at all about their valuable qualities. Perhaps you do not know what they are. Apart from the fact that they had the good taste to seek you out, you may know nothing at all about them. Cupid simply fired his dart and struck you squarely in the breast. Knowledge, if it comes at all, will come later. And, of course, in the thrill of it all it is possible to get the person's qualities wrong. In *Middlemarch* George Eliot's Dorothea falls in love with Casaubon, whom she sees as a man of creative genius and immaculate integrity. In fact, he is none of these things; he is a sad, cold mediocrity. Dorothea has got it wrong.

For Dorothea, there was no breakdown of reason between emotions and beliefs – they were perfectly in tune; if only her beliefs about her loved one were true her emotions, her love, would have been happily well-grounded. Unfortunately, the beliefs were false, and her irrationality is located here: she was given plenty of evidence of Casaubon's character and perversely failed to pick up the clues.

This kind of self-deception is very familiar. All the evidence is there, screaming to be heard, and reason battles, as it should, to pull beliefs into line with it. But the beliefs put up too strong a resistance. No doubt when there is such resistance it is emotionally based; the psyche, as it were, tries to align the beliefs, not with the evidence but with the emotions. Cupid's dart has done its work; you feel love, and you very much want your love to be worth it. This is a very different kind of breakdown from one in which you manage to see what the monster is truly like, yet cannot rid yourself of the feelings.

The price of Dorothea's kind of mistake is the impossibility of leading a happy life together. The mists of illusion are bound to lift, leaving only disappointed expectations. But other mistakes can be even more costly. If emotions and beliefs are out of step it can be devastating for the person's sense of emotional integrity. A woman I spoke to found this in her relationship with her first husband. 'I can't believe that I loved someone who treated me so badly. It wasn't just that he was unfaithful. He was brutal too. I had to have stitches in my face after one particular battering. But what was worse was that I loathed myself, not him. I felt sure I was sick – incapable of a healthy relationship with a man. It took me longer to get over that than it did to get over him.'

The breakdown in the rational process is fully exposed here: emotions and beliefs can be seen tugging in opposite directions. The wife feels for her husband, but she can see for herself that her loving is not justly elicited by such a man. In such a situation the psyche is divided against itself, and this generates an intolerable tension. Clearly, if love is to be a joy and not a blight, emotions and reason must be in harmony. This is most likely when love has a solid foundation, and the best foundation of all is a fixed and settled regard for the beloved, based in qualities he or she actually has.

Words like 'solid' and 'settled' are often greeted with scorn when they are applied to love. Many people glory in the very irrationality of passion and find the idea of a well-grounded love chilly and calculating. For them, love is not some kind of cognitive act. To the contrary, it is the essence of love that you are overwhelmed by feelings. It matters not one whit what the person is like; when love strikes, your heart is lost. As the crooner wails, 'I took one look at you. That's all I meant to do. And then my heart stood still.' It is no part of reasoning about love to cut out of human experience such delicious madness. The most rational thinker can be aware that when Cupid lets loose an arrow in your direction he does not expect you to settle down to a cool assessment of the good and bad qualities of your beloved.

But for my part, even as I relish the thrill of it all, I do not want my husband to love me despite himself. As he succumbs to the *coup de foudre* I want him to have some realistic view that I am lovable – not in the same breath, as it were, but eventually. Cupid's dart appears out of the blue, which is why we call it a *coup de foudre* – a thunderbolt; it does not have a lot to do with the real person. The mixing of love potions to win an unfeeling heart may be the stuff of romances, but even if it works, the caster of the spell must be aware that the love was caused by the potion, not by the person. It is the conviction that the love is about us, very personally, that we cherish. We want the loved one to believe in us. This, however dreary it may seem to the wild Byronic romantic, can be based only on knowledge of our personal qualities.

There has been a long romantic tradition of insisting that the love borne for a person is somehow independent of what the person is like. This tradition was exemplified in the medieval story of Patient Griselda, a tiresome goody-goody who loved the Marquis of Saluzzo. He wanted to be sure that she loved him for himself, not for his delightful personality, so he subjected her to appalling trials until finally, convinced by her patience and endurance, he married her and lived happily ever after – which is more than he deserved. Chaucer's prose just about managed to redeem the unremitting mush of this story. Nevertheless, it is mush. Yet it is mimicked in the game of 'Would you love me if . . . ' that lovers are so often tempted to play. Even great lovers do it: Mr Rochester, for example, assured Jane Eyre that he would love her even if she were mad.

A man of my acquaintance was more realistic. When his wife anxiously begged him to promise he would love her if she were different, he warily asked, 'How different?' She was mightily affronted. Yet why should anyone think it a mark of the beloved's esteem that he would love you if you were not the person you were? The game may, of course, have some point if you are anxious to find out whether you are loved for qualities you find valuable or qualities that will endure. If a man is rich he may justly want to be reassured that his beloved would love him if he were poor: 'If I were a carpenter, would you still love me?' If she is beautiful she may want to be certain that it is not her looks he is in love with – they fade, after all. Dorothy Osborne must have felt very secure in Sir William Temple's love when, at the end of the Civil War, he married her, even though the beauty which had first attracted him had been ravaged by smallpox.

People want to be loved for what they really are; they do not want a love that is based on too little. But people really are their qualities. If a woman has intelligence she really is intelligent. If a man has tolerance he really is tolerant. It makes no sense, then, to compile a list of one's qualities and complain, 'You only love me for my . . . ' intelligence, humour, or whatever, as though the love were thereby proved to be inadequate, not love for the 'real' you at all. The real person is not something mysterious lurking behind these qualities. It is an absurd game to try to prove you are loved for yourself by showing that you would have been loved if you had not been yourself.

Nor does it make sense to try to prove your love by insisting you would go on loving the beloved even if their character changed. We may justly ask that love survive changes in circumstances: if it is genuine, losing money should not destroy it. But we love people for the qualities they have that delight us. If those qualities disappear, leaving ones that are displeasing, love is very likely to fade. My father suffered a series of strokes that left him bed-ridden for several years before he died. From being a vigorous, good-humoured man he became an embittered despot. No one blamed him for being angry and bitter; perhaps we went on loving retrospectively the man he had been. But the unceasing bad-temper, the demands and the utter selfishness, made it impossible to love the man he had become.

Perhaps this seems rather cold. Certainly it is cold to think something like, 'When this person loses the things I value I'll cut myself off from them.' It is always cold to try and manipulate your affections. But anyone who loves is sensitive to what the loved one is like – and thus sensitive to changes. This does not mean they coldly calculate the grounds on which the love will survive. And it may also be true that a bit of change can be a shot in the arm to a wilting love. If a husband changes from being an inconsiderate oaf to showing a little tenderness – as all the songs advise – his wife may love him more.

All you may reasonably ask, then, is that your love comes with a guarantee against circumstantial change, not against personality change. So as the one you love gazes into your eyes and tells you they love you, squash the thought that if you were different they may not love you at all. Probably they would not, but this does not mean they do not love you now.

None of this means we have to abandon the idea that love is blind. Cupid, after all, is a little blindfolded god who fires off his darts more or less indiscriminately. It is what happens next that is important to reason's peace. I fell in love with my husband – head-over-heels and quite helplessly. I remember our hostess saying, 'I could see the laser beams, darling – laser beams everywhere.' Then, as I got to know him, I found there were all sorts of delightful and interesting things in him to which I could respond. Cupid's dart, as Shakespeare put it, 'knit our souls' and then, happily, my reason was able to follow and I could see that it was a happy chance that I had lost my heart to this man.

A common response to this is that the idea of the intellect checking out the person you love is very unappealing – it may be appropriate to check out those you work with, but rationally to assess a lover is to allow a crude intrusion of reason into what is essentially irrational. This seems to be a confusion, generated by running together what it is to be a turn-on, and what it is to be a valued loved one, which is something quite different. It is, of course, part of the romantic myth to fuse the two and make them inseparable: the person whose every touch is like a thousand-volt shock is the person most suitable for you to love. So far so good. There is no reason why you should not be both and no reason why you should not want both. The trouble is that the myth insists the irrational response of love at first sight and the rational response of loving esteem both happen at the same moment, that seeing someone as a turn-on and seeing someone as eminently valuable are somehow causally and inextricably fused. This is why the intellect cannot begin to do any appraising; if it is 'true' love it is all supposed to happen in that first look. This must be false. Indeed, it is a contradiction. The bolt from the blue just hits you – and that is it. The equivalent of a mortal blow cannot constitute a rational process of valuing and esteeming. You may look at that firm chin and sigh, 'He's wonderful' – and you may be wrong: he is a louse. But because falling in love is irrational, it does not follow that you may not become known and valued. The blindness of Cupid need not be permanent.

The whole process of falling in love does begin to seem like luck. If your beloved had met someone else, they might have fallen, just as irrationally, in love with them. That is certainly not an appealing thought: it is part of the charm of being in love that we are filled with the unshakeable conviction that no one else will do.

Does it follow also that if we love someone for their qualities, we will love anyone with the same qualities? To make the objections as strong as possible, suppose that you know J is not your beloved wife/husband, although they look the same, talk the same and move the same. J even has all your wife's/ husband's memories (a mad scientist fitted a memory bank into J's brain). So you could never tell, however closely you observed the substitute, that J was not your wife/husband. Would J do just as well for you? The most usual response to this is: 'No.' For when you are in love with a person, even a perfect replica of that person will not be satisfactory; you want your beloved.

Perhaps this seems no more than sentimentality. After all,

why should anyone care which of two indistinguishable people they love? The point is, we *are* sentimental. For instance, you will value the vase given to you on a special occasion and would not swap it even for an identical one. Similarly, if you are presented with two physically identical people with all the same qualities you may still love *this* person – not *that* one. It is the person you have shared things with you want, the person whose history is part of yours – even as short a history as your having a moment ago fallen for them. If the vase were given to you in a special ceremony you would not change it, even a moment later. Similarly, you are focused on a particular person, and no one else will do.

Of course, if Cupid's arrow is going to strike at all it is going to do so with anyone who is indistinguishable from the beloved. Unless you believe in magic, you must believe that whatever caused you to fall for your beloved in the first place was something about them. So, naturally, if someone has the same attribute they will have the same effect. This is what happens when people fall for a certain kind of person over and over again, or for someone who resembles a lost love. The reason for the fall is never, of course, explicable at a conscious level – it just seems to happen. Nevertheless, the person who caused the arrow to fly matters very much. Your love may indeed have fallen for your identical twin if you had not come along first. But if someone falls for you and then is given the choice, they are very unlikely to find your twin a satisfactory replacement. For your twin is not you.

With all this scope for reason, why is it that most people's love lives are a series of peaks and troughs as nerve-racking as a ride on the Big Dipper? Why do people go on falling for those who are quite unsuitable for them?

One reason is that we easily confuse 'true' love with infatuation. It may be simple to dismiss the schoolgirl's feelings for a teacher as a 'crush', or the married man's feelings for a nymphet as 'infatuation'. But when it comes to our own affairs such clear vision is inclined to desert us. Of course we all want the real thing rather than its false counterpart, infatuation – rather, even, than a sexual friendship which, as any romantic will tell you, is dull stuff when compared to the manic passion of romance. But can we ever distinguish love from infatuation? After all, one bewitching spell feels very much like another.

One common suggestion is that infatuation is short-lived, whereas love lasts. As everyone knows, the effects of Cupid's arrow are supposed to be short-lived. One friend recalled, 'I saw him on the back of a horse looking fantastic in hunt gear and I fell in love with him like a ton of bricks. Next minute he was off his horse and waddling towards me on bandy legs – and I smartly fell out again!' This is rather more rapid a transition than usual. But the relative brevity of the experience is not something to moan about: the whole psychedelic business would be exhausting if you had to put up with it for ever. I love the business of stars in my eyes and pavements moving beneath my feet. But only for a while. Then I want firm ground again – the firm ground of genuine love.

What makes this feeling last – unlike the rapture of a bolt from the blue – is that if there really are qualities in your beloved that you value, then your emotion will latch on to them. Love cannot be entirely transient since, on the whole, qualities do not change very rapidly. The sorts of qualities that your emotions hook into – kindness, humour, honesty – are not likely to fade, so they give a permanence to your feelings. By contrast, infatuation is not grounded in the person's qualities, and so it may disperse as rapidly as Cupid himself. On the other hand, I remember having a crush on my tennis teacher which lasted through several terms until I found out that his first name was 'Eric'. The *coup de foudre* cannot be described as necessarily having only a short-term effect; it is rather that – unlike infatuation – love has a certain long-termness built into it. This is why we make declarations like, 'I'll always love you,' or, 'My love will never die.' This makes perfect sense when your love is well-grounded, just as it makes sense to say, 'I'll always be afraid of man-eating sharks.' But although a particularly cunning arrow may get lodged in your breast and rankle there for some time it makes no sense to say, on the strength of that arrow, 'I'll always feel this way.' You very likely will not.

Any love we feel is bound to link with our wants. And those wants will reflect the quintessentially give-and-take nature of love. You love someone, and so you want to take an interest in them, to cherish and benefit them. You will also want them to

be interested in you, to cherish and care for you. Because
people are so very different, it will be impossible to spell out
precisely what wants any lover is going to have. But if you love
someone you must at least want to be with them. Perhaps even
more than this, wanting to be near the loved one actually
constitutes love. 'I love her but don't want to be with her' needs
explanation.

Part of the difficulty in disentangling love from infatuation is
that someone who is infatuated may want to be with the keeper
of their heart every bit as much as someone who is in love. So
wanting and the strength of it will not in itself distinguish the
two. There are, however, two different kinds of wanting which
may illuminate the difference between love and infatuation. In
the first kind an object is desired because it is seen as valuable,
worthwhile. It is not wanted as a means to an end – to power,
prestige or status; it is wanted simply because it is assessed as
intrinsically valuable. In the second kind the person simply
desires the object. The desire may be quite inexplicable in
terms of any value the object may have. The person who wants
it may not have thought about its value – or may even believe it
has no intrinsic value at all, that its only worth lies in its being
able to satisfy the desire.

Love will surely be made up of the first kind of wanting.
Desire for the beloved – wanting to be with them – will be
grounded in a conviction of their value as a person. However
wild, crazy, out of control your feelings may be, you can see
that it is rational to want to be with the one you love because of
all the good things they are. Perhaps they are kind, witty or
thoughtful. But whatever it is you value, it must consist of
qualities that make good sense of your wanting to be with that
person. In infatuation the wanting is of the second kind. The
person in the grip of desire need not see the cause of it as
having any value at all. They may see the one desired as trivial,
vain, silly, and still desire that person, against their better
judgment.

In theory, then, the distinction between love and infatuation
is that love recognises qualities in the beloved and sees those
qualities as valuable. Infatuation does not: it is utterly irrational
and, by definition, not well-grounded. In practice, of course,
the two may get hopelessly tangled. Infatuation can sometimes

turn to love, after all. But if you are in thrall yet cannot even specify what it is about someone that makes you want to be with them, you are probably the victim of infatuation. And if you can see only qualities that appal you – or bore you – and still want to be with them, then it is certainly infatuation.

It is precisely this feeling that Proust's unfortunate hero Swann has for the prostitute Odette. He knows she is incapable of loving, yet he cannot wrest himself away from her. Proust presents it as a terrible disease – a long-term infatuation that is Swann's profound misfortune. Infatuation, then, is where Cupid's arrow strikes and there is no other sustaining force whatsoever. If after the bolt there is a growing mutual esteem to keep the feeling going, you may be lucky enough to have found love.

None of this means that we should dismiss as infatuation a person's feelings for one who seems not to be worthwhile. The philosopher Jeremy Bentham once made a table in which each human desire is set out in three columns, according to whether it was to be blamed, praised or described neutrally. Thus in one column there is 'public spirit' and opposite it, in the blame column, there is 'spite'. The advantage of becoming familiar with Bentham's list is that it accustoms one to the idea that anything that will be disparaged by some people is likely to be praised by others. This is particularly so when we are observing other people's love affairs.

People often say things like, 'I suppose he loves her, but heaven knows why.' But it is surely a piece of great good fortune that what may to some people seem like a fault seems to others like a valuable attribute. You may, for instance, think one man a loudmouth; his lover may see him as wonderfully exuberant. When harsh Roman soldiers looked at Cleopatra, all they saw was a 'strumpet'. But for Antony, who loved her, 'every passion fully strives to make itself in thee fair and admired'. Love has its own special alchemy. And, luckily for all of us, tastes vary as to what qualities are desirable.

Just as it is easy to confuse love with infatuation, so it is easy to confuse love with need. The two can in theory be distinguished by the reflection that being loved is explicable only in terms of the beloved's worth. By contrast, being needed requires no good qualities at all. 'I need him' is easy to understand, even of one who is in all ways disagreeable. It was perhaps Baudelaire's fascination for decadence and evil that tied him in need to a mistress whom he saw as morally equivalent to a serpent. Need is perverse in a way that love is not.

In practice, however, it may be impossible to distinguish the two. You want to be with the one you need as much as – perhaps more than – the one you love. This desire, then, and the strength of it is no guide to what you are experiencing. And 'I need you' has a very similar resonance to 'I love you': it emphasises the irreplaceability of 'you'. Introspection about whether or not you can do without someone is not the way to discover whether it is love you have found. More often than not there may be no need to sort out this confusion, since need and love typically focus on the same person. But sometimes people find themselves locked into a miserable situation from which they cannot escape, and it is then that you hear the fatalistic, 'I suppose I must love him/her; I can't do without him/her.' It may help to see that the strength of that particular type of relationship is that it satisfies a need – one it might be as well to be rid of.

A guide in such a situation is that in love – unlike in need – there must be things that make you rejoice. If you can see nothing to celebrate in your partner's behaviour and character, then it is hard to believe you love them. However much you may want that person, however much you cannot do without them, the tie is surely one of need.

'I've always thought,' one woman said to me, 'that the real problem with love is that we all have an infinite capacity to idealise people. You really can be blind to their faults. So how on earth is love going to get grounded in qualities they really have?'

Love's blindness is celebrated in Cupid's blindfold, and in endless songs about smoke getting in your eyes. Shakespeare took the whole idea to its mad conclusion when Titania fell for the ass-headed Bottom. This inability to evaluate the beloved is of course a feature of the initial stages of love. It is part of the charm of falling for someone that you see them as special – the pick of the bunch. But does this want of sight carry over into the later stages? Is love in fact a screen which obscures the reality of the beloved while projecting a make-believe image?

Deliberately to embrace a falsehood – even in love – is to make a mockery of ourselves as essentially rational beings. People do it all the time, of course; the truth may be too hard to bear or the fiction too delicious to resist. Beliefs, then, may reflect the believer, not the object of belief. Thus when mystics fuse with God they often report an experience of Him that in fact reflects their own needs and desires: the resulting beliefs about God are totally spurious. Perhaps the same happens in romantic love. The lover creates a vision inside of the loved one and then represents it as objective. Yet, we cannot idealise just anyone: the person must have something that makes them suitable for such projection in the first place. Romeo may have idealised Juliet, but it is hard to imagine him doing the same with her mother. Love is not utterly blind: you do not fall for just anyone. This limitation is not, of course, imposed by reason. It seems to be more or less a matter of physiology, even though it operates below the level of any conscious awareness. We do not know what turn of a head or line of cheek strikes us like lightning. Nevertheless, whatever they may be, we need these 'unobservable' qualities to be present. This, I suppose, explains why someone apparently ideal simply strikes no spark: there is something vital missing.

Presumably, though, the reason for idealising the one you do fall for is to get your love well-grounded – to identify qualities that will sustain the effects of the *coup de foudre*. Your projections of the beloved as a being possessed of all human perfections is in fact an attempt to make your love rational. Even at the cost of a certain self-deception you want to display your good sense in loving this person. Our inclination to over-estimate the qualities of a loved one is not, then, evidence that love is essentially irrational. Rather, it shows that we may choose irrational means to get our love grounded.

This kind of deception will cost a great deal. Either the love will dissipate when the loved one is discovered to be mortal and imperfect. Or else, if you are to stay wrapped in the mists of illusion, all real intimacy of thoughts and feelings will have to be avoided. This, surely, is a mockery of love.

If self-deception mocks love, objective assessment, some

people argue, kills it. It is often thought that if you can see straight through to the reality of your partner – past the mystery, the thrill of discovery – then love will fade, rather as the subtle colours on a fish will fade if it is laid in sunlight. This is a doleful thought for anyone who is convinced that all knowledge is valuable. But is it a thought we need to accept?

It may be a killing blow to your love suddenly to perceive that your paragon is not all you had believed. It does not follow, though, that knowledge itself is inimical to love. Admittedly, knowledge is not a sufficient condition of love – you can know very well someone you loathe – but it is a necessary condition, for it is the qualities a person has that make him or her lovable. If you do not know what those qualities are, then either you will have nothing to harness your feelings to, or else you will harness them to qualities that do not exist. Either way, your love is likely to dim as rapidly as the moon in June.

I doubt, though, that there is any generalisation to be made about the dazzling power of love, or the destructive power of knowledge. Sometimes, far from blinding us, love can heighten our sensitivity to a person; we are aware of things in them that someone who did not care would miss. Love is sometimes described as making one flesh out of two persons, so that there is a kind of third individual, 'the couple', to which the relationship gives priority. Anyone identifying this closely with the beloved may indeed know more about them than one who keeps a little distance and, as it were, observes from the outside. It is a familiar thought that lovers see the best in each other.

If, then, you hold the romantic view that there is good in everyone, you may have a greater chance of seeing it through love. In love there can be a wonderfully moving process of stripping away defences to allow the beloved close to the reality of you. It is inevitably diminishing only to have contact with the façade that people present to the world. By contrast, the closeness of love can be extraordinarily enriching. It is also one of love's merits that it brings together people who would not have chosen each other as friends. Love leaps all sorts of boundaries of background, culture and taste, so that King Cophetua can fall in love with the beggar maid even though he would be unlikely to have a beggar as a friend. This is not because a beggar could not have the personal worth that would elicit friendship from the King. It is rather that friendship cannot provide the impetus to leap great gulfs. Love can; it is of inestimable value that through love we may become intimate with those we would otherwise have passed by.

Even if love is not entirely blind, it does tend to be generous. It would need quite a lot to make you believe badly of a loved one – considerably more than to make you feel the same of a mere acquaintance. The evidence that will persuade a jury of a stranger's guilt may be quite insufficient to persuade the man or woman who loves that stranger; this is one reason why a spouse cannot testify against their partner. Love, then, erects hurdles that must be surmounted before you can believe ill of the beloved. But what of the jealousy and possessiveness exemplified by Othello? There is nothing generous in choking the life out of the one you love on scant evidence of infidelity – not even on proof of it. Love did not protect Othello from suspicion by making him generous. To the contrary, it made him vulnerable.

Everyone has been racked by jealousy, the green-eyed monster, Dryden's 'tyrant of the mind'. In the grip of this ugly emotion you can become unrecognisable – you are no longer the kind of person you believed yourself to be. This madness is induced by the threatening of an important perception of yourself – the perception of yourself as unique – by a rival. In all other relationships you are replaceable – just another man or woman, doctor or lawyer. No one is indispensable. In love, however, that is precisely what is affirmed: you are irreplaceable, the best – the only one who will do.

It was suggested to me, however, that this was a reflection of a particularly invidious idea about love. 'Women have loved men as the only way of feeling worthwhile. But it can't be good to feel dependent.' To be loved is wonderful for anyone's self-esteem. There is no getting away from it – we do feel more valuable when we are in love; this is part of the radiance that love bestows. It does not follow from this that a person has no value at all before being loved. Indeed, love is a salute to that value. Nor is there anything demeaning in believing that, in the end, a person's value does not go beyond the effect they have on other people. A woman may be highly intelligent and wonder-

fully kind – qualities that have objective value independently
of being recognised – but if they do not impinge on others an
important potential has not been realised. What matters about
human beings is their responses to each other; and in love the
finest recognition is being bestowed in a very direct way.

If your loved one finds someone else, however, that perception of yourself as of inestimable value is shattered. You are,
after all, dispensable, and not only that – it is the most intimate
and valuable part of yourself that is dispensable. The affirmation of you as somehow special is poisoned; the rival proves
that you have nothing particular to offer. No wonder jealousy
can be so devastating to the integrity of the person. This is why
we so easily understand the *crime passionnel*, and why we
think it heroic if the lover sacrifices their love so that the loved
one can be happy with another. It is not something we expect:
we are much more familiar with, 'I'll never let you go!' So
although there may be limitations on love's generosity, according to the individual psyche of the lover, there must be some
element of it, for otherwise the love has surely gone wrong at
source. It might be added that since love is expansive and
generous, while jealousy is destructive, it must be rational to
learn control of the worse emotion rather than put limits on the
better.

One man I talked to thought that many people do not fall in
love with a person at all; they fall in love with love. 'Our
culture is a panegyric to romantic love. There's such pressure
to be "in" it – all the world loves a lover – that it's almost the
feeling that matters more than the person you feel for.' It is not
solely cultural conditioning that makes us believe that those in
love are enviable. Being in love is, in itself, such a deliciously
fevered state that it is hard not to want it for its own sake. If this
is a person's inclination, then within a fairly broad range of
people, they will almost certainly light on one who will supply
the occasion for them to fall.

The person in love with love will have no interest in getting
that love well-grounded. A lover may for a while be totally
concentrated on the person who has created the requisite
passion, but to try and hook that passion on to all that is good in
that person is by definition to be interested in *them* – not in
love alone. Inevitably, the lover will fall out of love because

they will become embroiled in the dynamics of the situation. Wanting only a romantic fling is something that cannot be fulfilled with the same person for more than a short time. Inevitably it modulates into something else, perhaps into a companionate kind of love ... or simply nothing. For the person in love with love it must be nothing. Companionate love intrudes the person as the object of desire, not the feelings and sensations. If all that is wanted is moonlit walks suffused with dark passion – a brief gaudy hour rather than a lifetime – 'occasion' will rapidly supplant 'occasion'.

In search of love we are constantly exhorted in magazines and newspapers to employ more modern methods than the arrows of an ancient Greek god, and to go shopping for lovers by computer. In computer dating you make your list of desirable qualities and a computer finds you the person who matches them. Then you set yourself to loving that person. This is surely the apotheosis of rationality; so why, if rational love is what we all should seek, does it so rarely work?

From everything that has been said about love being well-grounded, if you do specify the qualities you need you ought indeed to fall in love with the person who has them. Unfortunately there are many things that can go wrong. You may not specify what is important to you because although you know what you need in a friend you simply do not know what makes the ideal lover for you – which is why people are constantly falling for those they see as most unlikely life partners. It is also more or less impossible to programme Cupid, and, however much of an anachronism he may seem, impossible to do without him. The aim of the whole process is to fall in love. Regrettably few, if any of us, know precisely why we fall in love in the first place. So how are you to tell the computer what it is you want in a computer date? You may simply not know what moves you. Of course, you can tell *now* why you love someone, but it may be impossible accurately to spell out why you were so struck by them at the start of it all.

Most inimical to the success of the whole venture is that any properties you are likely to specify are bound to be wildly insufficient. You may just about manage to get down what is necessary to you – sharing common interests, perhaps – but not even begin to touch on what is sufficient. A friend of mine tried some computer dating when she became divorced. 'The agency was a good one in that the three men I met did have the interests I'd given as important – and they more or less looked as I said I wanted. But, for me, they had something missing. One man I remember couldn't stand silence. He had to fill every pause with chat. How are you supposed to know you must specify "being comfortable with silence"?' The project is made even more complex by the reflection that qualities like 'being able to get on with you without fighting' are impossible even for a computer to perceive in someone. However powerful computers may be, it is improbable that any puny, finite mind could construct a blueprint for love so that success is guaranteed. At the same time, you may rightly insist that if an infinite mind – God – had done the draughtsmanship then the love would be bound to blossom; He is omniscient after all. Marriages may be made in heaven but they are not likely to be made in the software of computing dating agencies.

Perhaps it seems sad – pathetic, even – that some people have to have recourse to such methods to find love. And, of course, it is sad when people are lonely or cannot find what they want in others. At the same time this is a testament – and a moving one – to the conviction that we are all the better for having loved. Not everyone can love; some people are too self-absorbed, or too mean-spirited, frightened or indolent. Yet we are convinced they are the worse for it. Imagine a special person, one who was the embodiment of all that was best in people who was yet unable to love another person. In the end, he or she is less of a person than one like the rest of us who is packed with human weaknesses yet does genuinely love another. And this is true even though our dark side may tarnish the love we feel; too often we are thoughtless or unkind. If the ideal person had been able to love I imagine that love would have been finer than the imperfect variety most of us manage. But if love never happens then the ideal is diminished. He or she is less of a person than those who are not ideal but do manage to love. We should never, then, say of any love that there is no point to it. It may be ill-advised, it may be illicit, but in love, for all our defects, we may display grand virtues. We are prepared to be involved, prepared genuinely to appreciate another, prepared to reveal what we are and to trust. We can only begin to do these things if we esteem the beloved, and have a perception of them as valuable. The love in which there is a conscious reciprocity of good can only be a rational love – a love which is well-grounded. Dante's love for Beatrice is a model of romantic love. He wrote:

> Again mine eyes were fix'd on Beatrice;
> And with mine eyes, my soul that in her looks
> Found all contentment.

His feelings were passionate and imaginative and they were ruled, he said, by 'the faithful council of reason'. There is nothing more to wish for in love than this.

SUGGESTIONS FOR FURTHER READING

Altman, Dennis, *Homosexual Oppression and Liberation*, Outerbridge, New York, 1971

Anscombe, G.E.M., *Ethics, Religion and Politics*, Blackwell, Oxford, 1983

Aquinas, St Thomas, *On the Truth of the Catholic Faith*, Doubleday, New York, 1956

Aristotle's 'Ethics' (ed. J. Ackrill), Faber & Faber, London, 1973

Augustine, St, of Hippo, *The City of God*, Penguin, London, 1972

Baker, Robert, and Elliston, Frederick, *Philosophy and Sex*, Prometheus, New York, 1975

Beauvoir, Simone de, *The Second Sex*, Penguin, London, 1972

Capellanus, Andreas, *On Love*, Duckworth, London, 1982

Crick, Bernard, *Crime, Rape and Gin*, Elek, London, 1975

Dworkin, Ronald, *Taking Rights Seriously*, Duckworth, London, 1978

Epictetus, *The 'Discourses' and 'Manual'*, Clarendon Press, Oxford, 1916

Feinberg, Joel, *The Problems of Abortion*, Wadsworth, California, 1974

Fichte, Johann Gottlieb, *The Science of Rights*, Routledge & Kegan Paul, London, 1970

Fortenbaugh, W.W., *Aristotle on Emotion*, Duckworth, London, 1975

Freud, Sigmund, *On Sexuality*, Pelican, London, 1977

Friday, Nancy, *My Secret Garden*, Virago, London, 1975

Friedan, Betty, *The Feminine Mystique*, Penguin, London, 1982

Greer, Germaine, *The Female Eunuch*, Paladin, London, 1971
— *Sex and Destiny*, Secker & Warburg, London, 1984
Hegel, G.W.F., *The Phenomenology of Mind*, Allen & Unwin, London, 1931
Honderich, T., and Burnyeat, M., *Philosophy As It Is*, Pelican, London, 1979
Hume, David, *Essays: Moral, Political and Literary*, Longman Green, London, 1875
Kant, Immanuel, *Lectures on Ethics*, Methuen, London, 1930
Kierkegaard, Søren, *The Diary of a Seducer*, Dragon Press, New York, 1932
MacMurray, John, *Reason and Emotion*, Faber & Faber, London, 1935
Marcuse, Herbert, *Eros and Civilisation: a Philosophical Inquiry into Freud*, Beacon Press, Boston, 1955–
Margolis, Joseph, *Values and Conduct*, OUP, London, 1971
Mill, John Stuart, *On Subjection of Women*, London, 1869
Moller Okin, Susan, *Women in Western Political Thought*, Virago, London, 1980
Morris, Desmond, *The Human Zoo*, Jonathan Cape, London, 1969
Nietzsche, Friedrich Wilhelm, *Thus Spake Zarathustra*, Penguin, London, 1974
Plato, *The Symposium*, Penguin, London, 1980
— *The Republic*, Penguin, London, 1974
Purtill, R.L., *Moral Dilemmas*, Wadsworth, California, 1985
Radcliffe Richards, Janet, *The Sceptical Feminist*, Pelican, London, 1982
Roberts, Yvonne, *Man Enough*, Chatto & Windus, London, 1984
Rolph, C.J., ed., *Does Pornography Matter?*, Routledge & Kegan Paul, London, 1961
Russell, Bertrand, *Marriage and Morals*, Unwin, London, 1929
— *The Conquest of Happiness*, Unwin, London, 1930
Sabini, Maury, and Silver, John, *Moralities of Everyday Life*, OUP, London, 1982
Sartre, Jean-Paul, *On Being and Nothingness*, Methuen, London, 1957
— *Sketch for a Theory of the Emotions*, Methuen, London, 1962

Scruton, Roger, *Sexual Desire*, Weidenfeld & Nicolson, London, 1986

Vannoy, Russell, *Sex Without Love*, Prometheus, New York, 1980

Williams, Bernard, *Morality*, Pelican, London, 1973

Wollstonecraft, Mary, *A Vindication of the Rights of Woman*, Norton, New York, 1967